DESCARTES' DEONT(

This book offers a new way of approaching the place of the will in Descartes' mature epistemology and ethics. Departing from the widely accepted view, Noa Naaman-Zauderer suggests that Descartes regards the will, rather than the intellect, as the most significant mark of human rationality, both intellectual and practical. Through a close reading of Cartesian texts from the *Meditations* onward, she brings to light a deontological and non-consequentialist dimension of Descartes' later thinking, which credits the proper use of free will with a constitutive, evaluative role. She shows that the right use of free will, to which Descartes assigns obligatory force, constitutes for him an end in its own right rather than merely a means for attaining any other end, however valuable. Her important study has significant implications for the unity of Descartes' thinking and for the issue of responsibility, inviting scholars to reassess Descartes' philosophical legacy.

NOA NAAMAN-ZAUDERER is senior lecturer in the Department of Philosophy at Tel Aviv University. She is the author of *Descartes: The Loneliness of a Philosopher* (2007) and co-editor of *Discourse and Dialogue: Multi-Perspective Philosophy* (2003).

DESCARTES'
DEONTOLOGICAL TURN

Reason, Will, and Virtue in the Later Writings

NOA NAAMAN-ZAUDERER

CAMBRIDGE
UNIVERSITY PRESS

CAMBRIDGE UNIVERSITY PRESS
Cambridge, New York, Melbourne, Madrid, Cape Town,
Singapore, São Paulo, Delhi, Mexico City

Cambridge University Press
The Edinburgh Building, Cambridge CB2 8RU, UK

Published in the United States of America by Cambridge University Press, New York

www.cambridge.org
Information on this title: www.cambridge.org/9781107692077

First published 2010
First paperback edition 2013

A catalogue record for this publication is available from the British Library

Library of Congress Cataloguing in Publication Data
Naaman Zauderer, Noa.
Descartes' deontological turn : reason, will, and virtue in the later writings /
Noa Naaman-Zauderer.
p.   cm.
Includes bibliographical references and index.
ISBN 978-0-521-76330-1 (hardback)
1. Descartes, René, 1596–1650.   2. Will.   I. Title.
B1878.W5N33 2010
194–dc22
2010033021

ISBN 978-1-107-69207-7 Paperback

To Yochai, Shira, Ella and Lihi

Contents

Preface

In his conversation with the young Dutch scholar Frans Burman in 1648, Descartes expressed his expectations about the future treatment of his metaphysical writings: "A point to note is that one should not devote so much effort to the *Meditations* and to metaphysical questions, or give them elaborate treatment in commentaries and the like. Still less should one do what some try to do, and dig more deeply into these questions than the author did; he has dealt with them quite deeply enough" (CB 48 = AT v 165: CSMK 346–47).

In the process of writing this book, I found myself recurrently wondering whether I was not acting against Descartes' expressed wish. Though I would certainly not credit myself with the sin of digging into Descartes' metaphysical questions more deeply than he had himself, I may have failed to comply with the first half of his wish. Fortunately, though, I am not alone in committing this sin, and we can only speculate about what the father of modern philosophy would have thought and felt had he been acquainted with the huge interpretive enterprise that his tree of philosophy has yielded. Three hundred and sixty years after Descartes' death, and despite the enormous wealth and diversity of interpretations that have since become available, the possibility of revealing new layers and striking perspectives in his thought was an exciting discovery in the course of my writing.

My endeavor in this book is to reconsider the place that the will occupies in Descartes' mature epistemology and ethics. Departing from the widely accepted view, I argue that Descartes regards the will, rather than the intellect, as the most significant mark of human rationality, both intellectual and practical. The overarching theme of the book is that the right use of free will, to which Descartes assigns obligatory force, constitutes for him an end in its own right and not only a means for acquiring true knowledge, happiness, or any other valuable end. My hope is that this study will invite scholars to reassess the legacy of Descartes' philosophical edifice as well as the dialogue that later philosophers have conducted with his thinking, either implicitly or explicitly – from Spinoza and Leibniz, through Kant and Nietzsche, and up to postmodern critics in the twentieth and twenty-first centuries.

I feel extremely fortunate and grateful for the invaluable encouragement and assistance I have received all along from colleagues, friends, students, and family. I extend my gratitude to Marcelo Dascal, who introduced me to the world of early modern philosophy, sparking my interest in the philosophy of Leibniz. Working with him, first as a student and then as a colleague, has privileged me with the lesson not to be deterred from posing difficult questions, yet at the same time to be rigorous in answering them. Zvi Tauber has been a constant source of intellectual enhancement and wisdom. I am deeply grateful for his thoughtful observations, caring involvement, and unfailing support all along. I am indebted to Martha Bolton for the fruitful and stimulating dialogue we have had over the years. Her inspiring responses and enduring encouragement were invaluable to the development of my ideas. I wish to thank Daniel Garber for stimulating me to pursue this project at its initial phase, and for his outstanding attentiveness and insights. I take great pleasure in thanking Hilary Gaskin, the philosophy editor at Cambridge University Press. Her thoughtful suggestions and supportive enthusiasm made the publication of this book an exciting and gratifying experience. I owe much to two anonymous referees for Cambridge University Press, whose insightful remarks helped me refine and clarify several important issues in an earlier version of this text. I am grateful to Amihud Gilead for his support and his enriching ideas. Thanks also to Saul Smilansky for his sound advice and his warm encouragement.

Several friends and colleagues have been engaged in this project over the years in various significant ways. I am deeply thankful to all of them. My intense conversations with Yaron Senderowicz have greatly contributed to the refinement of my ideas. His genuine concern and steadfast friendship were very meaningful to me. Hagi Kenaan and Vered Lev Kenaan were a continuing source of strength, accompanying me with their close friendship and inspiring ideas. Eli Friedlander helped me shape my main argument at the early stages of the writing, when I was still struggling to be clearer to myself. I am very grateful for his perceptive judgment and encouragement. Special thanks to Ilana Treston for her wholehearted assistance at the initial stage of the project and for her thoughtful comments. I also wish to thank Ilana Arbel, Ayelet Even-Ezra,

Hanoch Dagan, Tsilli Dagan, Ariel Meirav, and Galia Pat-Shamir for their personal and intellectual involvement.

I was fortunate in having had Batya Stein as my editor, who helped me navigate the manuscript with great wisdom, sensitivity, and skill. The contribution of her creativity, her keen intellect, and her unqualified commitment were invaluable to the writing of the book.

I wish to thank the Philosophy Department at Tel Aviv University, my colleague Ovadia Ezra, the head of the department, and especially Shlomo Biderman, Dean of the Faculty of Humanities, and Yoav Ariel, Dean of Students, for their unstinting support.

My immense love and gratitude to my parents, whose wisdom, care, and endless love have enriched my spirit and sustained me through this intellectual voyage. My mother, Oshra Zauderer, was a reassuring friend and a worthy philosophical partner at many crossroads. My father, Zvi Zauderer, the most giving person I have ever known, went out of his way to assist me during these long years of contemplation and writing. Thanks also to my brother, Arik Zidon, a close and loving intellectual companion, and to my uncle, Itzhak Gottlieb, my philosophical interlocutor since childhood.

I owe more than I can express in words to my husband, Yochai, an endless source of strength, love, and intellectual enthusiasm. I dedicate this book to him and to our three wonderful daughters, Shira, Ella, and Lihi, who never lost faith in their mother bringing this project to a close. Their wit, beauty, and love are for me the sweetest source of happiness and delight.

Abbreviations

AT   *Oeuvres de Descartes*, ed. Charles Adam and Paul Tannery, 12 vols. Paris: Vrin, 1964–76.

CB   *Descartes' Conversation with Burman*, trans. John Cottingham. Oxford: Clarendon Press, 1976.

CSM   *The Philosophical Writings of Descartes*, ed. and trans. John Cottingham, Robert Stoothoff, and Dugald Murdoch, 2 vols. Cambridge University Press, 1985.

CSMK   *The Philosophical Writings of Descartes: The Correspondence*, ed. and trans. John Cottingham, Robert Stoothoff, Dugald Murdoch, and Anthony Kenny. Cambridge University Press, 1991.

References to Descartes' works are made in parentheses in the main body of the text, by volume and page number of the original language edition (AT) and of the English translation, if available (CSM or CSMK). Two exceptions are Descartes' *Principles of Philosophy*, where parenthetical references are by part and article number, and *The Passions of the Soul*, where numbers refer to articles. Unless otherwise indicated, I adhere to the translation of these works by Cottingham, Stoothoff, and Murdoch (CSM), vol. I.

Introduction

One of the most challenging tasks that Descartes' philosophical corpus poses to interpreters is that of explaining the kind of responsibility we bear for our judgments and actions. This book offers a new way of approaching the issue of responsibility by bringing to light a *deontological* and *non-consequentialist* dimension of Descartes' later thinking, which credits the proper use of free will with a constitutive, evaluative role. The book explores prominent manifestations of Descartes' deontological approach, an aspect of his thinking that current interpretations have largely overlooked. Relying on a close reading of the *Meditations* and subsequent writings, I propose a new interpretation of several of Descartes' key epistemological doctrines and of the sense in which he considers human reason to be autonomous. Without denying the centrality of the intellect in the search for truth, or Descartes' deep interest in establishing the foundations of his science, I argue that he sees the right use of free will not merely as a means to some other, superior end but as an end in its own right. I claim, moreover, that Descartes views the will rather than the intellect as the most significant mark of human rationality, both intellectual and practical. I will then rely on this reading to interpret his statement that the human will constitutes the most prominent manifestation of our similitude to God.

The title, *Descartes' Deontological Turn*, alludes to the new sense that this book offers for Descartes' innovative "turn to the self." In *Sources of the Self*, Charles Taylor aptly characterizes the "turn inward" taken by the father of modern philosophy as the conversion of a "substantive" notion of reason – consisting in a proper understanding of the ontic *logos* – into a "procedural" notion defined by the standards used to construct internal orders between ideas in our minds (Taylor 1989: 143–58). While embracing this general perspective, my suggestion in this work is to view Descartes' turn inward as primarily rooted in the constitutive role he assigns to the duty to use free will correctly. My intention is to show that the conception of reason that Descartes' later writings portray, both in the speculative and practical domains, is deontological and non-consequentialist, placing at its very center the *pragmatic* distinction between the "right use" and the "misuse" of free will. This distinction, I suggest, depends exclusively on features pertaining to the process of deliberation that eventuates in an operation of the will, not on our power to distinguish truth from falsity. The rightness or wrongness of our judgments, as this book aims to substantiate, does not hinge on our power to distinguish the true from the false, which Descartes identifies in his earlier writings with human reason or *bon sens*.[1] Moreover, despite his reiterated proclamations, Descartes provides no conclusive criterion of falsehood, hence no conclusive criterion for discriminating the true from the false. The method exemplified in the *Meditations* enables us to discriminate only between what we perceive clearly and distinctly (which is undoubtedly true, given divine veracity), and what we perceive only confusedly or obscurely (which might be either true or false). The confusion or obscurity of an idea does not, in Descartes' thinking, entail its falsehood. The Cartesian method is therefore marked by an asymmetrical feature: it provides a conclusive means for the *verification* of ideas but no conclusive means for identifying falsehood. This feature must be taken into account when explaining several fundamental notions in Descartes' epistemology, of which the most notable are material falsity and error. Through the interpretation of these and other related epistemological notions, I show that the absence of a conclusive criterion for falsehood constitutes neither a deficiency nor a limitation of Descartes' system. Such a criterion is not needed for the main ends of his inquiry – from the search for truth, through the right exercise of free will, and up to the attainment of virtuousness and happiness in life.

The crux of the book is a new interpretation of Descartes' concept of error. Considering the wide variety of current views about Descartes' theory of error, I was surprised to learn that the meaning of the term "error" in his usage does not seem to be in dispute. Addressing various aspects of Descartes' theory of error, scholars appear to assume, explicitly or implicitly, that he considers error to be an affirmation of falsehood or a denial of truth. While acknowledging that Cartesian error can arise only

---

[1] *Discourse on the Method*, Part One (AT VI 1–2: CSM I 111). In Part Three of this treatise, Descartes argues that "God has given each of us a light to distinguish truth from falsehood" (AT VII 27: CSM I 124). This statement appears in later writings as well. In the Second Replies, for instance, Descartes writes that "we have a real faculty for recognizing the truth and distinguishing it from falsehood" (AT VII 144: CSM II 103).

when we let ourselves assent to matters we do not perceive clearly and distinctly, scholars tend to assume that error cannot occur unless the resultant judgment affirms what is false or denies what is true. My approach in this book takes a different course, claiming that Descartes equates not only the cause but the very essence of error with what he calls the "incorrect use of free choice" (*liberi arbitrii non recto usu*) (AT VII 60: CSM II 41). Any *act* of judgment that is not based on clear and distinct perception, regardless of whether the *content* being judged is true or false, is deemed a misuse of free will, hence an instance of error. In affirming or denying a confused or obscure idea, then, we are liable for a genuine, culpable error, regardless of whether the *content* to which we give credence is true or not. In establishing this reading, I inquire into Descartes' understanding of error as a *privation*. This notion, which has received relatively limited attention in the literature, proves to be crucial for our understanding of Descartes' position on the essence of intellectual error and its close affinity to moral wrong.

This reading invites the question as to what Descartes would count as an instance of "misuse of free will," and hence as an instance of error, when discussing speculative and practical issues that may not admit our clear and distinct apprehension. I show that when dealing with matters often precluding clear and distinct perception, Descartes "tempers" the content and scope of the duty to make "right use" of the will, but still retains his pragmatic and non-consequentialist conception of error as a misuse of free will.

Focusing on Descartes' account of intellectual error in the Fourth Meditation, I argue that rather than identifying error with a failure to discriminate the true from the false, he views error as a failure to comply with the precept dictated by the natural light of reason – never to make judgments unless on the basis of clear and distinct ideas. Any violation of this rational duty constitutes an instance of error, irrespective of its ensuing results. On these grounds I argue further that when Descartes speaks of erroneous (formally false) judgments, he does not confine himself to judgments whose propositional content fails to represent real objects or "things," as is usually maintained. Instead, I suggest that by "formally false judgment," Descartes denotes any *act* of judgment applied to matters we do not understand clearly and distinctly. This reading has important implications for the coherence of Descartes' position on the locus of falsity and truth. When he claims that "falsity in the strict sense, or formal falsity, can occur only in judgments" (Third Meditation, AT VII 43: CSM II 30), he does not deny that ideas can be bearers of truth or falsehood, nor does he mean that ideas are inherently true. Since formal falsity is a characteristic of voluntary *acts* of judgment rather than of the *content* to which these acts apply, it is not a feature of our ideas when "considered solely in themselves."

Descartes' "non-substantive"[2] notion of error provides an important insight into a deontological and non-consequentialist dimension of his thinking. The constitutive role he assigns to the duty to "use free will correctly" (or, in its negative form, to avoid misusing the will), clearly indicates that he considers compliance with this duty an independent end and not only a means of reaching other ends, even one as worthy as attaining true cognitions about reality. The boundary separating the right and the wrong, the rational and the irrational, overlaps the split between those circumstances where we refrain from misusing the will and those where we do not.

The principal merit of this deontological approach, as this study seeks to establish, is that of freeing rationality from "substantive" or extrinsic standards of falsity and truth without thereby abandoning the uncompromising commitment to truth. Descartes no doubt holds that insofar as we limit our judgments to clear and distinct perception, we not only avoid the guilt of error but also cognize the true nature of things. Yet, even if our clear and distinct ideas might ultimately be, absolutely speaking, false (AT VII 145: CSM II 103), we would still not be considered *irrational* for assenting to them. Indeed, through the correct use of our free will we become virtuous, despite the alleged possibility that the beliefs we are holding are false from an "absolute" (divine) point of view. In creating a new meaning and a new place for autonomous subjectivity, this conception entails crucial implications for the kind of responsibility we bear for our judgments and actions, independently of our prospects of attaining absolute truths.

The independent value of limiting our judgment only to clear and distinct ideas (in pure inquiry), or to the recommendations of reason (in the practical domain) lies in the very exercise of self-mastery, in judging and acting according to our internal standards rather than being activated from outside. By opting for an active stance toward the world while doing our utmost to reach the best (truest) judgment possible, we actualize in the fullest and most significant manner our rational essence, as well as our similitude to God.

---

[2] I borrow this expression from Charles Taylor (1989: 156). I consider "substantive" any conception or explanation that regards the standard for epistemic evaluation as depending on the conformity between the content of our mental states and the nature of their objects in reality.

Though I discuss some of Descartes' writings prior to the *Meditations*, I focus mainly on his later writings, from the *Meditations* onward. My main reason for this approach is that neither the conception of judgment as an operation of the will nor its underlying metaphysical doctrine of human freedom are expressly present in works that precede the *Meditations*. In the *Rules for the Direction of the Mind*, Descartes speaks of errors arising from conjoining things without being certain of their truth. He states that "it is within our power to avoid this error, *viz.* by never conjoining things unless we intuit that the conjunction of one with the other is wholly necessary ..." (Rule 12, AT x 425: CSM 1 48). Yet this early work refers the faculty of eliciting judgments to the intellect, as evidenced by its distinction "between the faculty by which our intellect intuits and knows things and the faculty by which it makes affirmative or negative judgments" (AT x 420: CSM 1 45). In the *Discourse on the Method*, the first rule of method prescribes "never to accept anything as true if [we] did not have evident knowledge of its truth" (AT vi 18: CSM 1 120). But this work does not expressly articulate a view of judgments as voluntary operations of the will either.[3] It is not until the *Meditations*, then, where Descartes sets his mature conception of judgment and his metaphysical doctrine of free will, that he assigns this precept its constitutive standing as a binding duty on which our rationality depends. On these grounds, I assume that the *Meditations* marks a genuine change in Descartes' conception of reason, though confirming this assumption is not part of my endeavor in this book.[4]

[3] See also the discussions in Beck (1952: 18–20) and references therein; Kenny (1972: 1–7); Rodis-Lewis (1998: 130); Curley (1978: 41–51); Menn (1998: 325–26); Alanen (2003: 29). For different interpretations of this issue see, for instance, Van De Pitte, (1988: 462 n. 40); Vinci (1998: 15–18); Davies (2001: 79, 87–91).

[4] My position on this issue is also inspired by Daniel Garber's analysis of the fundamental transformation that the *Meditations* and subsequent writings prove in Descartes' conceptions of method, of how knowledge is to be grounded, and of the order of reasons (Garber 1992, ch. 2, and 2001: 33–51). According to Garber, the *Meditations* and subsequent writings do not resort to the earlier method as outlined in both the *Rules for the Direction of the Mind* and the *Discourse*. Garber introduces two main changes in Descartes' thought that have made the earlier method largely inapplicable to his envisaged new system of knowledge. The first is "the change from a problem-solving conception of scientific activity to a system-building conception," and the second is "the adoption of the idea that intuition cannot be taken for granted and must be validated" (2001: 50). As Garber emphasizes (1992: 56–57), rather than merely reducing a given problem to simple intuitions, as suggested in the *Rules*, the first stage of the later program essentially involves *validation* of those intuitions (or clear and distinct perceptions) by the metaphysical doctrines of the soul and God. For different interpretations of the place assigned to the method of the *Rules* and the *Discourse* in Descartes' later writings see, for example, Gewirth (1943: 267ff.); Beck (1952: 272–307) and the references there given; Vinci (1998); Smith (2001: 280–91).

My general strategy in the present study is to explore the central motiv-ations and doctrines – epistemological, metaphysical, theological, and ethical – that lie behind Descartes' pragmatic and non-consequentialist conception of error. This strategy enables me to show that his conception of error, over and above its intrinsic innovative value, has significant elu-cidatory force. The reading offered here seeks to open up a new way of approaching a wide cluster of long-debated issues in Descartes' epistem-ology and ethics. I believe it may provide a distinctive key for acquiring a better understanding of some of his views and of his main motivations for holding them.

This strategy structures the general framework of this book. Chapter 1 focuses on Descartes' theory of ideas, setting the stage for the discus-sion of error and rationality in Chapter 2. The four subsequent chapters inquire into some of the main doctrines and motivations that lie behind Descartes' deontological approach: his notion of free will (Chapter 3), his conception of our similitude to God (Chapter 4), and his ethical thinking (Chapters 5 and 6).

Chapter 1 explores the notion of clear and distinct perception and the nature of true and false ideas. My intention in this opening chapter is to expound and substantiate my understanding of several key notions in Descartes' theory of ideas, locating myself within the wide spectrum of current interpretations. In particular, I seek to make sense of Descartes' crucial, yet often neglected distinction between confused or obscure ideas on the one hand, and false ideas on the other – a distinction that lies at the core of his philosophy in general, and specifically of his conception of error. My interpretation follows and reinforces Martha Bolton's thesis (1986) that an idea, however confused or obscure, cannot exhibit the thing it represents to immediate awareness as other than it is. Whether an idea is confused or obscure is a function of how the mind *regards* the content it exhibits (and represents). Through a close examination of the texts, I show that conformity between the idea's immediate content and the thing of which it is the idea is, for Descartes, an essential component of represen-tation. All and only ideas that, however confusedly, represent "things" (real objects) satisfy the "conformity" condition and are therefore *true* representations of the things of which they are ideas. A false idea, by con-trast, is one that fails to represent a thing or, in Descartes' wording, repre-sents a non-thing (AT VII 43–44: CSM II 30). Clarity and distinctness, in my reading, are features of the *act of perceiving* (of the "idea" taken in the *material* sense), not features of the idea's *content*. A perception being more or less clear and distinct does not affect the immediate content that the idea passively exhibits to the mind. An idea becomes clearer inasmuch as the mind's *attention* is directed to more of its elements, recognizing their interrelations when the idea is complex. The idea's distinctness depends on the extent to which the intellect, while immediately and involuntarily *interpreting* the idea's content *as* being such and such, recognizes the relations between the idea and other ideas (for instance, on whether the mind interprets pain *as* a mode of thinking or *as* a quality of the body). I conclude that the method of the *Meditations* for attaining clear and distinct perceptions, by withdrawing the mind from the senses and eliminating prejudice, is intended to remove various kinds of "disturbances" that may prevent us from "seeing" the true nature of things as they passively "reside in us," so to speak, in an "objective" mode of being.

On the basis of this reading, I analyze Descartes' notion of *material* falsity.[5] While many scholars hold that in the Third Meditation he equates materially false ideas with those representing non-things as things, I hold with others who claim, on various grounds, that he ascribes material falsity to sensory ideas on account of their inherent and irremediable obscurity and confusion. I further argue that Descartes' account of material falsity implies two senses in which ideas might be false. The first is the "ontological" sense mentioned above, which signifies the ideas' failure to represent "things," meaning *real* objects, but is still not the same as the *formal* falsity of judgments. The second sense, material falsity, is an *epistemic* category to which Descartes consigns ideas that are confused and obscure to such an extent that they do not enable him to judge *whether they are true or false* in the first, ontological sense. The chapter closes with a discussion of how confused and obscure ideas of sense provide "subject-matter for error."

Chapter 2 offers my reading of Descartes' concept of error and its implied deontological conception of rationality, whose essential features I have outlined above.

Chapters 3 and 4 explore the privileged status that Descartes assigns to the will as the most prominent manifestation of our likeness to God. As a first step, Chapter 3 analyzes Descartes' position on the essence of human free will, a topic which is the focus of a serious interpretive debate. While it is widely agreed that the spontaneity of the will is essential to our freedom, scholars disagree on whether Descartes also considers the positive two-way power of the will (the ability to do or not to do something) to be essential. Confronting several apparent inconsistencies in Descartes' writings on the topic, I argue that he consistently holds that

[5] Descartes discusses this issue both in the Third Meditation (AT VII 43–44: CSM II 30) and in the Fourth Replies (AT VII 231–35: CSM II 162–64).

only spontaneous self-determination is essential to our free will. I further show that Descartes' non-consequentialist notion of error rules out any interpretation that views him as a radical voluntarist, admitting the power of the Cartesian will to resist a clearly perceived truth or goodness while the mind's attention is directed to it.

Relying on these conclusions, Chapter 4 seeks to make sense of Descartes' doctrine, reiterated in various forms, that it is above all by dint of the will rather than the intellect that we understand ourselves to bear the image and likeness of God.[6] In the Fourth Meditation, Descartes goes so far as to claim that the will of God "does not seem any greater" than the human will "when considered as will in the essential and strict sense" (AT vii 57: CSM ii 40). The essential similarity that this statement suggests between divine and human free will appears to be at odds with Descartes' celebrated doctrine of the creation of the eternal truths, to which he remains faithful throughout his life. My endeavor in this chapter is to resolve the tension between the two fundamental doctrines by developing a coherent account of Descartes' position on the relation between divine and human free will. Prompted by Michael Della Rocca's reading of the Cartesian circle (2005), I suggest that the doctrine of the incomprehensibility of God allows Descartes to assign normative status to our *experience* of freedom, regarding it as an independent source of moral agency and responsibility. I conclude that although the human will is essentially different from the divine will, when our will's functioning is fully harmonious with its nature and optimally spontaneous and free, we *experience* it as unified with our intellect, thereby recognizing in ourselves "some trace" of the individual attributes of God.

Chapters 5 and 6 integrate some of the key themes developed in previous chapters by concentrating on Descartes' ethical thinking. These chapters highlight the deontological and non-consequentialist character of Descartes' view of practical reason, whose core merit is the duty to make right use of the will.

Recent years have exposed a growing interest in the writings on ethics that occupied Descartes toward the end of his life. The recent significant contribution of scholars such as John Cottingham, Lilli Alanen, Deborah Brown, Susan James, and Lisa Shapiro on the convergence of Descartes' epistemology and his ethics has enriched our vision of his

---

[6] See, for instance, the Fourth Meditation (AT vii 57: CSM ii 40); letter to Mersenne, December 25, 1639 (AT ii 628: CSMK 141–42); letter to Queen Christina, November 20, 1647 (AT v 83, 85: CSMK 325, 326); *Conversation with Burman* (CB 31 = AT v 159: CSMK 342); *Passions*, art. 152.

entire philosophical edifice. Building on these foundations, Chapters 5 and 6 proceed to articulate a new perspective on the deep connection between Descartes' views on practical and speculative reason. Chapter 5 concentrates on Descartes' initial steps toward his more developed conception of practical reason: his non-consequentialist outlook on religious activity and faith that appears in writings dated around 1641, and his early conception of moral action – the *morale par provision* – presented in the Third Part of the *Discourse on the Method*. This conception lays the foundations of what will later evolve into Descartes' mature morality of virtue, which is the focus of Chapter 6. In this final chapter, I show that Descartes' later ethical writings (notably his 1645–49 correspondence and the *Passions of the Soul* published in 1649) are intended to guide us on the correct use of our free will under conditions of imperfect knowledge. In order to judge well in the conduct of life, we are not obliged to judge indubitably and infallibly. Even when we fail to choose the best option, we shall still be virtuous and avoid the charge of error if, when deciding, we endeavor to use our reason as best we can and act resolutely according to our best judgment.

Descartes' ethical writings do not include an extensive set of first-order rules for action intended to govern particular decisions. Instead, Descartes sets at the core of his later morality a single, second-order duty to practice virtue, namely, to resolutely and constantly carry out whatever reason *recommends*. The practice of virtue, which Descartes reduces to the good use of the will, must not be taken merely as a means to happiness but as an independent end. In identifying virtue with our supreme good (*summum bonum*), Descartes equates it with "the final end or goal toward which our actions *ought* to tend" (AT IV 275: CSMK 261; my emphasis). The practice of virtue *qua* the good use of the will thus constitutes the highest good that we *ought* to set ourselves as the ultimate end of all our actions. On these grounds, I argue that the practice of virtue constitutes for Descartes a moral imperative and not something we are only recommended to pursue.

In considering moral action to emerge from our understanding of the good, Descartes is indeed to be seen as a virtue ethicist.[7] And yet, the most remarkable feature of his ethical reasoning, as this closing chapter aims to substantiate, is that he defines virtue in deontological terms. On these grounds, I suggest that no tension or self-contradiction is involved in the claim that Descartes' ethics of virtue is deontological.

---

[7] See Shapiro 2007: 32–34; and 2008.

CHAPTER I

Looking inward: truth, falsehood, and clear and distinct ideas

In the *Meditations on First Philosophy* published in Latin in 1641, Descartes aims to lay the metaphysical foundations of his science. To use his later "tree of philosophy" metaphor, he intended the *Meditations* to provide the metaphysical roots for the trunk of physics and for all the other sciences – the branches emerging from the trunk – which he reduces to medicine, mechanics, and morals.[1] In the waning days of 1640, Descartes writes to his friend Marin Mersenne that he meant the title of this work, *Meditationes de Prima Philosophia*, to indicate that it deals "not just with God and the soul, but in general with all the first things that can be discovered by philosophizing in an orderly way."[2] For this purpose, as he later writes to the same correspondent, "we have to form distinct ideas of the things we want to judge about, and this is what most people fail to do and what I have mainly tried to reach by my *Meditations*" (AT III 272: CSMK 165).

The *Meditations* offers a new method for acquiring clear and distinct perception by withdrawing one's mind from the senses and eliminating prejudice.[3] The First Meditation exemplifies the method of doubt, whose greatest benefit, Descartes contends, "lies in freeing us from all our preconceived opinions, and providing the easiest route by which the mind may be led away from the senses."[4] The first item of knowledge emerging from the method of doubt is the certainty of the Cogito – the paradigm of a clear and distinct perception. To validate the normative status of clarity

---

[1] Preface-Letter to the French edition of the *Principles* (AT IXB 14: CSM I 186).

[2] November 11, 1640 (AT III 239: CSMK 158). See also AT III 235: CSMK 157.

[3] As Daniel Garber points out (1992: 55), although the idea that we must reject our past beliefs in order to ground knowledge is a central theme of the earlier *Discourse on the Method*, the *Meditations* advances a new device for eliminating prejudice – the contemplation of skeptical arguments – and presents it as "a necessary first step in first philosophy." Garber's interpretation is to be viewed in the wider context of his perspective concerning the change that the *Meditations* and later writings display in Descartes' conceptions of method, of knowledge, and of order. See Garber (1992 ch. 2; 2001: 33–63).

[4] *Synopsis* of the *Meditations* (AT VII 12: CSM II 9).

and distinctness as reliable marks of the truth, Descartes proceeds to sub-stantiate the existence of God, the infinitely perfect being. This task, how-ever, is not fully accomplished until the end of the Fourth Meditation, where Descartes proves that the presence of error in human cognition is not incompatible with the veracity of God. The Fourth Meditation cul-minates in Descartes' pronouncement of our most fundamental rational duty – to limit our judgments solely to clear and distinct perceptions. Descartes counts compliance with this duty as "man's greatest and most important perfection" (AT vii 62: CSM ii 43).

Despite the pivotal role that clear and distinct perception plays in the *Meditations* and in Descartes' philosophy as a whole,[5] the precise mean-ing of the terms "clarity" and "distinctness" is far from clear. Typically, Descartes explicates these terms by means of examples, of which the most notable is, of course, the clarity and distinctness of the Cogito. In keep-ing with his general reservations about formal and abstract definitions, he advises his readers to acquire the particular knowledge needed for dis-cerning clear and distinct perceptions by way of examples rather than through abstract definitions and rules.[6] Nevertheless, Descartes provides a definition of these terms in Part One of the *Principles of Philosophy*: "I call a perception 'clear' when it is present and accessible (*praesens et aperta*) to the attentive mind ... I call a perception 'distinct' if, as well as being clear, it is so sharply separated from all other perceptions that it contains within itself only what is clear" (i, 45). Despite its apparent simplicity, however, this account is not very helpful either. As I show below, the notions it involves – such as "presence," "accessibility," and "attentiveness" – call for no less interpretation than those they are intended to explicate.[7]

---

[5] Notice that the notion of clear and distinct conception, proposition, or intuition appears in works that preceded the *Meditations*, such as the *Rules for the Direction of the Mind* (AT x 368: CSM i 14; AT x 407: CSM i 37; AT x 418: CSM i 44) and the *Discourse on the Method* (for example, AT vi 18: CSM i 120; AT vi 21: CSM i 121). In the *Discourse*, we find Descartes' first pronouncement of the principle that all clear and distinct conceptions are true (AT vi 33: CSM i 127).

[6] "I ask my readers to ponder on all the examples that I went through in my *Meditations*, both of clear and distinct perception, and of obscure and confused perception, and thereby accustom themselves to distinguishing what is clearly known from what is obscure. This is something that it is easier to learn by examples than by rules, and I think that in the *Meditations* I explained, or at least touched on, all the relevant examples" (Second Replies, AT vii 164: CSM ii 116).

[7] Aside from the meaning of the terms "clarity" and "distinctness," a closely related question is how clear and distinct perceptions are to be acquired and recognized so as to serve as marks of truth. Descartes was strongly criticized for the ambiguity associated with his criterion of truth. One of his most severe critics was Leibniz, who, a few decades later, argued that the axiom whereby whatever we perceive clearly and distinctly is true "is useless unless we use criteria for the clear and distinct, criteria which we have made explicit" (Ariew and Garber 1989: 26). In a later work, Leibniz writes that "there is not much use in the celebrated rule that only what is clear

The main task of this chapter is to explore the nature of clear and distinct perceptions or ideas. In particular, I seek to explain the possibility that ideas may be confused or obscure and at the same time true. The distinction between confusion or obscurity and falsehood is crucial for Descartes' project, from his method of doubt through his notion of material falsity and up to his account of error, as the next chapter will prove. Yet I show that a highly prevalent interpretation, which views confusion and obscurity as features of the *content* perceived, could face difficulties when attempting to explain this aspect of Descartes' thinking. I begin with a brief sketch of some lines of interpretation of the notion of clear and distinct perception, then turn to discuss some fundamental aspects of Descartes' theory of ideas, among them the notions of objective reality, objective being, and representation. I proceed to explore the nature of true and false ideas, and then turn to discuss the notions of clarity and distinctness. The chapter closes with a discussion of the material falsity of ideas, and of how obscure and confused ideas provide subject-matter for error.

I   INTERPRETING THE NATURE OF CLEAR
AND DISTINCT PERCEPTIONS

Descartes defines "thought" (*cogitatio*) in terms of consciousness. As he writes in the Second Replies, this term includes "everything that is within us in such a way that we are immediately aware of it. Thus all the operations of the will, the intellect, the imagination, and the senses are thoughts."[8] Doubting, affirming, denying, perceiving, imagining, sensing, or feeling – all are different modes of thinking, that is, different kinds of mental activity of which we are immediately conscious. In the *Principles* (1, 32), Descartes indicates that all the modes of thinking we experience within ourselves fall under two general headings: "perception, or the operation of the intellect, and volition, or the operation of the will."

---

and distinct shall be approved, unless better marks of clearness and distinctness are offered than those of Descartes" (Loemker 1969: 389). But Leibniz's expectations of "better [meaning abstract and formal] marks" of clarity and distinctness are thoroughly foreign to Descartes' way of thinking. Rejecting any kind of formalism, he opposes any attempt to subject human reasoning to abstract rules of thinking, consistently retaining his principal concern to beware from our reason taking a holiday while we investigate the truth (*Rules*, Rule 10, AT x 406: CSM 1 36). Descartes was criticized for the subjectivity of his criterion of truth by some of his contemporaries as well, among them Gassendi (AT VII 278: CSM II 194; AT VII 318: CSM II 221) and Hobbes (AT VII 191–92: CSM II 134).

[8] Second Replies, Geometric Exposition (AT VII 160: CSM II 113). See also *Principles*, 1, 9; Second Meditation (AT VII 28: CSM II 19).

While sensory perception, imagination, and pure understanding are various modes of perception, desire, aversion, assertion, denial, and doubt are various modes of willing.

When speaking of the operations of the intellect, Descartes often uses "thought," "idea," and "perception" interchangeably. But whereas "perception" in the strict sense denotes the operation of the intellect, the word "idea" signifies both the act of perceiving and the immediate content of this act. Descartes famously writes in the Preface to the *Meditations* that "there is an ambiguity here in the word 'idea'. 'Idea' can be taken materially, as an operation of the intellect, in which case it cannot be said to be more perfect than me. Alternatively, it can be taken objectively, as the thing represented by that operation" (AT VII 8: CSM II 7). Given the twofold meaning of "idea," the question arises as to whether clarity and distinctness are features of the act of perceiving or of the content perceived. Descartes' usage of the predicates "clear" and "distinct," or of their complements, "obscure" and "confused," can hardly help us decide on this point. He applies these predicates to a wide range of mental events, including perceptions, ideas, representations, notions, and conceptions, and also frequently speaks of perceiving, understanding, thinking, or conceiving things clearly and distinctly.

A prevalent interpretation of clarity and distinctness views them as features of the *content* perceived, that is, of "idea" taken objectively. On this interpretation, which we may call "intentional" (following Patterson 2008), the clarity and distinctness of an idea depend on the extent to which its content conforms to the nature of the thing it represents – the thing it is of. Kurt Smith, for example, suggests that an idea of A is clear only if it exhibits the element or elements that constitute the nature or essence of A, as well as the relations between them when A is complex. An idea is distinct if its elements are sharply separated from the elements of other ideas (Smith 2001: 294, 296). Sarah Patterson too proposes an intentional interpretation of the issue. She thus writes: "The perception of x becomes distinct through our ensuring that there is nothing included in it that does not belong to the nature of x. So a perception becomes clearer and more distinct by including in it more that belongs to the nature of its object, and excluding from it anything that does not belong to that nature" (Patterson 2008: 228). An intentional account of clarity and distinctness is also suggested by any interpretation viewing confused and obscure ideas as *misrepresentations* of their objects. A notable example is Margaret Wilson's later account of the representational character of sensory ideas (1990). She claims that Descartes' hybrid conception of representation involves two elements, one "presentational," the other "referential." Any idea, then, represents in two respects: it *referentially* represents the thing of which it is an idea, and it *presentationally* represents whatever it *appears* to be of, that is, whatever it *appears* to referentially represent (1990: 7–8).[9] Wilson argues that Descartes allows for an idea to present its object to the mind as other than it is: "an idea's being an idea of **n** – its representing **n** – does *not* preclude that the idea presents **n** as other than it is" (1990: 7). Such a disparity between the idea's presentational and referential objects occurs whenever the idea is obscure or confused. Referring to Descartes' statement in the Fourth Replies that the confused and obscure idea of cold "is referred to something other than that of which it is in fact the idea"(AT VII 233: CSM II 163), Wilson writes: "The idea is, referentially, the idea of *cold*; it presents, however, something else ... what the idea referentially represents is not what it presentationally represents: that is why Descartes can say that the idea of cold is referred to something other than that of which it is in fact the idea" (1990: 9).[10]

In explaining obscurity and confusion in terms of the conformity between the content the idea exhibits to the mind and the thing it actually represents, the intentional interpretation seems to conflate clarity and distinctness with truth. Since "truth" denotes for Descartes "the conformity of thought with its object,"[11] it is hard to see how a confused or obscure idea, *qua* a misrepresentation of its objects, can be other than false.

Alan Gewirth addresses another aspect of this difficulty: "if clarity and distinctness were qualities consisting in some direct relation between the idea and the thing it purports to represent, the mind, not knowing the thing without the idea, could never know whether it had attained these qualities" (1943: 254). Clarity and distinctness "cannot in their essential nature be the same as truth; it remains that they are qualities internal to ideas and perceptive acts" (1943: 254; see also 1941: 369–75). Gewirth's own interpretation is also intentional but, to avoid the above difficulty, he explains clarity and distinctness in terms of the relation between the idea's direct and interpretive contents. The situation where clearness and distinctness enter, he writes, "involves not merely the passive apprehension of a directly perceived content, but also some interpretation with

[9] Wilson indicates that an idea's presentational content "coincides with what the mind takes itself to be aware of ... regardless of what may actually be going on in the world or (otherwise) in me" (1990: 20 n. 10).
[10] For further versions of intentional interpretations of clarity and distinctness see, for instance, Danto (1978); Beyssade (1992); and Hoffman (1996).
[11] To Mersenne, October 16, 1639 (AT II 597: CSMK 139).

regard to that content" (1943: 258). "What is directly perceived may be other, or less, than what the mind interprets or wishes to interpret itself to be perceiving" (p. 260). An idea is clear, according to Gewirth, if its interpretive content includes all that is included in its direct content, and distinct if the interpretation includes nothing else (p. 260). "In most general terms," he concludes, "the clearness and distinctness of an idea may be said to consist in the 'equality' of its direct and interpretive contents" (1943: 260).[12]

While evading the obstacle of conflating clarity and distinctness with truth, Gewirth's interpretation might encounter another difficulty, quite similar to the one it intends to avoid. Given that a confused or obscure idea cannot be said to have two different contents of which the mind is simultaneously aware, how can the mind ever decide whether the idea's interpretive content (of which it is immediately aware) presents the idea's direct content as it really is? Moreover, if we explain the mind's immediate interpretive function (of perceiving things *as* being such and such) in intentional terms, namely, in terms of an extra interpretive *content* of which the mind is immediately aware, we might be led to accept that one and the same idea can have a long series of intentional objects. On Gewirth's interpretation, the mind's awareness of the idea's direct content is said to require the presence of an interpretive content mediating between the mind's gaze and the idea's direct content. But then, to attend to the idea's interpretive content, the mind would have to attend to an extra-interpretive content, awareness of which might require the presence of another interpretive content, and so forth. This may result in the mind's inability to ever become acquainted with the direct content of ideas that come before it.[13]

A different approach explains clarity and distinctness in terms of the way these ideas affect the mind. Peter Markie, for example, interprets clear and distinct perception in terms of psychological certainty (1986: 186–92). Harry Frankfurt alludes to a normative indubitability when he writes that "clear and distinct perception is a matter of recognizing that there are no

[12] Gewirth contends that in the context of science, which deals with the essence of things, the equality relation is logical, that is, the connection between the two contents must be necessary. The minimum requirement for an idea to be clear, he suggests, is that whatever the content taken as basic, the other should include the "formal nature" (*ratio formalis*) of its object, which Descartes describes in the *Principles* as the "leading property which constitutes its nature and essence" (I, 53). And the minimum requirement for an idea to be distinct, according to Gewirth, is "that nothing contradictory to the essence of its object be included in it" (1943: 261).
[13] For further reasons against treating the interpretive function of the intellect in terms of an auxiliary, secondary object, see Bolton (1986: 395).

reasonable grounds on which a proposition can be doubted" (1970: 135). A proposition is clearly perceived, according to Frankfurt, "when the perceiver recognizes that his evidential basis for it excludes all reasonable grounds for doubting it. A perception is distinct, on the other hand, when the perceiver understands what is and what is not entailed by the evidential basis that renders his perception clear" (p. 137).[14] Although Descartes does insist that the will cannot resist assenting to the intellect's clear and distinct perceptions,[15] neither the will's compulsion nor the intellect's recognition of it can explain what is it that clarity and distinctness consist in. Descartes writes in the *Principles* that "a perception which can serve as the basis for a certain and indubitable judgment needs to be not merely clear but also distinct" (I, 45). Given that the idea's clarity and distinctness are the basis for the evidence of the will, these features cannot consist in the intellect's awareness of the effect they have on the will.[16]

Martha Bolton suggests a different perspective on this issue. She offers several significant reasons to show that "it would be fatal for Descartes to hold that the cognitive content of an idea can diverge from the object of the idea, that it does so when the idea is confused or obscure" (1986: 393). Assuming that "an idea cannot falsely *exhibit* its object" (p. 394), Bolton explains obscurity and confusion in terms of the distinction between what an idea *appears* to exhibit (and represent), and what it *actually* does. A confused and obscure idea, she states, "seems to exhibit its object in a way in which it does not actually exhibit it" (p. 395).[17] In Bolton's

---

[14] Acknowledging that this account of clear perception precludes the possibility of any variations in degree of clarity, Frankfurt suggests another sense in which Descartes employs the term "clear perception." A perception is clear, in this second sense, "when it contains nothing of which [the perceiver] is ignorant" (1970: 141). Rather than referring to the perceiver's "appreciation of the state of his evidence" for the relevant proposition, this latter sense, which I endorse below, refers to the extent to which the perceiver understands what the proposition involves (p. 193).

[15] See, for example, Fourth Meditation (AT VII 58–59: CSM II 41); Fifth Meditation (AT VII 65: CSM II 45; AT VII 69–70: CSM II 48); Second Replies (AT VII 145–46: CSM II 104; AT VII 166: CSM II 117); Seventh Replies (AT VII 460: CSM II 309); to Regius, May 24, 1640 (AT III 64: CSMK 147); *Principles*, I, 43; to Mesland, May 2, 1644 (AT IV 115–16: CSMK 233–34).

[16] Edwin Curley appears to acknowledge these considerations when he claims that Descartes apparently does not wish to define clarity and distinctness in terms of the assent-compelling property of clear and distinct propositions (1978: 119). But the account he offers in a later work can hardly meet this requirement: "Having a clear and distinct idea of a thing, or of a kind of thing ... is a matter of seeing what is and what is not involved in being that thing or a thing of that kind. More precisely, it is a matter of recognizing that there are certain properties we cannot but ascribe to a thing of that kind (clarity) and others which we are not at all compelled to ascribe to it (distinctness)" (1986: 169–70). See also Carriero (2008).

[17] Bolton appears to be suggesting that when an idea is obscure or confused, the mind is undetermined about the object it actually exhibits and represents (1986: 396). On these grounds, she argues that a confused and obscure idea does not positively lead us to err but only "gives us opportunity to judge its object in the context of ill-considered assumptions" (ibid.; see also p.

reading, then, whether an idea is obscure and confused is a function of how the mind *regards* the content that the idea exhibits to immediate awareness, not of whether the idea truly exhibits whatever it represents. But unlike Gewirth, she holds that Descartes did not mean that what the idea *seems* to exhibit constitutes "a sort of second, phantom object of thought," accompanying and obscuring the actual object of the idea (p. 395). Instead, she suggests that a confused or obscure idea, though portraying its object correctly, "represents by means that are not evident from the idea itself." Owing to the obscurity of the means through which such an idea portrays its object, the mind may fail to recognize what it actually exhibits and represents:

To someone who makes a false assumption about its representative device ... a confused and obscure idea seems to represent something it does not. Such an idea portrays its object by obscure means. A person who understands the means correctly apprehends the idea's object; one who misunderstands them is likely to make errors about its object, but still has an idea that correctly exhibits it. (1986: 395)[18]

The interpretation offered in this chapter endorses Bolton's principal thesis that an idea cannot exhibit the thing it represents to immediate awareness as other than it is, pointing to the significant explanatory power of this thesis and its substantial textual support. To appreciate the force of this approach, we need first to take a closer look at Descartes' notions of objective reality and objective being.

2 OBJECTIVE REALITY IN THE THIRD MEDITATION

Early in the Third Meditation, Descartes classifies his thoughts into different kinds in order to find "which of them can properly be said to be the bearers of truth or falsity" (AT VII 37: CSM II 25). He introduces three successive classifications, of which the first marks off ideas from judgments, volitions, and emotions, on the grounds that only ideas have what Wilson calls "representational character." Descartes states that some of his thoughts are "as it were the images of things (*tanquam rerum imagines*), and it is only in these cases that the term 'idea' is strictly appropriate" (AT

390). I address this point below, when presenting my view of how obscure and confused ideas may provide subject-matter for error.

[18] Analyzing Descartes' account of sensory ideas in the Sixth Meditation, Bolton suggests that making wrong assumptions about how such ideas represent would be to treat each one of them in isolation as having representative character. By contrast, to understand these means correctly is to recognize that, in the present case, the relevant unit of representation is a more complex body of experience in which these ideas are elements (1986: 399–400).

VII 37: CSM II 25). By this statement, as Wilson points out, Descartes means not only that ideas have objects according to which they are classified (as ideas of God, of heat or cold, etc.), but also that "ideas are received by the mind *as if exhibiting to it* various things – or as if making things cognitively accessible" (1978: 102).

The distinctive feature of ideas that makes them the locus of truth and falsehood is that they "purport" to represent things (real beings) outside themselves.[19] Every idea is immediately received by the mind as a representation of a thing (*res*), that is, a possibly existing being, irrespective of whether it does in fact represent a thing (in which case it is true), or a non-thing (*non res*, in which case it is false). In saying that every idea is "as if of a thing," therefore, Descartes does not commit himself to the claim that every idea represents a real being. And since the reality of finite things entails their possible rather than their actual existence, to say of an idea that it represents a "thing" is not equivalent to saying that it represents an actual being.

When Descartes claims that ideas are "as it were the images of things," moreover, he does not mean that all ideas are images of the things they represent. He repeatedly indicates that the term "idea" does not signify the images of material things depicted in the corporeal imagination.[20] And besides denying the material character of ideas, he also clarifies that ideas do not necessarily bear a *pictorial* resemblance to their external objects.[21] And yet, even though *exact* resemblance is not necessary for representation, in order to be capable of informing the mind about the nature of things, as I show below, ideas taken objectively must resemble the things they represent.[22] Thus, in claiming that ideas are "as it were the images of things," Descartes might be willing to assert that ideas are immediately received by the mind as if resembling the things they purport to represent.

---

[19] In the next section, I address the question of how this reading is compatible with Descartes' subsequent statement that ideas "considered solely in themselves" cannot, strictly speaking, be false (AT VII 37: CSM II 26).

[20] Second Replies (AT VII 160–61: CSM II 113); Third Replies (AT VII 181: CSM II 127); Fifth Replies (AT VII 366: CSM II 253).

[21] In the *Optics*, for instance, Descartes says that "in order to have sensory perception the soul does not need to contemplate any images resembling the thing which it perceives" (AT VI 114: CSM I 166). Likewise, he writes in *The World* that "although everyone is commonly convinced that the ideas we have in our mind are wholly similar to the objects from which they proceed, nevertheless I cannot see any reason which assures us that this is so" (AT XI 3: CSM I 81). Ideas need not wholly resemble the objects from which they proceed any more than words need to resemble the things they signify or tears the sadness they express (AT XI 3–5: CSM I 81–82).

[22] See also Normore (1986: 235–37); Alanen (2003: 113–22).

Descartes' second classification in the Third Meditation is based on which of his thoughts can contain formal falsity or error. This classification, which I address later in this chapter, groups judgments into one class, and ideas, volitions, and emotions into another. In his third classification, Descartes sorts his ideas into three categories, according to their apparent origin: "some ideas appear to be innate, some to be adventitious, and others to have been invented by me" (AT VII 37–38: CSM II 26). While innate ideas "seem to derive simply from my own nature," Descartes explains, adventitious ideas – those I possess while hearing a noise, seeing the sun, or feeling the fire – appear to "come from things which are located outside me." Finally, some I take to be "my own invention," such as the idea of sirens, or of hippogriffs, and the like (AT VII 38: CSM II 37). Laying the foundations for his first proof of God's existence, Descartes focuses on the second, adventitious category of ideas and asks: "what is my reason for thinking that they resemble these things?" Descartes recognizes in himself a natural disposition to believe that these ideas are produced by external things and to regard these ideas as images of them. But since this natural disposition is but a blind impulse and is not derived from the natural light of reason, it might be thoroughly misleading. Not only could these ideas be produced by some mental faculty within himself of which he is ignorant, but even if these ideas do come from external things, as they purport to do, they might still not resemble these things (AT VII 38–39: CSM II 26–27). Descartes finds another way of investigating the issue, and this brings him to draw a distinction between the "formal" and the "objective" reality of ideas:

In so far as ideas are considered simply as modes of thought, there is no recognizable inequality among them: they all appear to come from within me in the same fashion. But in so far as different ideas are considered as images which represent different things, it is clear that they differ widely. Undoubtedly, the ideas which represent substances to me amount to something more and, so to speak, contain within themselves more objective reality than the ideas which merely represent modes or accidents. (AT VII 40: CSM II 27–28)

Formal reality, which Descartes also calls "formal being" (*esse formale*), generally refers to the *actual* existence of things, either mental or corporeal. Ideas possess formal reality by virtue of being modes of the mind, the thinking substance. Considered simply as modes of thought, or mental events, with no reference to their specific object or content, all ideas share the same degree of formal reality. But ideas also have objective reality (*realitas objectiva*), by virtue of their representative character. Considered "as images which represent different things," ideas may differ from one another in the degree of objective reality they contain, in accordance with the degree of formal reality they represent. An idea of a substance contains more objective reality than an idea of a mode, and the idea of God contains more objective reality than the idea of any finite substance.[23] When asked by Hobbes to consider afresh what "more reality" means, Descartes simply repeats the same ontological hierarchy of God, created substances, and accidents or modes (AT VII 185: CSM II 130). This suggests that an idea's degree of objective reality accords with its object's degree of ontological independence. As I show in the next section, moreover, an idea possesses objectively the same degree of reality that the thing of which it is an idea possesses formally. And when the object of the idea is a possible, non-actual existent, the idea possesses objectively the same degree of reality that the thing of which it is an idea would have possessed had it existed in actual reality.[24] In the Second Replies, accordingly, Descartes defines the objective reality of an idea, which he also calls "objective perfection" or "objective intricacy," as "the being of the thing which is represented by an idea, in so far as this exists in the idea" (AT VII 161: CSM II 113).[25]

While the *object* that an idea represents might be a non-actual, possible existent, the idea's objective reality must have a formally existing *cause*. Descartes embraces the scholastic causal principle that "there must be at least as much reality in the efficient and total cause as in the effect of that cause" (AT VII 40: CSM II 28).[26] Any effect must be produced by an actual cause that contains, either formally (actually) or eminently (in some higher form), everything to be found in the effect. Otherwise, if we admit that there can be something in the effect that was not previously present in the cause, we shall have to admit that this something was

---

[23] See also Second Replies (AT VII 165–66: CSM II 117); *Principles*, I, 17.

[24] See also Kaufman (2000: 393–94). Alanen appears to confine this to clear and distinct ideas (2003: 155). Cf. Nelson, who holds that "Descartes conceives objective reality as quantifiable into exactly three discrete degrees or levels": the modal level, the finite substantial level, and the infinite substantial level (that of the idea of God) (1996: 17). In virtue of their objective reality, says Nelson, ideas represent the amount of formal reality their efficient and total causes have, irrespective of their particular objects (1996: 16–18 and n. 9). For a recent critical analysis of Nelson's interpretation, see Brown (2008: 199–200).

[25] The phrase "objective perfection" appears also in the *Principles*, where Descartes states that "the greater the objective perfection in any of our ideas, the greater its cause must be" (I, 17). See also a letter to Regius, June 1642 (AT III 566: CSMK 214). For Descartes' use of "objective intricacy" see, e.g., First Replies (AT VII 103–05: CSM II 75–76).

[26] As Kenneth Clatterbaugh observes (1980: 382), Descartes does not specify in what conditions an efficient cause is total and, except for God, he does not give any examples of a total efficient cause. But since he also applies this principle to finite causes sufficient to produce an alteration in bodies or in the soul, we may assume that a total efficient cause, as used in this principle, signifies something whose presence is sufficient to bring about an alteration in the effect.

produced by nothing (Second Replies, AT VII 135: CSM II 97). A cause contains the reality of its effect formally when the reality of the effect exists in the cause in the same way it exists in the effect, and eminently when the cause does not exemplify the properties of its effect but still has some higher properties by virtue of which it can serve the same function as a cause that exactly resembles its effect. For example, God contains the extended substance eminently rather than formally because his nature differs essentially from that of the corporeal substance it produces, but still contains the nature of this effect in a higher form. Applying this causal principle to the objective reality of ideas, Descartes states that "in order for a given idea to contain such and such objective reality, it must surely derive it from some cause which contains at least as much formal reality as there is objective reality in the idea" (AT VII 41: CSM II 28–29).[27]

If we combine the Third Meditation discussion of formal and objective *reality* with the distinction in the Preface to the *Meditations* between the material and objective *senses* of "idea," Descartes' position may be stated as follows: insofar as we consider "ideas" in the material sense, namely, as operations of the intellect, they all have the same degree of formal reality. But taken objectively, as the things *represented* by this operation (AT VII 8: CSM II 7), ideas have an intrinsic representative function.[28] When we think of them as *representing* things outside themselves, ideas possess a certain degree of objective reality that cannot exceed the degree of formal reality they represent. In the Fourth Replies, moreover, Descartes tells Arnauld that when we think of ideas "as representing something we are

---

[27] The notion of eminent containment allows Descartes, *inter alia*, to account for the possibility that the content of an idea will not exactly resemble its actual object or cause but would still satisfy the correspondence condition. In the Second Replies, as Hoffman points out (1996: 375), Descartes refers to the eminent container not merely, as he does in the *Meditations*, as the cause of the idea, but as the idea's object: "Whatever exists in the object of our ideas in a way which exactly corresponds to our perception of it is said to exist *formally* in those objects. Something is said to exist *eminently* in an object when, although it does not exactly correspond to our perception of it, its greatness is such that it can fill the role of that which does so correspond" (Second Replies, AT VII 161: CSM II 114).

[28] This issue, I should note, is in dispute. Some scholars suggest, on various grounds, that objective reality is a feature of the act of thinking (idea taken materially) and not of ideas taken objectively. See, e.g., Wells (1990); Clarke (2003: 191); Wee (2006a: 44–45). Alanen also holds that Cartesian ideas are representational acts or modes of the mind that represent by virtue of the objective reality they contain or display to the mind (2003: 128). And according to Costa, while it is the perceptual act that is representative, the object of thought (as represented by this act) has objective reality (1983: 540). In the next section, I address this issue in the wider context of Descartes' notion of representation. I side with Chappell (1986: 189–90), Kaufman (2000: 386), and Hoffman (2002: 167–68, 178 n. 11), who hold that ideas taken objectively, apart from being the thing represented by ideas taken materially, are themselves representative and, as such, contain different degrees of objective reality.

taking them not *materially* but *formally*" (AT VII 232: CSM II 163). The formal *sense* of ideas should not be confused with the ontological notion of formal *reality*, which is an attribute of ideas in the material sense. Whereas formal reality is an attribute of ideas taken materially, objective reality is an attribute of ideas taken objectively or formally.

Let us now proceed to explore the kind of relation prevailing between ideas (taken objectively) and the things they represent. For this purpose, we need to examine Descartes' closely related notion of "objective being" (*esse objective*), which is the mode of being that things have in the intellect when known or conceived (that is, when represented by ideas).

3 OBJECTIVE BEING AND REPRESENTATION IN THE FIRST REPLIES

In the Second Replies, as noted, Descartes equates the objective reality of an idea (*realitas objectiva ideae*) with "the being of the thing (*entitas rei*) which is represented by an idea, in so far as this exists in the idea" (AT VII 161: CSM II 113). This formulation suggests that the objective reality of an idea coincides with the objective being of the thing it represents, which is the mode of being things have in the intellect when thought of (AT VII 102: CSM II 75).[29] As Steven Nadler rightly emphasizes (1989: 159), while objective *reality* is an attribute of *ideas* (those representing possible existents), objective *being* is not to be properly attributed to ideas (unless they are themselves the objects of other ideas) but rather to *things*, insofar as they are represented by ideas.[30]

To have objective being in the intellect, a thing need not be an actual existent. Every real being, either actual (such as the sun), or possible (such as geometrical figures having "true and immutable natures"), might exist objectively in the intellect by being thought of.[31] This objective mode of

---

[29] A similar reading is implied in Ayers' contention that "to be concerned with an idea in so far as it has objective reality, is to be concerned with its object in so far as it has objective being" (1998: 1067). Normore also suggests such a reading when he claims that "if an idea has objective reality, and is thus *of* a thing, that thing possibly exists. This suggests the equation of the objective reality of an idea with the objective existence (the *esse objectivum*) of its object and the objective existence of an object with the possible existence of that object" (1986: 238).

[30] Some Cartesian scholars use "objective being" and "objective reality" as equivalents (e.g., Nolan 1997: 192 n. 22; Wells 1990), whereas others insist on the need to distinguish between them, suggesting different accounts of this distinction. See, for example, Chappell (1986: 190); Normore (1986: 238); Nadler (1989: 159); Field (1993: 318–19 n. 10); Nelson (1996: 16–20); Kaufman (2000: 392); Alanen (2003: 122–37); Brown (2008: 200–01, 207).

[31] In the First Replies, Descartes accordingly argues that the objective being of true and immutable natures requires a formal cause: "even if the nature of the triangle is immutable and eternal, it is still no less appropriate to ask why there is an idea of it within us" (AT VII 104: CSM II 76).

being, Descartes clarifies, is of course much less perfect than that possessed by things existing outside the intellect, but it is not simply nothing and, as such, requires a cause (AT VII 103: CSM II 75). As he writes in the Third Meditation, "the mode of being by which a thing exists objectively or representatively in the intellect by way of an idea, imperfect though it may be, is certainly not nothing, and so it cannot come from nothing" (AT VII 41: CSM II 29).[32] The latter view was challenged by Caterus in the First Objections:

But what is "objective being in the intellect"? According to what I was taught, this is simply the determination of an act of the intellect by means of an object. And this is merely an extraneous label which adds nothing to the thing itself . . . So why should I look for a cause of something which is not actual, and which is simply an empty label, a non-entity? (AT VII 92: CSM II 66–67)

In his reply, Descartes concedes that thinking about a thing external to the mind adds nothing intrinsic to that thing. With respect to this external object, then, "objective being in the intellect" is indeed no more than an extrinsic denomination. But Descartes clarifies that in speaking of the objective being of the *res cogitatea* (the thing thought of), he "was speaking of the idea, which is never outside the intellect, and in this sense 'objective being' simply means being in the intellect in the way in which objects are normally there" (AT VII 102: CSM II 74). Descartes further illustrates this point:

By this I mean that the idea of the sun is the sun itself existing in the intellect – not of course formally existing, as it does in the heavens, but objectively existing, i.e., in the way in which objects normally are in the intellect. Now this mode of being is of course much less perfect than that possessed by things which exist

---

[32] The scholastic background of Descartes' distinction between the formal and the objective reality of ideas, and especially his debt to Francisco Suárez, has been widely discussed in the literature. See, e.g., Cronin (1966); Normore (1986); Nadler (1989: 147ff.); Wells (1990); Ayers (1998: 1062–69); Secada (2000). For further references, see Alanen (2003: 294–95 n. 15). Dealing with this controversial issue, however, exceeds the bounds of this study. For Suárez, roughly, when we think of a thing, the act by which we conceive of that thing is called the "formal concept" (1965: II, 1. 1). The formal concept is thus essentially or formally representative. The objective concept, by contrast, is the thing which is immediately known or represented by the formal concept (Suárez 1965: II, 1. 1). While the formal concept, *qua* an actual modification of the mind, is "a true and positive thing," the objective concept might be either a real thing (possible or actual) or a mere "being of reason" (*ens rationis*), which is a non-possible essence or existent. According to Suárez, moreover, things that are known or represented by the formal concept do not intrinsically inhere "in" the intellect in an objective mode of being. The thing known, as Wells points out (1990: 41), is characterized as a concept only by way of extrinsic denomination, as a way of talking about the thing represented by the formal concept. While inheriting the late scholastic terminology, Descartes insists, however, that the objective mode of being by which a thing exists in the intellect is a real mode of being, therefore requiring an efficient cause.

outside the intellect; but, as I did explain, it is not therefore simply nothing. (AT VII 102–03: CSM II 75)

Granted that by "the objective being of the sun" Descartes refers to the idea of the sun rather than (as Caterus has it) to the sun itself existing in the heavens, we may suggest that for Descartes to think of the *actual* sun, or to have an idea of it, is precisely to be immediately aware of the objective being the sun has in the intellect. Kenny locates a pitfall in Descartes' argument. He thinks it may imply that thinking about the sun or having an idea of the sun would amount to "thinking about the idea of the sun" (1968: 116). But for Descartes, as Kenny himself concedes, to be immediately aware of the objective sun or to have an idea of the sun is to think of the *actual* sun and not of its idea.[33]

But what exactly is it for the sun to exist objectively "in" the intellect and thus to have a mode of being different from that it has in the sky? The literature offers two major kinds of responses to this question, in accordance with two different readings of Descartes' notion of representation. The first, commonly called representationalism, holds that we perceive extra-mental objects by being immediately aware of ideas (taken objectively) as representative entities mediating between the mind and the world.[34] In this conception, Cartesian perceptions or mental acts are intentional by being directed to ideas (taken objectively) as their immediate objects. When I think of the actual sun, for instance, the sun exists objectively in my intellect as an internal, intentional *object* of thought. The objective sun has, in and by itself, a representational character through which it represents the actual sun existing in the heavens. The objective being of the actual sun resembles its formal being but still possesses a different ontological status. In Ayers' formulation (1998: 1068), the distinction between the formal sun and the objective sun is a real distinction rather than a distinction of reason. In recent years, however, the growing tendency among scholars is to read Descartes as holding a different conception of representation, usually called direct realism.[35] In this reading, when we perceive an extra-mental thing, the immediate object of our perception is the thing itself and not the idea of that thing

[33] Kenny proposes that "for Descartes, the *res cogitata* that exists in my mind when I think of the sun is not the sun itself, but some proxy for the sun" (1968: 114).
[34] For a defense of the representationalist reading of Descartes see, e.g., Gewirth (1943); Gilson (1967: 206); Kenny (1968: 114–16); Chappell (1986); Wilson (1994: 215ff.); Nolan (1997: 175ff.); Ayers (1998: 1067–68); Kaufman (2000); Hoffman (2002).
[35] See, e.g., Yolton (1984: 34–49); Nadler (1989: 157–65); Alanen (1990, esp. 355–62; 2003: 128–37); Clarke (2003: 190–95); Brown (2006: 109–15; 2008: 200ff.); Patterson (2008: 217–18).

as an entity mediating between the thing and the mind. John Yolton, for example, holds that ideas are simply acts of perception, mental activities, and not objects or "entities" intervening between the mind and the thing perceived. According to Yolton, the objective being of a thing in the idea is just the cognitive *meaning* of that thing (1984: 35). To speak of the objective existence of things "in the understanding" does not imply any ontic commitment. To say a thing is "in the understanding" simply means it is *understood* (1984: 37–38). Nadler also contends that, for Descartes, to say that the sun exists objectively in my idea is just to say that the sun is represented by the idea-act (1989: 161). What makes a mental act intentional is the content it possesses, which is an intrinsic feature of this act. Mental acts "are not aimed at a content, but possess a content within themselves" (1989: 146). According to Nadler, the objective reality of an idea *is* its representational content and, as such, confers intentionality on the idea-act, namely, makes it an idea-act *of* this or that particular object. The idea-act's representational content (or objective reality) is something inherent in or intrinsic to the idea-act itself (1989: 159–62).

Alanen, who also defends the direct realist interpretation, holds that the objective being of the thing thought of is not an entity or an object mediating between the external object and the mind, but she specifies the objective being of the *res cogitata* as "the thing itself as thinkable" (2003: 128). She states that the objective reality of an idea, or the idea taken objectively, is "the thing thought of in its objective (possible) being, without its formal (actual) being"; it is the "thinkability or possibility" of the thing the idea is of, "which remains what it is whether or not actually conceived" (p. 135). On these grounds, Alanen holds that ideas are *identical* with the things they represent: "My thought of, say, a particular goat is identical with the particular goat though having a different ontological status ... The goat as actual and the goat as thought of is the same entity but with different degrees of reality" (p. 128). Brown takes the identity thesis even further when she reads Descartes' replies to Caterus as suggesting that the distinction between the idea of the sun and the sun itself is only a distinction of reason rather than a real one (Brown 2006: 112–13, and 2008: 202, 213).

In a letter to an unknown correspondent, however, Descartes draws a real distinction between the objective mode of being that things have in the intellect and the mode of existence they have in the world: "if by essence we understand a thing as it is objectively in the intellect, and by existence the same thing in so far as it is outside the intellect, it is manifest that the two are really distinct" (1645 or 1646, AT IV 350: CSMK

281). Explaining Descartes' position in this passage could prove challenging for the "identity thesis" stating that ideas taken objectively are identical with the things they represent. This thesis, moreover, is not entailed by Descartes' replies to Caterus. As Hoffman rightly maintains (2002: 168), "to say that it is the same sun that has these two modes of existence does not imply that the sun as it exists objectively in the mind is identical to the sun as it exists formally in the heavens."[36] But even more significantly, the suggestion that the intentional objects of our perceptual acts are not ideas but external things themselves is incongruous with Descartes' reiterated statement that we know external things *by way of perceiving the ideas inhering in us*. Descartes resorts to this language, for instance, when he writes to Gibieuf: "I can have no knowledge of what is outside me except by means of the ideas I have within me; and so I take great care ... not to attribute to things anything positive which I do not first *perceive in the ideas of them*" (January 19, 1642, AT III 474: CSMK 201; my emphasis). Were Descartes to believe that we perceive external things directly, that is, that the idea-act is immediately directed to an external thing by means of the content it carries within itself, he would not have contended that his perceptual act is directed to the ideas inhering in his mind. I therefore think that in affirming he cannot have knowledge of external things except by *perceiving the ideas* he has of them, what Descartes has in mind is ideas (taken objectively) as the intentional *objects* of the perceptual act.

Indeed, in speaking of the mind's awareness of what exists "in it," Descartes does sometimes refer to the mind's immediate awareness of its mental *acts*. A case in point is his definition of "thought" in the Second Replies, as "everything that is within us in such a way that we are

---

[36] Hoffman suggests a very interesting argument to show that Descartes' theory of cognition is fundamentally Thomistic. In his account, while rejecting the Thomistic view that we have cognition of forms and that a species – a spiritual form – is somehow transmitted from the object and received in the soul, Descartes still accepts the most basic element of that theory: "that we have cognition of things in the world when they come to have another kind of existence – objective existence – in the soul" (2002: 167). What I take to be a most significant insight of Hoffman's interpretation is that it is not contradictory to say "that the same object can have two different ways of being such that as it exists in one way it is really distinct from itself as it exists in another way" (p. 179 n. 44). This interpretation is also found in Hoffman (2009: ch. 11). In an earlier paper, however, Hoffman suggests that, for Descartes, what our ideas seem to represent must exist in those ideas (or in the intellect) objectively (1996: 373). This reading leads him to hold that despite his endorsement of the most fundamental element of the Aristotelian–Thomistic theory of cognition, Descartes still leaves room for ideas containing objective reality to be misrepresentations (pp. 373ff.; see also his 2009: ch. 10). Descartes' thinking, as I will try to show, does not allow for the possibility that ideas containing objective reality would misrepresent the things they are of.

immediately aware of it" (AT VII 160: CSM II 113). The thing within us of which we are immediately aware here seems to be the mental act itself, the idea taken materially, as the explanation that follows confirms: "Thus all the operations of the will, the intellect, the imagination and the senses are thoughts" (AT VII 160: CSM II 113). Yet in the same passage from the Second Replies, Descartes proceeds to define "idea" as "the form [*forma*] of any given thought, *immediate perception of which* makes me aware of the thought" (AT VII 160: CSM II 113; my emphasis). The notion of ideas as "forms" is indeed ambiguous: it may refer to the formal reality of ideas (to "idea" in the material sense as an operation of the mind), or it may refer to the formal sense of "idea," which coincides with its objective sense, as representing this or that thing to the mind. In the Fourth Replies, as noted, Descartes tells Arnauld that "when we think of ideas as representing something we are taking them not *materially* but *formally*" (AT VII 232: CSM II 163). In the above definition, however, Descartes indicates that what makes us aware of any given thought is our *immediate perception of the idea* which is the form of that thought. Clearly, had Descartes believed we perceive external things directly and that what confers intentionality to the perceptual act is the content it intrinsically possesses, he would not have defined "idea" as the form of any given thought which we *immediately perceive.*[37] An idea, *qua* this form, can only be the intentional *object* of thought (of the perceptual act). On these grounds, I hold with Ayers (1998: 1066–68) that, in this definition, Descartes refers to ideas *qua* intentional objects (ideas taken objectively or formally). Descartes then proceeds:

Hence, whenever I express something in words, and understand what I am saying, this very fact makes it certain that there is within me an idea of what is signified by the words in question. Thus it is not only the images depicted in the imagination which I call "ideas." Indeed, in so far as these images are in the corporeal imagination, that is, are depicted in some part of the brain, I do not call them "ideas" at all; I call them "ideas" only in so far as they give form [*informare*] to the mind itself, when it is directed towards that part of the brain. (AT VII 160–61: CSM II 113)

In saying that ideas inform or give form to the mind itself, Descartes suggests that an "idea," *qua* the form of any given thought, confers on the thought its particular identity as a thought of this or that thing. And granted that the idea-as-form, in this definition, refers to the intentional

---

[37] In direct realism, recall, ideas are the perceptual acts themselves and not the intentional objects "which we immediately perceive" by these acts.

object of thought, we may infer that this intentional object structures the mind in a certain way that allows it to identify any of its thoughts as being *of* this or that object.

One of the most compelling reasons leading scholars to embrace a direct realist interpretation of Descartes is to "save" him from the destructive consequences of the notorious conception called "veil of ideas." In this conception, the mind is surrounded by ideas as mental objects standing between itself and the world, without ever being able to *directly* perceive the true nature of things in reality. In a recent paper, Nadler formulates the problem posed by this conception as follows: "since all we ever directly and immediately perceive are ideas, there would be no direct evidence for how things 'really' are – we certainly could not step outside the 'veil of ideas' and compare those things with the ideas – and thus ... no satisfying resolution to the skeptical puzzles with which the work begins" (2006: 90).

Indeed, Descartes attempts to elude this difficulty by adopting the doctrine that "idea" taken objectively is the thing it represents in its objective mode of being. As Hoffman aptly puts it, "the sun as it exists objectively is able to represent the sun as it exists formally in the heavens precisely because it is the same thing that has these two different modes of existence" (1996: 168). But rather than asserting an *identity* between the two modes of being of the *res cogitata* (for example, between the formal mode of being the sun has in the heavens and the objective mode of being it has in the intellect), this doctrine implies a "natural" correspondence between the two modes of being of the same thing. Every idea, as I show below, insofar as it represents a "thing" is a true (corresponding) representation of that thing. The idea taken objectively, as the objective mode of being of the thing thought of, exhibits to the mind the nature or the salient properties of that thing, regardless of whether we perceive it confusedly or distinctly. It is only on account of this conception that Descartes can say that by rendering our perceptions clear and distinct, we become acquainted with the true nature of things as they actually are, even though we cannot step outside the "veil of ideas" surrounding us.

4 TRUE AND FALSE IDEAS

In the Third Meditation, while classifying his thoughts into definite kinds to inquire "which of them can properly be said to be the bearers of truth and falsity," Descartes' first step was to show that only ideas, in the strict sense, are "as it were the images of things" (AT VII 37: CSM II 25). By this

he means, as noted, that only ideas are received by the mind as representations of things external to themselves, to which they bear some kind of
likeness. Other thoughts, which are reduced to volitions, emotions, and
judgments, have "various additional forms": although they apply to ideas,
they do not "purport" to resemble the objects to which they apply, meaning that they lack representational character. This may suggest that only
ideas, by virtue of their representational character, can qualify as the locus
of truth and falsehood. But Descartes then proceeds to argue that ideas,
insofar as they are considered solely in themselves and are not referred to
anything external, "cannot strictly speaking be false" (AT VII 37: CSM
II 26). He then clarifies that "falsity in the strict sense, or formal falsity,
can occur only in judgments" (AT VII 43: CSM II 30). Some scholars have
read these remarks as implying that ideas, strictly speaking, are *neither
true nor false*, and that judgments are the sole locus of falsity and truth.[38]
Others have suggested that these remarks only rule out that ideas could
be false so as to indicate that ideas, strictly speaking, cannot but be true.[39]
Contrary to both these options, I claim that the kind of falsity denied to
ideas in this passage is not propositional but formal. Descartes offers here
a new category for sorting his thoughts based on which of them can contain formal falsity or *error*.[40] The result is a new classification grouping
ideas, volitions, and emotions into one class, and judgments into another.
Descartes states: "Thus the only remaining thoughts where I must be on
my guard against making a mistake are judgments" (AT VII 37: CSM II
26). As I elaborate further in the next chapter, when speaking of erroneous or formally false judgments, Descartes refers to the *acts of judgment*
rather than to the propositional contents to which these acts apply. More
specifically, I will argue that Descartes denotes by "formally false judgment" any act of judgment applied to matters we do not perceive clearly
and distinctly, irrespective of whether the content being judged is in itself
true or false. In claiming that "falsity in the strict sense, or formal falsity,
can occur only in judgments," Descartes is not denying that ideas can
properly be said to be the bearers of truth or falsehood. Rather, formal
falsity cannot be found in ideas for the simple reason that it constitutes a

[38] See, for instance, Kenny (1968: 117); Curley (1975: 173); Williams (1978: 131, 167, 182); Wilson (1978: 108, 141); Gueroult (1984: I, 111); Rosenthal (1986: 409); Van De Pitte, (1988: 461ff.); Hoffman (1996: 359); Nolan (1997: 193 n. 43); Vinci (1998: 14); Nadler (2006: 100).
[39] See, e.g., Wells (1984: 33); Alanen (1994: 243–44, 248; 2003: 149, 160); Nelson (2008: 321).
[40] I thus hold with Gueroult (1984: I, 107–13) that, in this oft-cited passage from the Third Meditation, Descartes suggests three successive enumerations. Readings along these lines may also be found in Grene (1985: 9–12); and Field (1993: 313).

feature of our voluntary *acts of judgment*, not of the propositional contents to which these acts apply.[41]

With these considerations in mind, we may now turn to inquire into the nature of true and false ideas. In a letter to Mersenne of 1639, Descartes presents his nominal definition of truth in terms of "conformity": "the word 'truth,' in the strict sense, denotes the conformity of thought with its object [*denote la conformité de la pensée avec l'object*], but … when it is attributed to things outside thought, it means only that they can be the objects of true thoughts, either ours or God's" (AT II 597: CSMK 139). Strictly speaking, then, truth is an attribute of thoughts, not of things outside the mind. A true thought (idea) is one whose content (intentional object) conforms to the nature of the real object it is of. Yet, in line with his predecessors, Descartes does sometimes attribute truth to things to indicate that they are possible objects of true thoughts, whereby he means that these things are real. In the *Conversation with Burman*, for instance, Descartes is reported to have argued that "all the demonstrations of mathematics deal with true entities and objects," and that "the complete and entire object of mathematics and everything it deals with is a *true and real entity*" (CB 34 = AT V 160: CSMK 343). In the Fifth Meditation, he likewise says that all the properties of a triangle that he can clearly apprehend are true, which means that "they are something, and not merely nothing," irrespective of whether such a figure exists or has ever existed outside the mind: "for it is obvious that whatever is true is something" (AT VII 65: CSM II 45). In a similar vein, Descartes writes to Clerselier that "there is no distinction between truth and the thing or substance that is true" (AT V 355: CSMK 377). Even more explicitly, in the Third Meditation, when reflecting on sensible qualities such as cold, heat, light, and the like, which constitute the objects of his sensory ideas, Descartes treats the predicates "true" and "real" as synonymous. He says that he thinks of these qualities in a very confused and obscure manner, to the extent that he does not even know whether *these qualities* are true

---

[41] Newman makes a strong case for the view that Descartes regards the contents perceived by the intellect as having truth-value independent of the will's assent (see 2008: 339–40, and the textual evidence there referred to). Unlike the reading I propose, however, Newman takes the notion of formal falsity to refer to the proposition judged, not to the act of judging (p. 340). On his reading, when Descartes says that ideas, "provided they are considered solely in themselves and I do not refer them to anything else … cannot strictly speaking be false," he does not mean that *all* ideas without qualification lack truth-value, but only non-relational ideas, those lacking a propositional structure. The main drawback of Newman's reading, in my view, is that it sits uncomfortably with Descartes' subsequent contention in the Third Meditation that "falsity in the strict sense, or formal falsity, can occur only in judgments" (AT VII 43: CSM II 30).

or false, that is, whether the ideas he has of them are ideas of real things or of non-things (AT vii 43: CSM ii 30).

A true (real) object of thought may be an extra-mental existent, such as the sun and all other particular objects possessing formal being outside the mind, or a mode of thinking formally existing in the intellect, such as thinking, willing, fearing, and all other mental activities about which I can reflect by bringing them before my mind as objects of my thoughts. But a true object of thought may also be a non-actual possible existent, such as fictitious entities like Pegasus or the chimera. As opposed to true and immutable natures, fictitious entities "are invented and put together by the intellect" and, as such, "can always be split up by the same intellect, not simply by an abstraction but by a clear and distinct intellectual operation" (First Replies, AT vii 117: CSM ii 83). But insofar as they can be the objects of clear and distinct ideas, fictitious entities are real, possible existents. As Descartes tells Caterus, "possible existence, at the very least, belongs to such a [supremely powerful] being, just as it belongs to all the other things of which we have a distinct idea, even to those which are put together through a fiction of the intellect" (AT vii 119: CSM ii 85). And in a letter to Clerselier he writes that "not even chimeras contain falsehood in themselves" (AT v 354: CSMK 376).[42] Yet another kind of true (real) non-actual objects of thought includes mathematical objects that have "true and immutable natures," independently of whether they exist formally outside the mind and regardless of whether they exist objectively in the mind as intentional objects of occurrent thoughts. In the Fifth Meditation, Descartes finds within himself countless ideas of things that although they may not exist anywhere outside his mind, "still cannot be called nothing; for although in a sense they can be thought of at will, they are not my invention but have their own true and immutable natures" (AT vii 64: CSM ii 44). And in the Fifth Replies he states that there may not be any existing figures corresponding to the perfect figures conceived by the geometer (AT vii 381–82: CSM ii 262). But even if no perfect triangle actually exists anywhere outside thought, as the Fifth Meditation indicates, "there is still a determinate nature, or essence, or form of the triangle which is immutable and eternal, and not invented by me or dependent on my mind" (AT vii 64: CSM ii 45). These true and immutable natures are also independent of whether they are ever

---

[42] See also AT vii 362: CSM ii 250; *Conversation with Burman* (CB 34 = AT v 160: CSMK 343). Yet Descartes is inconsistent about the reality of chimeras. In the Fifth Replies, for instance, he tells Gassendi that the idea of a triangle is superior to the ideas of chimeras, "which cannot possibly be supposed to have existence" (AT vii 383: CSM ii 263).

being thought of. "It is not necessary for me ever to imagine a triangle," Descartes goes on to state, "but whenever I do wish to consider a recti-linear figure having just three angles, it is necessary that I attribute to it the properties which license the inference that its three angles equal no more than two right angles" (AT VII 67–68: CSM II 47). Descartes' theory of essences raises a series of problems that will not concern me here, nor will the interpretive debate concerning the ontological status of true and immutable natures.[43] I will confine myself to observing that their alleged thought-independent status rules out the possibility of under-standing them simply as actual objective beings, namely, as ideas taken objectively.[44] Although true and immutable natures may exist objectively in the mind as the contents of occurrent thoughts, they are still said to be independent of such existence.[45] In treating them as objects of innate ideas (AT III 383: CSMK 183), Descartes appears to regard them not as actual mental occurrences but as potential objective beings.[46] As he explains to Hobbes, "when we say that an idea is innate in us, we do not mean that it is always there before us. This would mean that no idea was innate. We simply mean that we have within ourselves the faculty of summoning up the idea" (Third Replies, AT VII 189: CSM II 132). In the *Comments on a Certain Broadsheet*, he writes that innate ideas "always exist within us potentially, for to exist in some faculty is not to exist actually, but merely potentially" (AT VIIIB 361: CSM I 305).

Possessing a certain degree of objective reality, even if only minimal, suffices for an idea to be true. A false idea, by contrast, is one representing a non-thing (a non-possible entity) and, as such, can have no objective reality. The following passage from the Third Meditation suggests such a

---

[43] Compare, e.g., Kenny (1968: 151–56; 1970: 692–93, 397); Gewirth (1970: 678); Schmaltz (1991); Chappell (1997); Nolan (1997); Cunning (2003); Doney (2005).

[44] Such a conceptualist interpretation of true and immutable natures appears in Chappell (1997: 122, 123), who argues that all universals are ideas in the objective sense. In an earlier work, however, Chappell expresses a more qualified view, whereby mathematical objects may have a mode of being distinct from objective being, in which case they are an exception to Descartes' general view that universals are merely ideas or concepts (1986: 196–97, ns. 20, 23).

[45] For Descartes' discussion of the stimulus that activates a disposition, see, for example, *Comments on a Certain Broadsheet* (AT VIIIB 360: CSM I 305); Fifth Replies (AT VII 382: CSM II 262). See also Jolley (1990: 36–39).

[46] To say that true and immutable natures are potential or possible objective beings surely does not explain what exactly their ontological status is *qua* possible objects of true thoughts: whether they inhere potentially in the mind (as in Wells 1990), or whether they constitute Third-Realm Platonic entities, which are neither extending beings nor objective beings in the mind (as in Kenny 1970). Other scholars suggest viewing these natures as identified with God's decrees (Schmaltz 1991: 137–39), or, alternatively, with the objects having those true and immutable natures (Cunning 2003).

reading. Discussing the ontological status of his sensory ideas, Descartes maintains:

For on the one hand, *if they are false, that is, represent non-things*, I know by the natural light that they arise from nothing – that is, they are in me only because of a deficiency and lack of perfection in my nature. *If on the other hand they are true, then since the reality which they represent* is so extremely slight that I cannot even distinguish it from a non-thing, I do not see why they cannot originate from myself. (Third Meditation, AT VII 44: CSM II 30; my emphases)

This passage clearly indicates that for an idea to be true, it is both necessary and sufficient for it to represent a thing possessing a certain degree of reality, even if extremely slight. And granted that a true idea contains objectively the same degree of reality or being that the thing of which it is an idea possesses formally (or would have possessed if it existed in actual reality), we may infer that all and only ideas containing a certain degree of objective reality are true, *qua* representations of "things."[47]

In reducing the truth of an idea to the reality of its object or, equivalently, to the objective reality of the idea itself, Descartes does not abandon his definition of truth in terms of the conformity of thought with its object. Rather, when telling Caterus that an idea representing a thing such as the sun is just that thing with a different (objective) mode of being, I take him to mean that insofar as an idea represents a thing, a real object, the objective being of that thing must conform to its actual being. This is tantamount to saying that every idea that represents a thing, however confusedly, cannot fail to exhibit to the mind the nature or essence of that thing *as it really is*. The objective being of the thing thought of, I suggest, is what Descartes has in mind when he writes to Mersenne: "by the term 'idea' I mean in general everything which is in our mind when we conceive something, *no matter how we conceive it*" (AT III 392–93: CSMK 185; my emphasis). Additional evidence is found in his letter to Gibieuf:

I am certain that I can have no knowledge of what is outside me except by means of the ideas I have within me; and so I take great care ... not to attribute to things anything positive which I do not first perceive in the ideas of

---

[47] I should note that the more common interpretation holds that Descartes identifies the representational character of ideas (their being *tanquam rerum imagines*) with their objective reality, and accordingly assumes that all ideas, by their very nature, have both (see, e.g., Gueroult (1984: I, 108); Nadler (1989: 162–64); Wilson (1990: 9–10, 12–14); Hoffman (1996: 373; 2009: 157); Nelson (1996: 16–17); Brown (2006: 94). Contrary to this view, I hold that all ideas have representational character, but only *true* ideas (those representing possible beings) can have objective reality. See also Wilson (1978: 106, 108–09, 111–14); Normore (1986: 230); Alanen (1990: 360); Wee (2006a: 44–45).

them. *But I think also that whatever is to be found in these ideas is necessarily also in the things themselves.* (January 19, 1642, AT III 474: CSMK 201; my emphasis)

Descartes writes in a similar vein to Clerselier: "if one has no idea, i.e., no perception which corresponds [*réponde*] to the meaning of the word 'God,' it is no use saying that one believes that *God* exists" (AT IXA 210: CSM II 273). And he tells Gassendi that "an idea represents the essence of a thing, and if anything is added to or taken away from the essence, then the idea automatically becomes the idea of something else" (AT VII 371: CSM II 256). I take these passages to indicate that every idea that represents a thing (and, as such, contains objective reality) exhibits to the mind the nature or essence of its object as it really is. The conformity between an idea and the thing it represents lies at the very essence of representation. The clarity and distinctness of an idea, by contrast, are features of the act of perceiving rather than of the content (intentional object) perceived, as the next section will show.

To conform to the nature or essence of the thing it represents, however, an idea need not contain objectively *all* the essential properties of that thing. Otherwise, we could not possibly have a true idea of God, the infinite being. Descartes thus writes to Gassendi: "You repeat the same mistake in this section when you deny that we have a true idea of God. For even though we do not know everything which is in God, nonetheless all the attributes that we do recognize to be in him are truly there" (AT VII 368: CSM II 254). A true idea must contain a sufficient number of salient or essential properties of the thing it represents so as to enable the mind, whenever its perceptions are clear and distinct, to recognize the nature of that thing and to discriminate it from others.

The objective mode of being that a thing has in the intellect when being thought of, which I take to be the intentional object of which the mind is immediately aware when thinking of that thing, is not to be confused with what the mind takes itself to be aware of – what Wilson calls the idea's "presentational content."[48] In speaking of the objective being of the thing thought of, I suggest, Descartes is referring to the content that the idea actually exhibits rather than to that it *appears* to exhibit and represent. The content or immediate object that the idea *actually* exhibits,

---

[48] According to Wilson (1990: 20 n. 10), the idea's presentational content roughly "coincides with what the mind takes itself to be aware of … If I think I see a tanager, then I can be ascribed a presentational representation of a tanager, regardless of what may actually be going on in the world or (otherwise) in me." As noted, Hoffman also holds that what our ideas seem to represent must exist in those ideas objectively (1996: 373).

qua the objective being of the thing it represents, cannot fail to correspond to the formal being of that thing. What the idea *actually* exhibits, however, may differ from what it *appears* to exhibit, as is true of confused and obscure ideas (Bolton 1986). Another way to articulate this point is to say that the thing with which the idea (taken objectively) *conforms* might differ from that to which the idea is *referred*. This discrepancy, as I will show in the next two sections, allows for an idea to be true and yet confused or obscure. Moreover, it allows for the same true idea to become more or less clear and distinct.

A false idea, by contrast, is one representing a non-thing (*non res*). Since a false idea fails to represent a real object or a "thing," it must lack objective reality according to Descartes' causal principle. A false idea cannot be said to objectively contain the formal being of the thing it is of, for there is no such thing. But false ideas, like all other ideas, do have representational character, by virtue of which they are immediately received by the mind as if presenting to it various things (real objects) outside themselves. For this reason, Descartes states in the Third Meditation that false ideas are those representing non-things as if they were things (*non rem tanquam rem repraesentant*) (AT VII 43: CSM II 30). By this statement, as Bolton contends, "Descartes did *not* mean that a false idea exhibits something real and represents nonentity; he means instead that a false idea *seems* to exhibit something positive, but *actually* exhibits nonentity" (1986: 394–95).[49]

Descartes argues that "we cannot conceive of anything except as existing. Possible or contingent existence is contained in the concept of a limited thing, whereas necessary and perfect existence is contained in the concept of a supremely perfect being" (Second Replies, AT VII 166: CSM II 117). But if every idea, by its very nature, "purports" to represent a possibly existing object outside itself, how can we ever ascertain that our ideas do represent real beings and not only pretend to do so? How can we know, in other words, which of our ideas has objective reality? For Descartes, an idea's degree of objective reality has a bearing on the possibility to perceive clearly and distinctly the object it exhibits to the mind. Only ideas that possess some degree of objective reality can

---

[49] Brown contends that "on the representationalist reading, when there is a mismatch between the intentional and real object, an idea may be mistaken and lead to mistaken judgment when we infer from the properties of the intentional object what properties are possessed by the real object" (2006: 90). Although most representationalist readings of Descartes do hold or imply such an account of false ideas and of the way they may lead us to error (e.g., Wilson 1990 and Patterson 2008), representationalism, as such, does not entail this account, as I try to show in this chapter.

be perceived clearly and distinctly. And ideas possessing a very slight degree of objective reality, such as those of particular sensible qualities, are said to be inherently and irremediably confused and obscure as a result of the original union between body and soul.⁵⁰ Descartes therefore writes that "possible existence is contained in the concept or idea of everything that we clearly and distinctly understand" (AT VII 116: CSM II 83). Granted that all and only ideas that represent real objects are true, we may regard the above statement as an equivalent formulation of Descartes' general principle that all clear and distinct ideas are *true*.⁵¹ And just as not *only* clear and distinct ideas are true (represent possible beings), so also not only clear and distinct ideas have objective reality and, as such, entail the possible existence of their objects. But only insofar as our perceptions are clear and distinct can we legitimately ascertain or judge that our ideas are true, namely, that they represent something capable of existing outside thought to which they must correspond. Descartes makes this point explicit in the Sixth Meditation, when he writes: "I know that everything which I clearly and distinctly understand is capable of being created by God so as to correspond exactly with my understanding of it" (AT VII 78: CSM II 54). Granted that an idea cannot fail to conform to the thing it actually represents, we may

⁵⁰ Toward the end of the *Principles*, Descartes writes that the images we have in our thought of color, sound, and all other tactile qualities "are always confused, and we do not know what they really are" (*Principles*, IV, 200). See also *Principles*, II, 3; letter to Hyperaspistes (AT III 424: CSMK 189–90); Sixth Meditation (AT VII 81: CSM II 56). Descartes does affirm that "pain and colour and so on are clearly and distinctly perceived when they are regarded merely as sensations or thoughts," that is, as modes of thinking rather than as corporeal qualities existing outside our mind (*Principles*, I, 68). Yet by this statement he seems to be referring to sensible qualities as generally or abstractly understood by means of the intellect rather than to particular sensible qualities we perceive by sense. See also Frankfurt (1970: 136); Wilson (1993: 163–64).

⁵¹ To affirm that an idea is true, therefore, is not to affirm the *actual* existence of its object, with the exception of the idea of God. Descartes argues that the essence or idea of every finite thing contains its *possible* rather than its *actual* existence, whereas only the essence of God contains its necessary existence. "[A]part from God, there is nothing else of which I am capable of thinking such that existence belongs to its essence" (Fifth Meditation, AT VII 68: CSM II 47). And in the *Comments on a Certain Broadsheet*, he likewise maintains that absolutely necessary and actual existence is contained only in the concept of God, "and not just possible or contingent existence, as in the ideas of all other things" (AT VIIIB 361: CSM I 306). Granted that actual existence is not contained in the idea of any finite being, it becomes clear why Descartes argues that the idea of an existing lion represents a fictitious (and yet real) entity, one "invented and put together by the intellect" (First Replies, AT VII 117: CSM II 83–84). Even if we could perceive clearly and distinctly the essence of a lion or of any other particular being, to infer from this essence an actual existence would be impossible. Given that no necessary connections link the components "lion" and "existence," we can split up the idea of an existing lion into these components through the intellect, "not simply by an abstraction but by a clear and distinct intellectual operation" (AT VII 117: CSM II 83). The idea of an existing lion, like the idea of a winged horse or of the chimera, represents a fictitious but real entity, not a "true and immutable nature."

be sure that whenever our perceptions are clear and distinct we cognize the true nature of the things they are of.

The intentional object of any given thought, *qua* the objective mode of being of the *res cogitata*, is what gives this thought its identity as a thought of this or that thing, regardless of what the idea is referred to (what it *appears* to exhibit and represent). The following passage from the Fifth Replies, cited earlier, is especially revealing concerning this point: "An idea represents the essence of a thing, and if anything is added to or be taken away from the essence, then the idea automatically becomes the idea of something else" (AT VII 371: CSM II 256). Descartes' examples of such cases are the ideas of Pandora and of all false gods, which are formed "by those who do not have a correct conception of the true God" (ibid.). Rather than being confused or obscure ideas of the true God, the idolaters' ideas neither exhibit nor represent the essence of God and, as such, are ideas of something else (of false entities, namely, of non-things). "But once the idea of a true God has been conceived," Descartes proceeds,

although we may detect additional perfections in him which we had not yet noticed, this does not mean that we have augmented the idea of God; we have simply made it more distinct and explicit, since, so long as we suppose that our original idea was a true one, it must have contained all these perfections. Similarly, the idea of a triangle is not augmented when we notice various properties in the triangle of which we were previously ignorant. (AT VII 371: CSM II 256)

As this passage suggests, our becoming increasingly attentive to the intentional object of the idea renders it progressively clear and distinct. Yet this does not mean that we have augmented the idea itself and have thereby changed its identity into an idea of something else. *Qua* a representation of a thing, such an idea contains objectively the properties of that thing, regardless of whether we have noticed them fully or only in part.[52] Obviously, were we to extend the content of an idea by rendering it more clear and distinct, we could not be said to have rendered *the same idea* more clear and distinct.

An important source for investigating the nature of clear and distinct ideas, and the relation between the truth-value of an idea and its degree

---

[52] Kenny thinks that Descartes "cannot give a consistent answer to the question about the criterion for the object of an idea" (1968: 121). Addressing Descartes' exchange with Arnauld about the idea of cold, Kenny asks: "What is it that makes a particular idea the idea *of cold*? Is it the idea's resembling cold? Or is it the idea's being meant by its possessor to resemble cold?" (p. 120). This difficulty, I believe, rests mainly on a typical confusion between the content of the idea and the thing the idea is referred to by the mind. I discuss this issue in more detail in the next section.

of clarity and distinctness, is Descartes' account of the material falsity of sensory ideas. This account, as I will argue below, implies a distinction between two senses in which Cartesian ideas can be considered "false." The first sense is the one discussed so far, denoting the non-reality of the idea's object. The second sense, "material falsity," is an *epistemic* category that Descartes applies to ideas, notably ideas of sense confused and obscure to such an extent that we cannot possibly judge whether they are true or false in the former, "ontological" sense. Before addressing this issue, however, I present my reading of the nature of clear and distinct perceptions.

5 CLARITY AND DISTINCTNESS

When Descartes introduces his definition of clear and distinct perception in the *Principles*, he employs an analogy with a visual perception of a tangible object: "I call a perception 'clear' when it is present and accessible to the attentive mind – just as we say that we see something clearly when it is present to the eye's gaze and stimulates it with a sufficient degree of strength and accessibility" (1, 45). A perception is clear, then, when the mind is fully attentive to its content – just as a tangible object is "present and accessible" to our sight, strongly stimulating our eyes and grabbing our attention. An idea is obscure (unclear) when the mind is ignorant of some of its elements. As Descartes writes in the Second Replies, "Whenever we call a conception obscure or confused this is because it contains some element of which we are ignorant" (AT VII 147: CSM II 105). An idea becomes clearer inasmuch as the mind's attention is directed to more of its elements: "the more attributes we discover in the same thing or substance, the clearer is our knowledge of that substance" (*Principles*, 1, 11).

Recall, however, that Descartes insists that there can be nothing within us of which we are not in some way aware.[53] This implies that every perception or idea enjoys a certain degree of clarity, which is the same as saying that the intentional object of an idea cannot be wholly veiled from recognition (Bolton 1986: 395). But to be aware or conscious of an idea is not synonymous with being attentive to it. Wilson describes the distinction between being merely conscious of *x* and being attentive to *x* as one between implicit and explicit knowledge, which she rightly counterposes to another distinction suggested by Descartes, that between actual and potential consciousness.[54] We are potentially conscious of *x* when we have

---

[53] First Replies (AT VII 107: CSM II 77); Fourth Replies (AT VII 246: CSM II 171).
[54] Wilson (1978: 157–60). Cf. McRae (1972: 61ff.); Jolley (1990: 48–49).

an innate idea of *x*, which means that we have in us the faculty of knowing *x* (Wilson 1978: 157). As mentioned, Descartes states that innate ideas "always exist within us potentially, for to exist in some faculty is not to exist actually, but merely potentially" (*Comments on a Certain Broadsheet*, AT VIIIB 361: CSM I 305). In light of this, we should be careful not to confuse cases where Descartes speaks of rendering his obscure ideas clearer by becoming more attentive to them[55] with cases where he speaks of rendering his potential consciousness actual by becoming aware of the objects of his innate ideas, actually perceiving them with whatever clarity and distinctness.[56]

Before we delve into the question of what it is for the mind to be "attentive" to the idea's intentional object, we need to address Descartes' notion of distinctness. "I call a perception 'distinct,'" he writes, "if, as well as being clear, it is so sharply separated from all other perceptions that it contains within itself only what is clear" (*Principles*, I, 45). While the clarity of a perception hinges on the mind's ability to attend to all that is included in its content, the distinctness of a perception depends on the mind's ability to distinguish its content from the contents of other ideas by recognizing the relations that hold between them. A perception is confused (not distinct) when the mind conflates (confuses) its content with elements of other ideas, and becomes more distinct inasmuch as the mind, while being attentive to its content, recognizes more of these relations. The fuller the mind's attentiveness to the idea's content, the greater its ability to recognize its relations to other ideas: "A concept is not any more distinct because we include less in it; its distinctness simply depends on our carefully distinguishing what we do include in it from everything else" (*Principles*, I, 63).

---

[55] A case in point is the Second Meditation example of the piece of wax (AT VII 30–32: CSM II 20–21), which I discuss below.

[56] In the Fifth Meditation, for example, Descartes writes: "It is not necessary that I ever light upon any thought of God; but whenever I do choose to think of the first and supreme being, and bring forth the idea of God from the treasure house of my mind as it were, it is necessary that I attribute all perfections to him, even if I do not at that time enumerate them or attend to them individually" (AT VII 67: CSM II 46–47). A few paragraphs earlier in the same Meditation, he writes: "there are countless particular features regarding shape, number, motion and so on, which I perceive when I give them my attention. And the truth of these matters is so open and so much in harmony with my nature, that on first discovering them it seems that I am not so much learning something new as remembering what I knew before; or it seems like noticing for the first time things which were long present within me although I had never turned my mental gaze on them before" (AT VII 63–64: CSM II 44). See also letter to Hyperaspistes, August 1641 (AT III 424: CSMK 190; AT III 430: CSMK 194); Third Replies (AT VII 189: CSM II 132); Fifth Replies (AT VII 381–82: CSM II 262). But keeping apart the two distinctions that Descartes has in mind when he speaks of "paying attention" to things inhering "in his mind" is not always easy, nor is he always consistent on this issue, as Wilson points out (see 1978: 162–63 and references therein).

This account implies that no perception can ever be absolutely or entirely distinct. Indeed, Descartes' notion of "adequate knowledge" suggests that in order for a perception to be clear and distinct, the mind need not be attentive to all there is in its content nor need it recognize all the relations it holds with other ideas. Descartes reserves the term "adequate knowledge" for the highest possible level of clarity, characterizing it as one containing "absolutely all the properties which are in the thing which is the object of knowledge" (Fourth Replies, AT vii 220: CSM ii 155). Note that Descartes does not rule out the possibility that a created intellect would possess adequate knowledge of many things, and even adds that "this can easily occur" (ibid.). Yet he insists that "only God can know that he has adequate knowledge of all things," while a created intellect can never be sure of that "unless God grants it a special revelation of the fact." Descartes explains that "in order for the intellect to know it has such knowledge, or that God put nothing in the thing beyond what it is aware of, its power of knowledge would have to equal the infinite power of God, and this plainly could not happen on pain of contradiction" (ibid.). In the *Conversation with Burman* (CB 14), Descartes hints that adequate knowledge of a thing contains not only all there is in the nature of that thing but also all the properties that are logically deducible from it. Although we can never ascertain that our knowledge is adequate, we can render an idea more adequate by enhancing its clarity and distinctness. In so doing, we are neither augmenting the idea itself nor transforming it into an idea of something else (AT vii 371: CSM ii 256), but only expanding our understanding of the thing our idea exhibits and represents.

Descartes clarifies that one can have "sufficiently clear" knowledge of a thing without grasping all that is included in its nature. He writes to Mersenne: "I do not deny that there are things in God which we do not understand, just as even in a triangle there are many properties which no mathematician will ever know – which does not prevent everyone knowing what a triangle is" (AT iii 274: CSMK 166). As Frankfurt comments, however, deciding how clear and distinct a perception must be in order to be justifiably accepted as true is not an easy task (1970: 143–45). In the Second Replies, Descartes seems to suggest that "sufficient clarity" is attained whenever we are able to assert the reality (possible existence) of the thing of which we have an idea:

But even if we conceive of God only in an inadequate or, if you like, "utterly inadequate" way, this does not prevent its being certain that his nature is possible, or not self-contradictory. Nor does it prevent our being able truly to assert that we have examined his nature with sufficient clarity (that is, with as much clarity as is necessary to know that his nature is possible and also to know that necessary existence belongs to this same divine nature). (AT VII 152: CSM II 108; see also AT VII 140: CSM II 100)

Yet Descartes could not mean in this passage that we should regard the reality of the thing of which we have an idea as a mark of the idea's "sufficient" clarity. Mixing up things in this manner is tantamount to suggesting that we regard truth as a mark of sufficient clarity and distinctness. To know that a thing is real requires us to know not only that its idea is not self-contradictory but also that it is compatible with a whole body of true ideas we possess. To meet this requirement, we must have an entirely distinct idea of that thing as well as recognize ourselves having it. The infeasibility of satisfying this requirement is indeed what brought Descartes to provide a criterion for truth or reality – clarity and distinctness. In the above quotation, then, Descartes might be willing to suggest that sufficient clarity and distinctness is attained whenever the will, on the basis of the intellect's clear and distinct understanding, cannot resist affirming that the idea is true (namely, that its object is possible). Even though our clear and distinct perception of God is inadequate, he states, "this does not prevent its being certain that his nature is possible." Although clarity and distinctness are not reducible to the certainty of the will, the only mark that Descartes can offer for "sufficient" clarity and distinctness, I think, is the will's irresistible inclination to assent to those perceptions that satisfy this preliminary postulation.[57]

A perception or an idea cannot be distinct without being clear (*Principles*, 1 46). For, unless the mind is fully attentive to the content of an idea, it cannot sharply separate it from the elements of other ideas (Nadler 2006: 99). A distinct perception, Descartes argues, "contains within itself only what is clear" (*Principles*, 1, 45). But a perception can be clear without being distinct, as Descartes illustrates by the example of pain (*Principles*, 1, 46). When we experience severe pain our perception is very clear, meaning that the mind's attention is fully directed to its immediate object – the sensation of pain. But this perception may be confused: "For people commonly confuse this perception with an

---

[57] This line of thought is also implied by Stephen Menn's remark that a perception is not clear enough to be included within the scientific system "if I have the liberty of indifference not to assent to it" (1998: 315). For an analysis of how clear and distinct perceptions are "rationally compelling," see Carriero (2008). Compare to Vinci, who suggests three criteria for identifying clear and distinct perceptions (1998: 23–30), among them what he calls "the criterion of psychological certainty." On Vinci's reading, divine guarantee is required to establish assent-compulsion as a reliable mark of clarity and distinctness rather than to ensure that our clear and distinct ideas are true (1998: 21–30).

obscure judgment they make concerning the nature of something which
they think exists in the painful spot and which they suppose to resemble the sensation of pain; but in fact it is the sensation alone which they
perceive clearly" (*Principles*, I, 46). What confuses this clear perception is
the mind's failure to discriminate the content actually presented to it –
the sensation of pain, which is a mode of thinking – from other ideas it
possesses (that of the bodily spot to which it refers the pain). This "failure" amounts to the mind regarding the pain as existing in the foot, for
instance, which is tantamount to saying that the mind is *referring* the
pain to the foot. In the Fourth Replies, Descartes tells Arnauld that "it
often happens in the case of obscure and confused ideas … that an idea
is referred to something other than that of which it is in fact the idea."
But this does not apply to the clear and distinct idea of God, "since it
cannot be said to refer to something with which it does not correspond"
(AT VII 233: CSM II 163). I suggest, then, that the function of "referring"
or "regarding as," which involves the immediate *interpretive* working of
the intellect, affects only the idea's degree of distinctness and determines
neither the content that the idea immediately exhibits *nor* the thing it represents, as some scholars assume.[58] Descartes accordingly states that ideas
of "pain and colour and so on are clearly and distinctly perceived when
they are regarded merely as sensations or thoughts" (namely, as modes of
thinking) (*Principles*, I, 68). But insofar as we regard them "not as being
in the mind alone, or in our perception, but as existing in the objects
outside us they are clear but confused" (*Principles*, I, 67). Had the function of referring determined the thing that the idea exhibits or represents,
we could not possibly perceive the same sensation (of pain, for instance)
clearly and distinctly on one occasion – by referring it to the mind – and
confusedly on another when referring it to the body.

To gain a keener grasp of the interpretive function of the intellect, which
determines the perceptions' degree of distinctness, we need to address the

---

[58] My interpretation thus opposes Wilson's suggestion that what an idea appears to be *of*, namely,
what it appears to referentially represent, is part of the idea's presentational content (1990: 4, 20
n. 10). It also differs from the view that the "regarding as" or "referring" function of the intellect
determines the objective being of the thing thought of (as in Hoffman 1996: 373ff.), as well as
from the reading suggested by Brown that what a perception is referred to coincides with what it
represents. According to Brown, "there is a clear link between what the perception is referred to
and what it represents. The tinkling sound is referred to the bell and is of the bell. Pain is referred
to the foot and represents the foot as afflicted" (2006: 100; see also her 2008: 209–11). If in referring the pain to the foot the idea is said to represent the foot as afflicted, the question arises as
to what makes such an idea a confused idea *of pain* (regarded as a bodily quality) as opposed to a
confused idea of *the foot* (regarded as painful). I elaborate on this issue and discuss further relevant textual sources in the next section.

account of sense perception in the Sixth Replies. This immediate interpretive "activity" involves unnoticed and non-volitional judgments that the *intellect* is habituated in making since childhood, as opposed to the volitional judgments elicited by the will.[59] Descartes distinguishes three grades of sensory response. The first is limited to the stimulation of nerves and sense organs by external bodies, which produces certain movements in the brain (AT VII 436–37: CSM II 294). Descartes says that the "movement in the brain, which is common to us and the brutes, is the first grade of sensory response" (AT VII 437: CSM II 295). This leads to the second grade, which "comprises all the immediate effects produced in the mind as a result of its being united with a bodily organ which is affected in this way. Such effects include the perceptions of pain, pleasure, thirst, hunger, colours, sounds, taste, smell, heat, cold and the like, which arise from the union and as it were the intermingling of mind and body" (AT VII 437: CSM II 294). The third grade, Descartes proceeds, "includes all the judgments about things outside us which we have been accustomed to make from our early years – judgments which are occasioned by the movements of these bodily organs" (AT VII 437: CSM II 295). Such is, for example, our habitual and non-volitional judgment that a stick located outside us is colored. Since we make these judgments "at great speed because of habit," we do not distinguish them from simple sense-perceptions (AT VII 438: CSM II 295). But Descartes insists that nothing more than the first and second grades "should be referred to the sensory faculty, if we wish to distinguish it carefully from the intellect" (AT VII 437: CSM II 295).

This account indicates that involuntary judgments belonging to the third grade of sense are *not* an intrinsic part of the content of our sensory ideas, pertaining to the second grade (see also Alanen 2003: 90). As such, they determine neither the idea's truth-value nor its identity as an idea of a certain object. To "refer" a sensation of pain to the foot, for instance, is to confuse the idea of pain (whose object, the sensation of pain, is a mode of thinking) with the idea of the foot. This confusion affects only what the idea *appears* to exhibit and represent, not the object it actually does.[60]

---

[59] See also the discussions in Alanen (1994: 243, 245; 2003: 91–93, 160–62); Nelson (1996: 23–26); Clarke (2003: 65ff.); Brown (2006: 98–99). On the difference between non-volitional judgments and those elicited by the will, see Gewirth (1943: 262–64); Beyssade (1992: 17).

[60] As Alanen points out (1994: 244), as a result of the unnoticed and involuntary judgment we are used to making about their origin and objects, these ideas come to the mind in connection with other ideas (with which they are confused). For Alanen's later Leibnizian interpretation of Descartes' notion of clear and distinct perception, see 2003: 65–70. Cf. Nelson (1996: 23–26).

Descartes argues, accordingly, that "no falsity can occur" in the first and second grades of sensory response (AT VII 438: CSM II 295–96). Ideas of sense are thus true in themselves, *qua* representations of real modes of thinking. The falsity that Descartes ascribes to the third grade of sense, as the next section will show, is the *material* falsity consisting in the inherent confusion and obscurity of these ideas and *not* in the non-reality of their objects.

To sum up, clarity and distinctness are features of the operation of the mind rather than intrinsic characteristics of the content perceived. While the clarity of an idea depends on the mind's attentiveness to its content, its distinctness hinges on the mind's ability to recognize its relations to other ideas. When the idea is confused, the mind refers its content to something other than that to which the idea corresponds. When the idea is clear and distinct, the mind, while interpreting its content as being such and such, cannot fail to refer this content to the thing with which it conforms. The discussion of the piece of wax example in the Second Meditation supports this reading. Realizing that all the features he recognizes in the wax by means of his senses, such as taste, color, shape, and so forth can alter while the wax persists, Descartes infers that none of these features truly belongs to the wax. To arrive at the true nature of the wax he embarks on an elimination process: "Let us concentrate, take away everything which does not belong to the wax, and see what is left: merely something extended, flexible and changeable" (AT VII 30–31: CSM II 20). And since this potentiality of the wax to undergo countless changes in shape and extension cannot be captured by his faculty of imagination, Descartes concludes that only his intellect can reveal to him the true nature of the wax. Descartes' own reflection on this process is highly revealing:

> But what is this wax which is perceived by the mind alone? It is of course the same wax which I see, which I touch, which I picture in my imagination, in short the same wax which I thought it to be from the start. And yet, and here is the point, the perception I have of it [or rather the act whereby it is perceived (added in French version, AT IX 24)] is a case not of vision or touch or imagination … but of purely mental scrutiny; and this can be imperfect and confused, as it was before, or clear and distinct as it is now, depending on how carefully I concentrate on what the wax consists in. (AT VII 31: CSM II 21)

As this passage indicates, in transforming his obscure and confused idea of the wax into a clear and distinct idea of the same wax, no change has occurred in the objective being of the wax. What has changed is *the mental act* by which this intentional object was perceived or the mental scrutiny of the same cognitive content: only the pure intellect rather than the senses and the faculty of imagination can capture the essence of the wax. This change in the *perceptual act*, as Descartes clarifies, its transition from being imperfect and confused to being clear and distinct, depends "on how carefully I concentrate on what the wax consists in." As Wilson concludes in her earlier reading (1978: 155), "the difference between having a confused idea of x and having a distinct idea of x is drawn in terms of our *awareness or perception* of what is in the idea, rather than in terms of what is in the idea."[61]

Clarity and distinctness are thus to be properly assigned to the mind's gaze rather than to the object immediately perceived. In keeping with Descartes' dominant metaphor of light – the natural light of reason – we may think of the self-clarification process through which our perceptions become clearer and more distinct in terms of self-illumination. This light, when properly directed inward, illuminates elements of the obscure idea that are concealed, thereby revealing the true nature of things as they really are. As the wax example clarifies, however, besides the mere "attentiveness" or focusing of the mind on whatever exists "in it," what is essential to this process are the withdrawal of the senses and the elimination of prejudice. In the Sixth Replies, Descartes identifies the intellect's habitual and non-volitional judgments (of the third grade of sense) with preconceived opinions that we have become accustomed to accepting from our earliest years (AT VII 438–39: CSM II 296). Since only the pure intellect can reveal the true essence of things, we must eliminate all the distorting influences of prejudice, the senses, and the passions by subjecting our precipitate and non-reflective judgments to critical evaluation (Alanen 1994: 245). As the following chapters will show, this process of "purifying" our intellectual activity by eliminating whatever is "extrinsic" to it requires *voluntary* intellectual effort, constant practice, and good habits (or virtues).[62]

In suggesting that clarity and distinctness are features of the mind's perceptual activity rather than of the content it perceives, I am not denying that intrinsic features of the idea taken objectively have a bearing on the mind's capability to perceive the idea's object clearly and distinctly. By "intrinsic features" I mean, in particular, the idea's degree of objective reality which is equivalent to the degree of reality that its object possesses formally (or

---

[61] This account may equally apply to the Third Meditation discussion of the two ideas of the sun: the one acquired from the senses and the other based on astronomical reasoning (AT VII 39: CSM II 27).

[62] See also Hatfield (1986: 56ff.); Alanen (1994: 245; 2003: 106); Garber (2001: 283–88); Patterson (2008: 220, 226).

would have possessed had it existed in actual reality). But the clarity and distinctness of an idea are not *determined* by the object it exhibits and represents, since we can perceive the same object at different times with different degrees of clarity and distinctness. This invites the question as to what makes an intentional object more or less prone to be perceived obscurely and confusedly, except for the mind's attentiveness to it. Descartes writes that "we know size, shape and so forth in quite a different way from the way in which we know colours, pains and the like" (*Principles*, I, 69). The inherent confusion and obscurity of sensory ideas is a result of the mind's intimate conjunction with the body, so that it is affected by the latter's movements.[63] Sensory ideas that, as noted, constitute the second grade of sense, are "the immediate effects produced in the mind as a result of its being united with a bodily organ" (AT VII 437: CSM II 294). What is more, our habitual, unnoticed judgments, which render our sensory ideas confused, are themselves products of our embodiment. Because of the intimate connection between body and soul, we are accustomed to – wrongly – referring mere sensations to extended things located outside us. The case is different with ideas of size, shape, motion, number, and all other "primary qualities," to use Locke's terminology (1995, book II, ch. viii), which are capable of being perceived by the intellect. When clearly perceived, these qualities are "actually or at least possibly present in objects in a way exactly corresponding to our sensory perception or understanding" (*Principles*, I, 70).[64] As Wilson points out (1993: 165), even when we are not considering them generally or abstractly but as particular figures of actual bodies affecting us, we know clearly, with respect to a given body, what being figured is: "our knowledge of what it is for the body to have a shape is much clearer than our knowledge of what it is for it to be coloured" (*Principles*, I, 69).

6 MATERIALLY FALSE IDEAS

Material falsity in the Third Meditation

The notion of material falsity first arises in the Third Meditation in connection with Descartes' attempt to inquire whether any of his ideas contain a degree of objective reality so great as to make it impossible that they originated in himself, thereby proving the existence of things beyond

---

[63] Sixth Replies (AT VII 437: CSM II 295). See also *Principles*, IV, 200.
[64] Descartes proceeds to claim that when the mind perceives sizes, shapes, motions, and so forth, these qualities are "presented to it not as sensations but as things, or modes of things, existing (or at least capable of existing) outside thought" (*Principles*, I, 71).

his thoughts. Examining his ideas of corporeal things, Descartes finds that the things he perceives clearly and distinctly in them are very few in number. This category includes "primary qualities," such as size, shape, position, and motion that apply only to bodies, and also substance, duration, and number that apply to both mental and corporeal things (AT VII 43: CSM II 30).[65] Descartes then continues:

> But as for all the rest, including light and colours, sounds, smells, tastes, heat and cold and the other tactile qualities, I think of these only in a very confused and obscure way, to the extent that I do not even know whether they are true or false, that is, whether the ideas I have of them are ideas of real things or of non-things. (AT VII 43: CSM II 30)

In this preliminary passage, Descartes does not as yet introduce the term "material falsity" but does outline the essence of his position on the nature of sensory ideas. He claims that he can think of tactile qualities such as light, colors, sounds, smells, and the like only in a confused and obscure manner, so much so that he cannot decide whether *these qualities* are true (real) or false (non-real), meaning he cannot know whether the ideas he has of them represent real things or non-things. Since Descartes does not refer material falsity to things but only to ideas, he clearly employs the terms "true" and "false" in this passage in their standard, ontological sense as synonymous with "real" and "non-real." Another important insight emerging from this passage is that our sensory ideas are not to be identified with the sensations themselves, as some scholars have suggested.[66] Mere sensations, such as light, sounds, colors, and so forth, are the *objects* of our sensory ideas but not ideas in themselves.[67] As such, sensations are not to be taken as representations nor as (mis)representations of the corporeal qualities that cause them. Only ideas represent, and sensory ideas are indeed confused representations *of* sensations.[68] This

---

[65] As Wilson points out, Descartes appears to be referring here to "primary" qualities understood generally or abstractly, as opposed to sensory perceptions of primary qualities of particular, actual bodies around us (1993: 163–64).

[66] See, for instance, Kenny (1968: 120); Wilson (1978: 110–19; 1990); Gueroult (1984: I, 151ff.); Normore (1986: 229); Beyssade (1992, esp. pp. 6–7); Simmons (1999, esp. pp. 348–50).

[67] See also Beyssade (1992: 17); Field (1993: 323–24); Wee (2006a: 55, 66). According to Beyssade, "sensation is but a non-representational thought, which deserves to be called a feeling rather than an idea" (1992: 17). In his reading, all sensory qualities are connected with geometrical qualities, so that whenever we are aware of sensations of heat, cold, and so forth, we simultaneously possess ideas of figures, motions, and the like. The representational character of sensations, Beyssade suggests, consists in "the native link between a (non-representational) content of various sensations and a represented content (of geometrical ideas)" (p. 16).

[68] The Sixth Replies discussion of the three grades of sensory response does not support the reading I am offering. Associating the first grade of sense with brain movements, Descartes identifies

point is significant for our understanding of the nature of material falsity, and should be taken into account when considering the objective reality and the truth-value of our (materially false) ideas of sense. Descartes then proceeds:

For although, as I have noted before, falsity in the strict sense, or formal falsity, can occur only in judgments, there is another kind of falsity, material falsity, which occurs in ideas, when they represent non-things as things. For example, the ideas which I have of heat and cold contain so little clarity and distinctness that they do not enable me to tell whether cold is merely the absence of heat or vice versa, or whether both of them are real qualities, or neither is. And since there can be no ideas which are not as it were of things, if it is true that cold is nothing but the absence of heat, the idea which represents it to me as something real and positive deserves to be called false; and the same goes for other ideas of this kind. (AT vii 43–44: CSM ii 30)

The opening sentence in this passage has led to the widely accepted view that, at least in the Third Meditation, Descartes *identifies* materially false ideas with those representing non-things as things.[69] On this reading, which I call "substantive," materially false ideas cannot be true.[70] Embracing a substantive reading of this type, Wilson holds that Descartes "was determined at all costs to maintain that the ideas of sense, even if

the resultant second grade with perceptions of pain, colors, and so forth, without mentioning the sensations themselves as something different from these perceptions or ideas. This second grade of sense, as I understand it, is supposed to include both the mental ideas of sense and the internal objects to which these ideas apply, meaning the feelings or sensations themselves that, just like emotions, judgments, and volitions, are non-representative modes of thinking. On other occasions, however, Descartes quite explicitly states that sensory ideas are *of* sensations. Apart from the above quotation from the Third Meditation, he further asserts that "if it is true that cold is nothing but the absent of heat, the idea which represents it to me as something real and positive deserves to be called false" (Third Meditation, AT vii 44: CSM ii 30). And in the Fourth Replies he likewise argues that the obscure idea of cold has "something positive as its underlying subject, namely the actual sensation involved" (*ens aliquod positivum habet pro subjecto, nempe sensum ipsum*) (AT vii 234: CSM ii 164). I hold with Wee (2006a: 66) that this statement clearly indicates that the materially false idea of cold is not to be identified with the sensation of cold. This means that materially false ideas of sense, rather than exhibiting themselves (Vinci 1998: 180–87), exhibit and represent sensations, which are real modes of thinking.

[69] See, e.g., Kenny (1968: 118–20); Cottingham (1976: 67); Wilson (1978: 109, 111–14; 1990: 1, 9, 20 n. 12); Bolton (1986: 392); Field (1993: 313 n. 5, 314ff.); Hoffman (1996: 358–59; 2009: 145); Vinci (1998: 27, 180–87); Brown (2006: 91, 106; 2008: 203, 206); Wee (2006a: 3–4, 22–24, 48–49). Some scholars hold that, in the Fourth Replies, Descartes changes his view of the nature of materially false ideas (e.g., Wee 2006a: 12ff.). Bolton's suggestion, by contrast, is to read the Fourth Replies as broadening the notion of materially false ideas in the Third Meditation to include not only "those that both represent nonentity and represent it as something other than it is," but also all ideas that "provide material for error." On this broader view, she writes, "all confused and obscure ideas are false (although Descartes insists ideas of heat, cold, and so forth, provide more opportunity for error than others do)" (1986: 392).

[70] For my use of the term "substantive," see Introduction, n. 2 above.

they are *tanquam rerum*, nevertheless fail to exhibit to us any possibly existent quality in an intelligible manner ... In an important ('*de re*') sense they are *not* 'of things'" (1978: 114). In a later paper, where Wilson modifies her view about Descartes' notion of representation, she still holds that "in the Third Meditation, he seems to construe such sensations as 'ideas of' cold and the like, which *misrepresent* 'what cold is' to the mind. Their 'falsity' consists in representing what is not a real physical quality as if it were" (1990: 1).

Considering the analytic order of the *Meditations*, however, Descartes would probably be reluctant to make any definite assertion at this early stage of his argument as to the objective reality of the ideas occurring in his mind, and commit himself to the non-reality of the objects of his sensory ideas. Indeed, only by the Sixth Meditation does he reach resolution on this issue when he affirms the reality of sensations in general in the context of his argument for the existence of bodies (AT VII 79–81: CSM II 55–56).[71] Notice also that, in the above quotation, Descartes repeats his initial position that sensory ideas, such as those of heat and cold, contain so little clarity and distinctness that they do not enable us to decide *whether* any of them is true or false: "whether cold is merely the absence of heat or vice versa, or whether both of them are real qualities, or neither is." Clearly, had Descartes regarded all sensory ideas as materially false while identifying their material falsity with the representation of nothingness, he could not have allowed for the possibility that heat and cold might both be real qualities or that one of them might be real and the other non-real.[72] This point is well brought out by Richard Field:

[I]f cold were simply the absence of heat, cold could not exist as a mode, but only as the absence of a mode, and consequently it would not have the reality that would be contained objectively in the idea of heat. But since this account of the material falsity of the idea of cold presumes the material truth of the idea

---

[71] See also Bolton (1986: 396ff.); Hoffman (1996: 361–62). Wilson does acknowledge this difficulty (1978: 111, 114), but still insists that Descartes is determined to maintain that ideas of sense are not "of things" and, as such, lack objective reality (1978: 111, 114).

[72] As some scholars remark, what Descartes has in mind when raising the possibility that cold is simply a privation of heat is not entirely clear. "Privation" in this context may signify either a non-thing or a non-existing thing or, instead, a negative but still real quality, just like rest as the negation of motion or darkness as the negation of light. On other occasions, Descartes affirms the reality of negative qualities such as nothing, or instant, or rest, counting them among the simple natures (*Rules*, Rule 12, AT X 420: CSM I 45; *The World*, AT XI 40: CSM I 94; *Principles*, II, 27). But in the present context, when raising the false hypothesis that coldness is but the absence of heat, he equates being positive with being real (AT VII 44: CSM II 30), and therefore seems to regard cold-as-an-absence or privation as a non-thing. Cf. Wilson (1990: 19 n. 6); Beyssade (1992: 9–10).

of heat, it still does not explain in what way all ideas of sense may be materially false, that is, how they all might represent unreal things. (1993: 319–20; see also Kaufman 2000: 397)

To resolve this difficulty, some scholars have suggested that, in the Third Meditation, Descartes defines materially false ideas as those representing "non-things as things" but does not *assert* that sensory ideas are materially false. Rather, he only suspects them to be so, raising the possibility that they fail to represent real qualities (or "things").[73] This "moderate" substantive reading fits well with Descartes' contention, cited above, that "since there can be no ideas which are not as it were of things, if it is true that cold is nothing but the absence of heat, the idea which represents it to me as something real and positive deserves to be called false" (AT VII 43–44: CSM II 30). And yet, while in the Third Meditation Descartes nowhere explicitly states that sensory ideas are materially false, he does affirm that this had been his original position when readdressing this issue in the Fourth Replies:

But my critic asks what the idea of cold, which I described as materially false, represents to me. If it represents an absence, he says, it is true; and if it represents a positive entity, it is not the idea of cold. This is right; but my only reason for calling the idea "materially false" is that, owing to the fact that it is obscure and confused, I am unable to judge whether or not what it represents to me is something positive which exists outside of my sensation. And hence I may be led to judge that it is something positive though in fact it may merely be an absence. (AT VII 234: CSM II 164)

Rather than rejecting Arnauld's understanding that the Third Meditation regards the idea of cold as materially false, Descartes reaffirms that in describing this idea as materially false, he had not meant to rule out the possibility that this idea might be true. The identity of an idea depends on what it actually represents: assuming that cold is but an absence of heat rather than something positive, an idea that represents an absence is a true idea of cold, whereas an idea that represents something positive must be a true idea of something else (rather than a false, non-true idea of cold). The main point of this passage is thus to indicate that no tension or contradiction is involved in affirming that the materially false idea of cold might be true in itself. Arnauld was simply wrong in identifying the *material* falsity of the idea of cold with an absence of truth! To be even more precise, Descartes explains that his only reason for calling

---

[73] Readings along these lines are found in Bolton (1986: 396); Beyssade (1992); Field (1993: 316, 323, 331–32); Hoffman (1996: 357–58, 361–62, and 2009: 145–46, 148).

the idea "materially false" is that "owing to the fact that it is obscure and confused, I am unable to judge whether or not what it represents to me is something positive which exists outside of my sensation."

With these considerations in mind, we may return to Descartes' statement in the Third Meditation, that "if it is true that cold is nothing but the absence of heat, the idea which represents it to me as something real and positive deserves to be called false." This statement does not display the conditions necessary for the idea of cold to be *materially* false. Rather, it displays the conditions wherein the materially false idea of cold would not unjustly be called false (*non immerito falsa dicetur*) in the standard, *ontological* sense of falsehood: the representation of a non-thing as if it were real. In both the Third Meditation and the Fourth Replies, I argue, material falsity is an *epistemic* category applying to ideas of sense, whose inherent and irremediable obscurity and confusion do not enable us to tell whether they are ontologically true or false.[74] This reading implies that Descartes' account of material falsity involves two different senses of "false ideas." Whereas the standard, ontological sense is to be understood as the negation of truth, there appears to be no direct evidence that Descartes thinks of ideas that do not fall under the category of material falsity as being "materially true."[75]

Descartes concludes the Third Meditation account of material falsity with the recognition that his materially false sensory ideas, regardless of whether they are ontologically true or false, do not require him to assume any formally existing cause distinct from himself:

Such ideas obviously do not require me to posit a source distinct from myself. For on the one hand, if they are false, that is, represent non-things, I know by the natural light that they arise from nothing – that is, they are in me only because of a deficiency and lack of perfection in my nature. If on the other hand

---

[74] For various non-substantive readings of Descartes' notion of material falsity, in both the Third Meditation and the Fourth Replies, see Gueroult (1984: 1, 153); Wells (1984); Alanen (1994: 238–48; 2003: 156–64); Nelson (1996; 2008: 321); Nadler (1989: 164–65; 2006: 100–03); Kaufman (2000: 396ff.). Vinci also considers obscurity to be "a distinct variant" of material falsity in both the third Meditation and the Fourth Replies (1998: 181, 195–205). But as opposed to non-substantive interpretations, he insists on two additional distinctive properties of materially false ideas: (a) failing to (re)present a real thing (*res*) and, (b) mis(re)presenting something that is not a real thing as a real thing (p. 181. See also pp. 27, 182–87). Materially false ideas, according to Vinci, *"are* ideas but they have no objects and thus have no intentional objects" (p. 27).

[75] In the Second Replies, Descartes does refer to an argument as "materially true" (AT vii 151: CSM ii 107; see also AT iv 685, mentioned by Wee 2006a: 153 n. 3). But in both references material truth is not applied to ideas. Scholars still tend to speak of Cartesian ideas as being materially true. See, for example, Frankfurt (1970: 129ff.); Curley (1975: 187 n. 41); Clatterbaugh (1980: 390); Gueroult (1984: 1, 204, 221); Field (1993: 319–20); Alanen (1994: 238, with reference to clear and distinct ideas); Davies (2001: 298 n. 22); Wee (2006a: 20, 34–36, 73); Brown (2008, 203).

they are true, then since the reality which they represent is so extremely slight that I cannot even distinguish it from a non-thing, I do not see why they cannot originate from myself. (AT VII 44: CSM II 30)

Descartes thus realizes that he cannot reject the possibility that he himself might be the source of his materially false sensory ideas. For if they are ontologically false, and thus represent non-things, they must originate from nothing, from a mere absence of perfection in his own nature. And if, despite their material falsity, these ideas are true (represent real qualities), the degree of reality they represent is so slight that he cannot distinguish it from a non-thing and so, again, he cannot rule out the possibility that he is their origin.

My reading of this passage departs from the more common view that *materially* false ideas must arise from nothing.[76] Combined with the assumption that Descartes takes sensory ideas to be materially false, this interpretation results in a serious puzzle about his position on the objective reality of sensory ideas. Insofar as these ideas arise from nothing, they must lack objective reality; yet the Sixth Meditation expressly affirms that sensory perceptions arise from bodies existing outside the mind (AT VII 79–81: CSM II 55–56). Confronting this difficulty, Wilson suggests that sensory ideas, when considered as modes of thoughts, have positive *formal* reality and, like any other real occurrence, must have an equally real cause. From an objective point of view, however, these ideas are caused by nothing and, as such, lack objective reality (Wilson 1978: 111, 114).[77] Yet this reading may run contrary to Descartes' response to Arnauld's supposition that materially false ideas are said to issue from nothing. Arnauld contends:

What is the cause of the positive objective being which according to you is responsible for the idea's being materially false? "The cause is myself," you may answer, "in so far as I come from nothing." But in that case, the positive objective being of an idea can come from nothing, which violates the author's most important principle. (AT VII 207: CSM II 146)

Descartes replies: "I do not claim that an idea's material falsity results from some positive entity; it arises solely from the obscurity of the idea – although this does have something positive as its underlying subject, namely the actual sensation involved" (AT VII 234: CSM II 164). This reply affirms that in ascribing material falsity to ideas of sense, Descartes

---

[76] See, e.g., Wilson (1978: 111); Field (1993: 318–19); Brown (2006: 92; 2008: 203); Wee (2006a: 4, 17). For a critical discussion of this reading, see Nelson (1996).

[77] See also MacKenzie (1994: 264).

does not deny the presence of something real and positive underlying them – the sensation, which is a formally existing mode of being.

Material falsity in the Fourth Replies

In the Fourth Objections, Arnauld charges Descartes with inconsistency in speaking of materially false ideas. Construing the Third Meditation account in substantive terms, namely, as identifying materially false ideas with those representing non-things as things, Arnauld's main point is to show that every idea, by its very nature, is true, and that falsity can occur only in judgments. Arnauld begins by paraphrasing Descartes' statement cited above that "'if it is true that cold is nothing but the absence of heat,' the idea which represents it to me as something real and positive deserves to be called false." He assumes, though Descartes does not say so explicitly, that this statement characterizes *materially* false ideas:

The author says that "if cold is merely the absence of heat, the idea of cold which represent it to me as a positive thing will be materially false."
   But if cold is merely an absence, then there cannot be an idea of cold which represents it to me as a positive thing, and so our author is here confusing a judgment with an idea. (AT VII 206: CSM II 145)

Arnauld correctly assumes that what an idea represents must exist objectively in the intellect. But he also incorrectly assumes that for an idea to represent a certain thing (for example, a privative quality) *as* something else (a positive quality), the positive quality must exist objectively in the intellect. For this reason, Arnauld insists that an idea cannot represent one thing and, at the same time, represent it *as something else*, which for him means to represent one thing and objectively contain quite another:

What is the idea of cold? It is coldness itself in so far as it exists objectively in the intellect. But if cold is an absence, it cannot exist objectively in the intellect by means of an idea whose objective existence is a positive entity. Therefore, if cold is merely an absence, there cannot ever be a positive idea of it, and hence there cannot be an idea which is materially false. (AT VII 206: CSM II 145)

According to Arnauld, then, if cold is simply an absence of heat, for an idea to be an idea *of cold* it must contain objectively the allegedly negative quality of coldness. Any idea containing objectively a positive entity is a true idea of this positive entity and not a false idea of cold: "Lastly, what does the idea of cold, which you say is materially false, represent to your mind? An absence? But in that case it is true. A positive entity? But in that case it is not the idea of cold" (AT VII 207: CSM II 146).

Descartes begins by pointing out Arnauld's mistake in construing the material falsity of ideas in substantive terms. He writes: "The first point is that certain ideas are materially false. As I interpret this claim, it means that the ideas are such as to provide subject-matter for error. But M. Arnauld concentrates on ideas taken in the formal sense, and maintains that there is no falsity in them" (AT VII 231: CSM II 162). This remark is revealing: while Descartes interprets a materially false idea as one providing "subject-matter for error," Arnauld misinterprets material falsity as pertaining to ideas taken formally or objectively, that is, with reference to the truth or falsity of their objects. Descartes then writes:

When M. Arnauld says "if cold is merely an absence, there cannot be an idea of cold which represents it as a positive thing," it is clear that he is dealing solely with an idea taken in the *formal* sense. Since ideas are forms of a kind, and are not composed of any matter, when we think of them as representing something we are taking them not *materially* but *formally*. If, however, we were considering them not as representing this or that but simply as operations of the intellect, then it could be said that we were taking them materially, but in that case they would have no reference to the truth or falsity of their objects. So, I think that the only sense in which an idea can be said to be "materially false" is the one which I explained. (AT VII 232: CSM II 162–63)

This passage clarifies that material falsity is not to be ascribed to ideas taken formally or objectively, that is, with reference to the truth (reality) or falsity (non-reality) of their objects. Material falsity, however, is not to be ascribed to ideas taken materially (in their formal reality) either, considering them as mere operations of the mind with no reference to their intentional objects. Recall that Descartes notes: "in so far as the ideas are considered simply as modes of thought, there is no recognizable inequality among them: they all appear to come from within me in the same fashion" (AT VII 40: CSM II 27–28). What, then, could Descartes have in mind when telling Arnauld that "the only sense in which an idea can be said to be 'materially false' is the one which I explained"? Insofar as material falsity consists in the obscurity and confusion of ideas, I suggest, it has to do with how the mind "reads" and interprets the idea's immediate content, not with this content or intentional object *per se* nor with the mere operation of the intellect. I therefore hold with Beyssade (1992: 13) that the material falsity of ideas concerns the borderline between the ideas' formal and objective realities.

With this view in mind, we may now examine Descartes' reply to Arnauld's objection:

When my critic says that the idea of cold "is coldness itself in so far as it exists objectively in the intellect," I think we need to make a distinction. For it often happens in the case of obscure and confused ideas – and the ideas of heat and cold fall into this category – that an idea is referred to something other than that of which it is in fact the idea. Thus if cold is simply an absence, the idea of cold is not coldness itself as it exists objectively in the intellect, but something else, which I erroneously mistake for this absence, namely, a sensation which in fact has no existence outside the intellect. (AT VII 233: CSM II 163)

Descartes' main objective in this passage is to explain what precisely confusion and obscurity consist in. The ideas of heat and cold are obscure and confused because they refer to something other than that of which they are ideas. To refer an idea to something, as I have argued, affects neither the idea's intentional object nor the thing the idea represents. But what might be the grounds for Descartes' assertion that "if cold is simply an absence, the idea of cold is not coldness itself as it exists objectively in the intellect"? If an idea of a thing, such as the idea of the sun for instance, is the thing itself as it exists objectively in the intellect (AT VII 102: CSM II 75), why should it work differently for the idea of cold? When Descartes says "we need to make a distinction," I take him to distinguish ideas of "things" from ideas of "non-things." Assuming that cold is an absence and thus, presumably, a non-thing, it cannot exist objectively in the intellect any more than the non-thing that the idea represents can exist formally in the world. And yet the idea's obscurity and confusion does not lie in its misrepresenting the thing of which it is an idea, but in the fact that we *regard* the privative object (coldness) it exhibits and represents *as* something other than it is.

Interpreting this passage, Wilson suggests that the obscure and confused idea of cold referentially represents cold and is, as such, an idea *of cold*, but presentationally represents something else, a positive sensation. This kind of disparity between the idea's referential and presentational objects is what Descartes has in mind, according to Wilson, when he claims that the idea of cold is referred to something other than that of which it is in fact the idea:

The idea is, referentially, the idea of *cold*; it presents, however, something else: a mere, if "positive," sensation. It thus "provides the material" for my error of judging that what is (positively if obscurely) presented to me is what the idea refers to, namely cold (which is in fact, in the real world, a privation). What the idea referentially represents is not what it presentationally represents: that is why Descartes can say that the idea of cold is referred to something other than that of which it is in fact the idea. (1990: 9)

Wilson's suggestion that an idea presenting a positive quality to the mind can be a confused and obscure idea of a negative quality is ruled out by

Descartes himself a few paragraphs later in the Fourth Replies. Reinforcing the view that an idea cannot misrepresent its object in the manner Wilson suggests, Descartes fully accepts Arnauld's contention that if cold is simply an absence, an idea that exhibits a positive entity to the mind cannot be the idea of cold (AT VII 234: CSM II 164).[78] Commenting on this statement, Wilson writes that "although Descartes seems to give away the store here ... he has merely expressed himself ineptly. He does not really intend to retract his position that a particular 'positive' sensation counts as the 'idea of cold,' even if cold is in fact a privation" (1990: 10). She holds that Descartes "is not *categorically* accepting Arnauld's claim that if cold is a privation, a positive idea is not the idea of cold. He is merely agreeing that the idea would not be *presentationally* the idea of cold as it 'is' in nature, or *quam res* (namely, a privation)" (Wilson 1990: 10). For the reasons I have introduced so far, however, I hold that the above statement should indeed be taken literally.[79]

In discussing these passages, we must recall that Descartes eventually rejects the hypothesis he had followed both in the Third Meditation and in the Fourth Replies that cold is simply an absence, as opposed to something "positive and real." Ultimately, as noted, he thinks that sensory ideas exhibit and represent real modes of thinking caused by external bodies existing outside us. Being inherently obscure and confused, however, sensory ideas provide a high degree of material for error.

To provide material for error in judgment (*judicio materiam praebeant erroris*) or "opportunity for error" (*dant occasionem erroris*), ideas need not be ontologically false. In the next chapter, I will argue further that an idea to which a formally false *act* of judgment applies may be true in itself, but must still be obscurely or confusedly perceived by the mind. Ideas provide subject-matter for error by being obscure or confused. But whereas

---

[78] Except for one brief remark, Wilson does not confront directly the question of how her interpretation might fit with Descartes' position in the First Replies (AT VII 102: CSM II 75). She states only that, in the First Replies, Descartes does not "address the question of whether, or under what circumstances, a *misrepresentation* of the sun can count as "the sun itself existing in the understanding" (1990: 20 n. 11).

[79] See also Bolton (1986: 394); Hoffman (1996: 369). Hoffman suggests an alternative reading of Descartes' assertion that "if cold is simply an absence, the idea of cold is not coldness itself as it exists objectively in the intellect, but something else, which I erroneously mistake for this absence." He claims that Descartes is saying here that the idea of cold both exhibits and represents a positive entity, and is therefore not the idea of cold (pp. 369–71). In Hoffman's reading, since Descartes accepts the Aristotelian view that an idea is the thing represented in a different mode of being, he must agree that if the idea we call the idea of cold is not coldness itself existing in the intellect, it cannot be the idea of cold (1996: 371; 2009: 154–55). Despite the temptation to accept Hoffman's reading, I think that Descartes quite explicitly states in this passage that the idea is an obscure and confused idea *of cold*.

every confused or obscure idea provides *some* opportunity for error, not all confused or obscure ideas deserve to be called materially false. Ideas "which give the judgment little or no scope for error do not seem as much entitled to be called materially false as those which give great scope for error" (AT VII 233: CSM II 163). Descartes clarifies that "confused ideas which are made up at will by the mind, such as the ideas of false gods, do not provide as much scope for error as the confused ideas arriving from the senses" (AT VII 233–34: CSM II 163). The greatest scope for error, he states, "is provided by the ideas which arise from the sensations of appetite. Thus the idea of thirst which the patient with dropsy has does indeed give him subject-matter for error, since it can lead him to judge that a drink will do him good, when in fact it will do him harm" (AT VII 234: CSM II 163–64).

Descartes thus views the involuntariness of our confused sensory ideas as a weighty reason for considering them particularly misleading. And since these ideas are inherently and irremediably confused on account of the slight degree of formal reality they represent, we are unable to judge whether they exhibit something real.[80] Some scholars read this statement concerning our inability to judge as implying that confused and obscure ideas of sense can only be said to provide us with opportunity for error and cannot be said to positively lead us or tempt us to err.[81] But rather than asserting our psychological or phenomenological inability to decide, this statement suggests only that our sensory ideas, owing to their inherent confusion, do not allow us to judge *correctly* whether they exhibit something real or non-real. And even though these ideas do not determine the *pure intellect* to ascribe certain properties to their objects as do clear and distinct ideas, they might still be said to *positively* lead us to make erroneous judgments in their regard. Because of the involuntary judgments that our *intellect* is accustomed to making about their external causes, when we unconsciously refer the color to the stick or the pain to the foot, for instance, our *will* may be strongly inclined to judge the color as existing in the stick or the pain as existing in the foot. One may object, however, as does Nelson (1996: 23–26), that the intellect's involuntary judgments about the causes of our sensory ideas are not intrinsic features of the ideas themselves. As I argued in section 5 above, moreover, the involuntary judgments belonging to the third grade of sense are

---

[80] Third Meditation (AT VII 43–44: CSM II 30); Fourth Replies (AT VII 234: CSM II 164).

[81] For instance, Wilson (1978: 115–16); Bolton (1986: 396). Cf. Nelson (1996) and Vinci (1998: 152ff.) who, for different reasons, also reject the idea that intrinsic features of sensory ideas positively incline us to make erroneous judgments.

not an intrinsic part of the *content* of our sensory ideas, which Descartes assigns to the second grade. But although these involuntary judgments, or the confusion they produce in the mind, determine neither the idea's truth-value nor its identity as an idea of this or that object, they do affect what the idea *appears* to exhibit and represent. And insofar as these involuntary judgments, as well as the confusion they produce, have their roots in the slight degree of objective reality that sensory ideas possess, we may pin the blame for our positive inclination to make erroneous judgments about their objects on intrinsic features of the ideas themselves.

Recall that Descartes claims, in the Third Meditation, that we have a natural, blind impulse to judge that the ideas our senses provide resemble or correspond to things located outside us (AT vii 38–39: CSM ii 26–27). In the Sixth Meditation, however, he refines his view of the "teachings of nature," referring this inclination not to nature but to "a habit of making ill-considered judgments" about the external causes of our sensory perceptions: "There are, however, many other things which I may appear to have been taught by nature, but which in reality I acquired not from nature but from a habit of making ill-considered judgments" (AT vii 82: CSM ii 56).[82] The examples he gives of things he is inclined to believe by his habitual "ill-considered judgments" indicate that what he has in mind are the unnoticed judgments that the intellect is accustomed to making from our earliest years (third grade of sensory response), rather than the voluntary judgments made by the will.[83]

Descartes further explains that when speaking of things he is taught by nature (or by *his* nature), he employs "nature" in a narrow sense to signify "what God has bestowed on me as a *combination of mind and body*," and not in the broad sense as "the totality of things bestowed on me by God" (AT vii 82: CSM ii 57; my emphasis). But then, since our habit of making unnoticed judgments itself originates in our embodied nature, in the mind–body union, how can Descartes deny that our nature (in the narrow sense) is responsible for the deceptive effect of our sensory ideas?[84]

---

[82] I thank an anonymous reviewer for Cambridge University Press for bringing this point to my attention. See Vinci (1998: 152).

[83] "Cases in point are the belief that any space in which nothing is occurring to stimulate my senses must be empty; or that the heat in a body is something exactly resembling the idea of heat which is in me; or that when a body is white or green, the selfsame whiteness or greenness which I perceive through my senses is present in the body; or that in a body which is bitter or sweet there is the selfsame taste which I experience, and so on; or, finally, that stars and towers and other distant bodies have the same size and shape which they present to my senses, and other examples of this kind" (AT vii 82: CSM ii 56–57).

[84] As Descartes writes in the Sixth Replies, "as s result of being affected by this sensation of colour, I judge that a stick located outside me is coloured" (AT vii 437: CSM ii 295). See the discussion in this chapter, section 5.

The key to answering this question lies in the explanation that follows about what our nature teaches us and what it does not: "My nature, then, in the limited sense, does indeed teach me to avoid what induces a feeling of pain and to seek out what induces feeling of pleasure, and so on."[85] But as opposed to these practical teachings necessary for the preservation of the mind–body union, our nature "does not appear to teach us to draw any conclusions from these sensory perceptions about things located outside us *without waiting until the intellect has examined the matter*. For knowledge of the truth about such things seems to belong to the mind alone, not to the combination of mind and body" (AT VII 82–83: CSM II 57; my emphasis).

In line with the strategy of the Fourth Meditation, Descartes seeks to show that our God-given embodied nature is not directly responsible for our tendency to make erroneous judgments about things outside the mind. Rather, it is *we* who misuse the teachings of nature by putting them into a direct theoretical use "without waiting until the intellect has examined" the information they provide. Descartes writes:

For the proper purpose of the sensory perceptions given me by nature is simply to inform the mind of what is beneficial or harmful for the composite of which the mind is a part; and to this extent they are sufficiently clear and distinct. But I misuse them by treating them as reliable touchstones for immediate judgment about the essential nature of the bodies located outside us; yet this is an area where they provide only very obscure information. (AT VII 83: CSM II 57–58)[86]

We may conclude, then, that our spontaneous inclination to regard sensory perceptions as resembling corporeal qualities, unless suppressed or corrected by reason and well-considered judgments, positively leads us to believe our sensations inhere in external objects. But the case might be different with regard to confused ideas of abstract entities such as justice, happiness, and the like, or even regarding a confused idea of God. While misinterpreting these objects, our intellect can still recognize itself, at least

---

[85] Notice that even the practical teachings of nature may positively mislead us: "it is not unusual for us to go wrong even in cases where nature does urge us toward something," as in the case of the thirst felt by someone who suffers from dropsy. "The resulting condition of the nerves and other parts will dispose the body to take a drink, with the result that the disease will be aggravated" (AT VII 84: CSM II 58). Notwithstanding the immense goodness of God, Descartes claims, "the nature of man as a combination of mind and body is such that it is bound to mislead him from time to time" (AT VII 88: CSM II 61). See also Second Replies (AT VII 143: CSM II 102).

[86] As Cottingham suggests, an impulse in this context counts as "natural" only if the inclination to believe is a result of clear and distinct intellectual perception and rational deliberation (1997: 216). See also the discussions in Loeb (1990: 13–14 and n. 16); Menn (1998: 317, 366–80); Garber (2001: 107–10); Clarke (2003: 118–20).

in some cases, to be undetermined about them, which would mean that the confused ideas we have of them provide us only opportunity for error without tempting us to judge. Another reason for considering sensory ideas materially false, then, could be the strong inclination they produce in the will to make erroneous judgments about their objects, namely, to affirm or deny what we fall short of perceiving clearly and distinctly.

CHAPTER 2

Error in judgment

By the end of the Third Meditation, Descartes establishes the existence of a veracious God and the resultant credibility of clear and distinct perception as a reliable mark of the truth. To complete this task, however, he must also show that the presence of error in human cognition is compatible with God's omnibenevolence. In the analytic order of the *Meditations*, as Martial Gueroult has admirably shown, the theodicy of error is required to safeguard divine veracity and thereby validate the Cartesian criterion of truth – clarity and distinctness – upon which the possibility of a firm and systematic science depends.[1] Not surprisingly, therefore, Descartes asserts in the Synopsis of the *Meditations* that he has proven the truth of our clear and distinct perceptions in the Fourth Meditation (AT VII 15: CSM II 11), and that "it was not possible to prove this before the Fourth Meditation" (AT VII 13: CSM II 9). For the same reason, it is only in the concluding paragraph of the Fourth Meditation that he invokes the validity of his criterion of truth.[2]

Clearly, then, when Descartes states at the outset of the Fourth Meditation that God cannot be a deceiver and therefore cannot be the author of his errors, he does not intend this assertion to serve as a *premise* of his argument but rather as the main conclusion he undertakes to substantiate. Descartes writes:

To begin with, I recognize that it is impossible that God should ever deceive me. For in every case of trickery or deception some imperfection is to be found; and although the ability to deceive appears to be an indication of cleverness or

---

[1] Gueroult (1984: 1, 8–11, 203–32, see esp. pp. 204, 221). See also Bordo (1987: 78); Gibson (1987: 323); Tierno (1997: 27).

[2] Descartes writes: "every clear and distinct perception is undoubtedly something, and hence cannot come from nothing, but must necessarily have God for its author. Its author, I say, is God, who is supremely perfect, and who cannot be a deceiver on pain of contradiction; hence the perception is undoubtedly true. So today I have learned not only what precautions to take to avoid ever going wrong, but also what to do to arrive at the truth" (AT VII 62: CSM II 43).

power, the will to deceive is undoubtedly evidence of malice or weakness, and so cannot apply to God.

Next, I know by experience that there is in me a faculty of judgment which, like everything else which is in me, I certainly received from God. And since God does not wish to deceive me, he surely did not give me the kind of faculty which would ever enable me to go wrong while using it correctly. (AT VII 53–54: CSM II 37–38)

The concluding sentence of this paragraph encapsulates the cornerstone of Descartes' argument in the Fourth Meditation: God has endowed him with such a faculty of judgment that will never allow him to err insofar as he uses it correctly. The main objective of the Fourth Meditation is thus to shift the burden of accountability for error from God to human beings. Descartes aims to prove that God has not placed in us any positive imperfection that renders our errors inescapable, and has instead given us the power to avoid error by exercising rational control over our judgments and beliefs. Descartes holds that God has granted us unlimited freedom of choice (*arbitrii libertas*), allowing us to refrain from making ill-considered judgments about objects we do not perceive clearly and distinctly. This God-given power renders us the sole authors of our erroneous judgments, when we fail to use this power correctly by making voluntary judgments about issues we do not fully understand. This doctrine enables Descartes to exempt God from any responsibility for human error, and thereby establish God's absolute veracity. It also allows him to prove that we are able to free ourselves from the blindness and culpability of error and attain true knowledge, despite the essential finitude of our intellect.

Descartes' theory of error has been the subject of extensive interpretation and criticism. Views on many aspects of this issue and its related topics, including its underlying theory of judgment and its conception of free will, extend over a broad range. One question, however, has not been given much consideration: the exact meaning of the term "error" in Descartes' usage. Scholars commenting on this matter ordinarily assume, either explicitly or implicitly, that Descartes takes error to be (or at least to be reducible to) an affirmation of falsehood or a denial of truth. In asserting that Cartesian error can arise only when we let ourselves assent to matters we do not perceive clearly and distinctly, most commentators find this condition necessary but not sufficient. The usual assumption is that error cannot occur unless the resultant judgment is an affirmation of falsehood or a denial of truth.[3] I call this commonly held interpretation

---

[3] Two notable exceptions are Hiram Caton's remark that "the argumentative structure of the text (AT VII 60) shows that chance hitting on the truth is not a true judgment, i.e., that any

"substantive," since it construes Cartesian error as a failure to discriminate between falsity and truth.[4] Note that scholars tend to take this substantive interpretation for granted, without considering the possibility that Descartes gives the term "error" quite a different meaning in his writings. Margaret Wilson's critical discussion of Descartes' theory of judgment is but one example of this prevailing trend. She appears to regard the substantive notion of error that she unhesitatingly attributes to Descartes as the only one he could possibly embrace:

But clearly, what we affirm or deny are not "images of things," but propositions or propositional contents – and these are true or false independently of our affirmations or denials. (*After all, what could error be but the affirmation of what is false, or the denial of what is true?*) (1978: 141; my emphasis)

A substantive reading of Descartes' notion of error has recently been suggested by Della Rocca, who contends that "error occurs only when the mind gives its assent to a representational content that is false" (2006: 146; see also p. 147). Kenny, too, appears to suggest a substantive reading when he states that "error is a matter of falsehood and sin of badness" (1972: 10), and does so even more explicitly in his statement that "the truth and falsehood which belongs to a judgment ... belongs to it not in so far as it is an assent, but in so far as what is assented to – what is presented by the intellect – corresponds or does not correspond to reality" (p. 15). Gueroult also suggests a substantive reading when he argues that Cartesian error is an affirmation of what is nothingness as being, or a "confusion of being and nothingness."[5] Similarly, Evans asserts that "a person cannot be in error and yet that which he takes to be true be true" (1963: 141), and that "when we are in error the proposition accepted must be false" (p. 142).[6] Readings along these lines are also found in McRae (1972: 67–68); Danto (1978: 291); Williams (1978: 170, 171, 179); Wells (1984: 37), and others.[7]

affirmation of unclear ideas is a false judgment" (1975: 94 n. 10), and Ferdinand Alquié's annotation to *Oeuvres Philosophiques de Descartes*: "La vérité trouvée par hasard est donc assimilable à l'erreur" (Truth found by chance is thus assimilable to error) (1967: 464 n. 2, mentioned by Caton).
[4] See Introduction above, n. 2. Cf. Chapter 1, section 6.
[5] Gueroult (1984: 1, 221, 231). See also pp. 214, 217, 228, 318 n. 7.
[6] What seems to underlie Evans' substantive reading is the assumption that the confusion and obscurity of ideas indicates their semantic falsehood. This is how I read his following assertion: "Descartes' recipe is to affirm or deny only what we clearly understand; if we persist in assenting to what we do not clearly understand the penalty is that we assert as true what is in fact false" (1963: 138). See also pp. 138–39, 142–44.
[7] See also Rosenthal (1986: 409); Cress (1994: 145–46); Tierno (1997: 79); Davies (2001: 94); Wee (2006a: 61, 121–22); Friedman (2008: 82). Tierno appears to allude to a non-substantive reading when he writes: "When we give our assent to propositions we do not adequately understand we

The widely accepted substantive reading does not lack textual support. Descartes does at times speak of error as a failure to discriminate the true from the false.[8] Despite a number of indications to the contrary, however, his fullest account of error in the Fourth Meditation takes quite a different route. My main concern in this chapter is to show that Descartes equates the very essence of error, not just its cause, with what he calls "the incorrect use of free choice" (*liberi arbitrii non recto usu*) (AT VII 60: CSM II 41). In contexts of pure inquiry, I suggest, he considers erroneous any *act of judgment* not based upon clear and distinct perceptions of the intellect, irrespective of whether the *content* to which we give credence is true or false.[9]

I ERROR AS A MISUSE OF FREE WILL

Recalling Descartes' general disapproval of formal or abstract definitions, the absence of any explicit definition of the term "error" in his writings is not surprising. Moreover, his discussion of the *nature* of error, both in the Fourth Meditation and in the first part of the *Principles*, is often intertwined with his analysis of the *causes* of error and of the cognitive mechanism that brings about error in the human mind. To take just one example, early in the Fourth Meditation, Descartes reflects on his own experience in order to explore the nature of his errors. He thus writes: "When I look more closely at myself and inquire into *the nature* of my errors ... I notice that they depend on two concurrent *causes*, namely on the faculty of knowledge which is in me, and on the faculty of choice or freedom of the will" (AT VII 56: CSM II 39; my emphases). Descartes is not accidentally binding together the issues of *essence* and *cause* of error. In this chapter, I attempt to show that a distinctive mark of his nonsubstantive conception of error is that the deficiency that *yields* error in the human mind is precisely what constitutes the *essence* of error: the incorrect use of free will.

To inquire into Descartes' conception of error, we first need to examine his account of judgment as an operation of the will. The doctrine that the will, not the intellect, is the faculty that elicits judgments does not

---

act defectively. This is nonetheless true even if we happen to judge truly. What is of paramount importance, then, is not that our judgments be true, but that they be made on the basis of reliable methods of arriving at the truth" (1997: 40).

[8] See, for example, Synopsis of the *Meditations* (AT VII 15: CSM II 11); Fourth Meditation, French version (AT IX 46); *Principles*, I, 42.

[9] Parts of section I appear, in earlier versions, in Naaman-Zauderer 2000, 2004 (50–53), 2007 (ch. I).

become explicit until the *Meditations*. In the early *Rules for the Direction of the Mind*, when distinguishing between "the faculty by which our intellect intuits and knows things and the faculty by which it makes affirmative or negative judgments" (Rule 12, AT x 420: CSM 1 45), Descartes assigns both faculties (intuiting and judging) to the *intellect*. In his later *Discourse on the Method*, he acknowledges our ability to make "a strong and unswerving resolution never to fail to observe" his four Rules of Method, of which the first is "never to accept anything as true if [we] did not have evident knowledge of its truth" (AT vi 18: CSM 1 120). As Kenny (1972: 5) notes, however, Descartes mentions judgments only in passing throughout this essay, making no explicit claim that judgments are operations of choice (namely, voluntary operations of the will). At this juncture in his philosophical career, Descartes had not yet established the metaphysical foundations for his program, nor had he developed his mature theory of judgment and conception of free will.[10]

In his later writings, Descartes famously distinguishes between the mind's mere awareness of a certain content (for which he uses the general term "perception" or "idea") and the operation of judgment that affirms or denies the truth of the idea. Whereas the intellect passively perceives ideas, the will actively and voluntarily elicits judgments (that is, affirmations and denials).[11] Characterizing the will as the "faculty of choosing" (*facultas eligendi*) (AT vii 56: CSM ii 39), Descartes considers every operation of judgment, as a mode of willing, to be an operation of choosing between accepting a given proposition as true or denying it as false. Affirming, denying, and withholding assent are thus possible mental attitudes of the will toward a given propositional content exhibited to the mind ("ideational attitudes," to use Danto's phrasing).[12]

In his *Comments on a Certain Broadsheet* (*Notae in Programma quoddam*), a work Descartes published in 1648, he introduces his reason for diverging from his predecessors in considering judgments to be oper-

---

[10] See also Introduction above and references therein (n. 3).

[11] In the *Principles*, the distinction between the operations of the intellect and those of the will is said to be exhaustive. Descartes writes: "All the modes of thinking that we experience within ourselves can be brought under two general headings: perception, or the operation of the intellect, and volition, or the operation of the will. Sensory perception, imagination and pure understanding are simply various modes of perception; desire, aversion, assertion, denial and doubt are various modes of willing" (i, 32).

[12] Danto (1978: 289). See, for instance, Third Meditation (AT vii 37: CSM ii 26); Fourth Meditation (AT vii 60: CSM ii 41); Fifth Replies (AT vii 337: CSM ii 259); letter to Hyperaspistes, August 1641 (AT iii 432: CSMK 195); *Principles*, i, 32, 34. For Descartes' characterization of the intellect as the mind's passivity and of the will as the mind's activity, see his letter to Regius, May 1641 (AT iii 372: CSMK 182). Cf. *Passions*, art. 17. See also n. 14 below.

ations of the will. Descartes says this doctrine allows him to account for our freedom to withhold assent to matters that our intellect fails to perceive clearly:

> For I saw that over and above perception, which is a prerequisite of judgment, we need affirmation and negation to determine the form of the judgment, and also that we are often free to withhold our assent, even if we perceive the matter in question. Hence I assigned the act of judging itself, which consists simply in assenting (i.e., in affirmation or denial) to the determination of the will rather than to the perception of the intellect. (AT viiib 363: CSM i 307)

Not until the *Meditations*, then, where Descartes develops his mature theory of judgment and conception of free will, is he able to work out his theory of error based on the distinction between the intellect and the will.[13]

For Cartesian error to occur, two simultaneous conditions must obtain: a confused or obscure perception or idea, and a voluntary act of judgment that affirms or denies its truth. Error thus requires the concurrence of both faculties: the intellect, which is "the faculty of knowledge," and the will, which is "the faculty of choice" (AT vii 56: CSM ii 39).[14] A fundamental postulate of Descartes' epistemology is that the mere apprehension of ideas, even the most confused and obscure, cannot bring about error: "Now all that the intellect does is to enable me to perceive ['... without affirming or denying anything' (added in French version, AT ix 45)] the ideas which are subject for possible judgments; and when regarded strictly in this light, it turns out to contain no error in the proper sense of the term" (AT vii 56: CSM ii 39). A confused or obscure perception, taken by itself, provides us with a certain degree of material or opportunity for error, an issue discussed in Chapter 1. But error is impossible so long as we abstain from making judgments on matters we apprehend confusedly or obscurely. For Descartes, when the ideas occurring in the mind are confused or obscure, the will in their regard is undetermined (indifferent). In such cases, the will can assent to or dissent from the ideas (and in both

---

[13] I discuss Descartes' conception of free will in Chapter 3 below.

[14] In this context, as Kenny points out (1972: 12–13), Descartes employs the term "intellect" in a broad sense, to refer to the general capacity of the mind to recall and combine ideas. This broad sense of "intellect" is also the one Descartes refers to when he states that "all the intellect does is to enable me to perceive the ideas which are subjects for possible judgments" (AT vii 56: CSM ii 39). But on occasion, Descartes uses "intellect" in a narrower sense, to signify the power of producing clear and distinct ideas (what he often calls "pure intellect" or, in earlier works, *vis cognoscens*). Descartes refers to a narrow sense of "intellect," for instance, when he claims, in the Fourth Meditation, that the scope of his intellect is much more limited than that of his will (AT vii 56–57: CSM ii 39–40); (AT vii 58: CSM ii 40); (AT vii 60: CSM ii 42).

cases, as I will soon show, it will incur a state of error) or, alternatively, the will can suspend judgment with regard to them (and thereby avoid error). By contrast, when the ideas that come before the mind are clear and distinct, the will cannot resist assenting to them. As Descartes writes to Regius, "our mind is of such a nature that it cannot help assenting to what it clearly understands."[15] As long as our ideas are clear and distinct, the judgments we are irresistibly inclined to make upon them can contain no error. As Descartes states in the *Principles*, error arises "only when, as often happens, we make a judgment about something even though we do not have an accurate perception of it" (I, 33).

The discussion so far may not seem to challenge the standard, substantive reading of Descartes' notion of error. One may argue that Descartes does not *equate* error with the affirmation or denial of confusedly or obscurely perceived propositional content, but only takes error to be *possible* under these conditions. Scholars usually tend to argue that by passing judgment on matters we do not apprehend clearly and distinctly we only *run the risk of error*, implying that error will occur if and only if the ideas to which we assent are false in themselves.[16]

The following passage from the Fourth Meditation, however, which includes Descartes' fullest account of the essence of error, casts serious doubt on the widely held substantive interpretation. For ease of discussion, I divide this passage into two parts, numbered (1) and (2):

(1) If, however, I simply refrain from making a judgment in cases where I do not perceive the truth with sufficient clarity and distinctness, then it is clear that I am behaving correctly and avoiding error. But if in such cases I either affirm or deny, then I am not using my free will correctly.

(2) If I go for the alternative which is false, then obviously I shall be in error; if I take the other side, then it is by pure chance that I arrive at the truth, and I shall still be at fault since it is clear by the natural light that the perception of the intellect should always precede the determination of the will. In this incorrect

---

[15] May 24, 1640 (AT III 64: CSMK 147). See also Third Meditation (AT VII 36: CSM II 25); Fourth Meditation (AT VII 57–58: CSM II 40); (AT VII 58–59: CSM II 41); Fifth Meditation (AT VII 65: CSM II 45); (AT VII 69–70: CSM II 48); Second Replies (AT VII 145–46: CSM II 104); (AT VII 166: CSM II 117); Seventh Replies (AT VII 460: CSM II 309); letter to Mesland, May 2, 1644 (AT IV 116: CSMK 233). In the *Principles*, Descartes also maintains that "the minds of all of us have been so moulded by nature that whenever we perceive something clearly, we spontaneously give our assent to it and are quite unable to doubt its truth" (I, 43).

[16] See, for instance, Wilson (1978: 148); Wells (1984: 37); Tierno (1997: 79); Wee (2006a: 122). Gassendi is also implying such a reading of Descartes' notion of error when he asks: "is it not still an imperfection not to perceive clearly matters which you need to decide upon, and hence to be perpetually liable *to the risk of error*?" (Fifth Objections, AT VII 312–13: CSM II 217; my emphasis).

use of free will may be found the privation which constitutes the essence of error. (AT vii 60: CSM ii 41)[17]

The full passage examines possible attitudes of the will toward confused and obscure perceptions occurring in the mind. Insofar as I refrain from making a judgment, as Descartes maintains in part (1), I am clearly behaving correctly and avoiding error. But if I choose *to affirm or deny* my confused or obscure perceptions, I will be blamed for not using my free will correctly, irrespective of whether the content of my judgment is true or false. Descartes allows for an idea to be confused or obscure and at the same time true.[18] Hence, in asserting that any *affirmation or denial* of a confused and obscure idea amounts to an incorrect use of free will, he implies (without as yet asserting so explicitly) that he does not restrict error to the affirmation of what is false and to the denial of what is true. Rather, he considers any *assent* to a confusedly or obscurely perceived *truth*, as well as any *denial* of a confusedly or obscurely perceived *false-hood*, an incorrect use of free will (and hence, I will argue, an instance of error).

The second part of the passage lends this reading even stronger credence. Descartes goes on to state: "If I go for the alternative which is false, then obviously I shall be in error." This statement suggests that the falsity of the content to which we assent in a judgment is a sufficient condition for the occurrence of error; but this falsity is not a necessary condition, since it does not constitute part of the essence of error. As Descartes explicitly maintains, "if I take the other side" and assent to a confusedly or obscurely perceived *truth*, "then it is by pure chance that I arrive at the truth." In this case "I shall still be at fault" (*non ideo culpâ carebo*; *je ne*

---

[17] Because the second part of this paragraph is central to my discussion, I am including in this note the original Latin (1641) as well as its French rendering of 1647: "*Atque si in eam partem quae falsa est me convertam, plane fallar; si verò alteram amplectar, casu quidem incidam in veritatem, sed non ideo culpâ carebo, quia lumine naturali manifestum est perceptionem intellectûs praecedere semper debere voluntatis determinationem. Atque in hoc liberi arbitrii non recto usu privatio illa inest quae formam erroris constituit*" (AT vii 60).

"*Et si j'assure ce qui n'est pas vrai, il est évident que je me trompe, même aussi, encore que je juge selon la vérité, cela n'arrive que par hasard, et je ne laisse pas de faillir, et d'user mal de mon libre arbitre; car la lumière naturelle nous enseigne que la connaissance de l'entendement doit toujours précéder la détermination de la volonté. Et c'est dans ce mauvais usage du libre arbitre, que se rencontre la privation qui constitue la forme de l'erreur*" (AT ix 47–48).

[18] As I argued in Chapter 1 above, the confusion and obscurity of an idea indicates the mind's failure to fully and accurately "read" and interpret the idea's immediate content, but this by no means entails the non-reality of the object the idea is *of*. Confused and obscure ideas *might* indeed be "ontologically" false; for they might represent non-beings. Yet these ideas might also be true in themselves, namely, ideas of "things" whose immediate content corresponds to the nature of the things they represent.

laisse pas de faillir), that is, I shall incur an error accompanied by guilt, "since it is clear by the natural light that the perception of the intellect should always precede the determination of the will." The guilt, as this statement makes clear, lies in what constitutes *the very essence* of error, not just its cause: the misuse of free will, that is, our failure to comply with the precept of our natural light of reason – never make judgments on the basis of confused or obscure perceptions. Any violation of this rational precept, internally imposed upon every human being, constitutes an instance of error, irrespective of the content to which we apply the operation of our will. Accordingly, Descartes writes in the *Principles*: "when we give our assent to something which is not clearly perceived, this is always a misuse of our judgment, even if by chance we stumble on the truth" (I, 44).

The concluding sentence of the passage we have been discussing thus far provides a further important insight into Descartes' non-substantive concept of error. Descartes explicitly stipulates that the privation that constitutes the essence of error *is found* in the incorrect use of free will (*Atque in hoc liberi arbitrii non recto usu privatio illa inest quae formam erroris constituit*). Cottingham, Stoothoff, and Murdoch have translated this crucial sentence as follows: "In this incorrect use of free will may be found the privation which constitutes the essence of error." This translation may result in a misunderstanding: rendering *inest* as "may be found" (and not "is found") could give the impression that the *locus* of the privation that constitutes the essence of error is not necessarily the incorrect use of free will. As the original Latin confirms, however, Descartes takes the privative essence of error to *inhere* in the incorrect use of free will.[19] The subsequent sentence in the Fourth Meditation reinforces this line of thought. Descartes writes:

The privation, I say, lies in the operation of the will in so far as it proceeds from me, but not in the faculty of will which I received from God, nor even in its operation, in so far as it depends on him. (AT VII 60: CSM II 41; my emphasis)

In this sentence, Descartes clarifies that the privation he identifies with the essence of error lies in the operation of judging (which he considers an operation of the will). Therefore, to think that the deficiency that constitutes the essence of error lies in the propositional content to which the operation of the will applies is, in my view, groundless.

---

[19] Note that the French version is also unequivocal on this point: "*Et c'est dans ce mauvais usage du libre arbitre, que se rencontre la privation qui constitue la forme de l'erreur*" (AT IX 47).

Later in this chapter, I discuss more extensively the notion of "privation" that Descartes identifies with the essence of error. I show that the privative essence of error constitutes an absence of clear and distinct *cognitio* that the agent should have possessed while exercising her power of judgment, rather than an absence of truth. At this point, however, it should suffice for us to recognize that Descartes takes the essence of error to lie in our incorrect use of free will, that is, in a deficiency in the operation of our will rather than in the *propositional content* to which this operation applies.

I therefore suggest that when speaking of erroneous (formally false) judgments, Descartes does not confine himself to judgments whose propositional content fails to represent real objects or "things." Rather, by "false judgment," Descartes denotes any *act* of judgment we apply to matters we do not perceive clearly and distinctly. In claiming that "falsity in the strict sense, or formal falsity, can occur only in judgments" (Third Meditation, AT VII 43: CSM II 30), Descartes is referring to our *acts of judging*, not to the content of our judgments and beliefs.[20] As I argued in the previous chapter, it is for this reason that he holds that falsity in the strict sense, or formal falsity, cannot occur in ideas "when considered solely in themselves" (AT VII 37: CSM II 26). In this perplexing statement, Descartes does not deny that ideas can properly be said to be the bearers of truth or falsehood, as is often assumed,[21] nor does he suggest that ideas are inherently true.[22] Rather, I argue, formal falsity cannot be found in our ideas since it is a characteristic of our voluntary *acts* of judgment, not of the *content* to which these acts apply.[23]

Descartes' non-substantive conception of error differs from the substantive conception in both extension and intension. Cartesian error is

[20] The kind of falsity that Descartes assigns to acts of judgment is called "formal," I suggest, because these acts apply to "ideas" in the formal sense, that is, with reference to the truth or falsity of the objects they represent (Fourth Replies, AT VII 232: CSM II 163).

[21] See, e.g., Kenny (1968: 117); Curley (1975: 173); Williams (1978: 131, 167, 182); Wilson (1978: 108, 141); Gueroult (1984: I, 111); Rosenthal (1986: 409); Van De Pitte, (1988: 461ff.); Hoffman (1996: 359); Nolan (1997: 193 n. 43); Vinci (1998: 14); Nadler (2006: 100). As most scholars emphasize, however, it is unquestionable that Descartes does often speak of ideas as being true or false.

[22] See, for instance, Wells (1984: 33); Alanen (1994: 243–44, 248; 2003: 149, 160); Nelson (2008: 321).

[23] Notice that Gueroult (1984: I, 221), while embracing a substantive reading of Descartes' concept of error, still holds that Descartes refers formal falsity to the act of judgment (when this act affirms what is nothingness as being). For a different reading, see Newman (2008: 340), who argues that formal falsity is referred to the propositions judged rather than to the acts of judging (see also Chapter 1 above, section 4, n. 41). Vinci's interpretation also implies such a view, though for very different reasons. Reading the conception of the *Rules* into the *Meditations* and later writings, he holds that the immediate objects of ideas are properties rather than propositions,

wider in its range than the substantive conception, applying not only to affirmation of falsehood or denial of truth but also to cases where we affirm what is true or deny what is false *without being justified in our judgments.* But even more important, Descartes' concept of error shifts the focus from the truth-value of the content being judged to the question of how we employ our faculty of judgment. This conception of error is pragmatic rather than substantive, dynamic rather than static; its key notions are "use" and "misuse" of free will rather than the substantive notions of falsity and truth. The notion of justification, which plays no role in the standard, substantive concept of error, plays an essential role in that of Descartes. To avoid error, we are obliged to be *justified* in our judgments: never accept anything as true without having *sufficient reasons* for doing so.

The prescription to limit our judgments and beliefs to issues on which we have evident knowledge is already set forth in writings preceding the *Meditations.* Already in the *Rules*, Descartes holds that "we should attend only to those objects of which our minds seem capable of having certain and indubitable cognition" (Rule 2, AT x 362: CSM 1 10). Descartes indicates that "in accordance with this Rule, we reject all such merely probable cognition and resolve to believe only what is perfectly known and incapable of being doubted" (AT x 362: CSM 1 10). This prescription has a later counterpart in Part II of the *Discourse on the Method*, where it appears as the first of Descartes' four Rules of Method:

The first was never to accept anything as true if I did not have evident knowledge of its truth: that is, carefully to avoid precipitate conclusions and preconceptions, and to include nothing more in my judgments than what presented itself to my mind so clearly and so distinctly that I had no occasion to doubt it. (AT vi 18: CSM 1 120)

And yet, however important the rule of evidence may have been for the method of the *Rules* and of the *Discourse*, it was not given the same standing and meaning assigned to it in the *Meditations* and in subsequent writings. Only after the doctrine of judgments as operations of the will has been worked out, along with its underlying metaphysical conception of freedom, does the rule of evidence become an absolutely binding duty – in contexts of rigorous inquiry – to exercise rational control over our judgments and beliefs. Any violation of this duty, as noted, constitutes a

and that an act of judgment is required to impart propositional form to the idea's content (1998: 14–19, 63–64, 143–55). Vinci's approach appears to suggest that formal falsity is a feature of the content of any judgment ascribing a property to a thing or to a substance that does not possess this property, either formally or eminently (1998, esp. chs. 1, 5, and 7).

culpable instance of error, irrespective of the content to which we assent by our operation of judgment.[24]

In Chapters 5 and 6, I show that Descartes' account of error as a misuse of free will applies not only to the purely intellectual regime but also to extra-theoretical decision-making pertaining to the religious, moral, and practical affairs of everyday life. And yet, what he counts as a misuse of free will, and hence as an instance of error in the extra-theoretical domain, does not coincide with assenting to ideas we perceive less than clearly and distinctly. In this respect, his account of error in the Fourth Meditation is confined to metaphysical and other purely theoretical issues that admit to our clear and distinct apprehension. In practical matters that might not be susceptible to our clear and distinct perception, as I will argue, it is incumbent upon us to judge and act on the basis of the right reasons, a notion to be specified for each domain separately. Descartes appears to hold a similar approach when discussing *speculative* matters that cannot be perceived clearly and distinctly. To illustrate this point, let me address Daniel Garber's intriguing discussion of the relation between reason and experience in the *Meditations*.

Garber emphasizes the essential role that sense experience and experiment play in Descartes' method for constructing knowledge.[25] On these grounds, he suggests that we reconsider Descartes' *apparent* recommendation in the Fourth Meditation "to limit ourselves to knowledge derived from the light of reason" so as to "guarantee that we do not stray into intellectual sin, that is, error" (2001: 104–05). For, "if we are to limit ourselves to clear and distinct perceptions, then there would seem to be no room for *any* appeal to experience *at all*" (p. 105). Rejecting a "narrow" perspective of Descartes' notion of reason, Garber analyzes the strategy employed in the Sixth Meditation of subordinating the teaching of the senses to reason.[26] His analysis of the argument for the existence of bodies in the Sixth Meditation (AT VII 79–80: CSM II 55), by which he

---

[24] This issue should be viewed in its larger context, as part of the foundational place that epistemological inquiry occupies in the *Meditations*, and in light of the new conception of method that this work provides for withdrawing the mind from the senses and eliminating prejudice. See Garber (1992: 48–62). Compare the discussion in Curley (1978: 44–45), who appears to group the *Discourse* together with the *Meditations* as Descartes' later writings, contrasting both with the *Rules*.

[25] Garber (2001: ch. 5). See also Clarke (1982); Cottingham (2008a: 289ff.) and references therein.

[26] Garber's analysis proves the close connection between the Sixth Meditation's treatment of sensations and Descartes' later notion of rational mastery of the passions as present in the *Passions of the Soul*, an issue I address in Chapter 6 below. See also Brown (2006, esp. ch. 3).

exemplifies his claim, may help me illustrate the above suggestion that judging well in these domains will amount to judging on the basis of the right reasons. Garber emphasizes (2001: 106) that the conclusion (that bodies exist) "is established not because we have a clear and distinct perception that bodies exist," but rather by virtue of our clear and distinct apprehension that God would be a deceiver if it turned out that our ideas of bodies do not come from the bodies themselves. Since God has given us a "great propensity" to believe that our ideas of sense come from corporeal things while he has given us "no faculty at all" for learning that this propensity might be mistaken, we must conclude that, given divine veracity, bodies exist. We see, then, that though lacking a clear and distinct perception of this conclusion, we shall still be regarded as having used our free will correctly by virtue of perceiving clearly and distinctly the *reasons* supporting its truthfulness.

Descartes' use of the word *culpâ* when speaking of the misuse of free will suggests the ethical import he assigns to one incurring a state of error. Indeed, throughout the Fourth Meditation he asserts an essential affinity between intellectual error and moral sin. Not only does he state that both kinds of error have the same cause, but he also asserts that they share the same privative essence: the misuse of free will. In the Fourth Meditation he writes: "As for the privation involved – which is all that the essential definition of falsity and wrong (*culpâ*; *péché*) consists in – this does not in any way require the concurrence of God" (AT VII 60–61: CSM II 42). This assertion might seem at odds with Descartes' repeated cautions against a strict application of his conception of intellectual error to the practical sphere. In the Synopsis of the *Meditations*, for instance, he explicitly proclaims that he intends to discuss only intellectual errors that occur "in distinguishing truth from falsehood," and not errors we commit "in pursuing good and evil" (AT VII 15: CSM II 11). Nevertheless, as I elaborate in Chapter 6 below, the close connection that Descartes assumes between intellectual error and moral wrong lies in the non-substantive, privative essence he assigns to both. More specifically, I will argue that intellectual and moral error do not differ essentially from one another, since the privative essence of both inheres in our exercising the faculty of choice without having sufficient reasons for doing so, and not in the content of the choices we make, nor even in their resultant outcomes.

What Descartes means by asserting, in the Fourth Meditation, that the *privation* that constitutes the essence of error is found in the misuse of free will is the subject of the next section.

2 ERROR AS PRIVATION

The notion of privation, which Descartes identifies with the essence of error, needs to be placed in the context of its first appearance in the Fourth Meditation. At the beginning of this Meditation Descartes argues that God cannot be the cause of his errors, since "error as such is not something real which depends on God, but merely a defect" (AT VII 54: CSM II 38). Since error is not a real or positive being but rather a mere *absence* of being or of perfection, it cannot originate in the Supreme Being that creates only what is real. Descartes thus realizes that the cause of his errors must be found in himself, insofar as he is "something intermediate between God and nothingness, or between supreme being and non-being" (ibid.). He then claims: "in so far as I participate in nothingness or non-being, that is, in so far as I am not myself the supreme being and am lacking in countless respects, it is no wonder that I make mistakes" (ibid.).

But Descartes remains displeased with this solution. He goes on to assert that error is not a pure negation but rather a privation or lack of some knowledge (*cognitio*)[27] that somehow *should be in him*. The occurrence of error, when understood as *a positive* imperfection, might appear incompatible with God's omnipotence and ultimate veracity. In Descartes' formulation:

> But this is still not entirely satisfactory. For error is not a pure negation [... i.e., not simply the defect or lack of some perfection to which I have no proper claim (added in French version, AT IX 43–44)], but rather a privation or lack of some knowledge which somehow should be in me. And when I concentrate on the nature of God, it seems impossible that he should have placed in me a faculty which is not perfect of its kind, or which lacks some perfection which it ought to have. (AT VII 55: CSM II 38)

Descartes acknowledges that God, who "always wills what is best" (AT VII 55: CSM II 38), should have given him a nature ensuring he would

---

[27] Descartes distinguishes between knowledge as *cognitio*, which is a clear and distinct apprehension of a certain matter, and knowledge as *Scientia*, which denotes a complete, well-ordered, and firm body of knowledge based on intuitively grasped first principles (Alanen 2003: 7). In *The Search for Truth*, he characterizes *Scientia* as "a body of knowledge (*doctrine*) which was firm and certain enough to deserve the name 'science' (*science*)" (AT X 513: CSM II 408). And in the *Rules*, he argues: "the whole of human knowledge (*scientia*) consists uniquely in our achieving a distinct perception of how all these simple natures contribute to the composition of other things" (Rule 12, AT X 427: CSM I 49). In the Second Replies, Descartes states that the kind of awareness (*cognitio*) possessed by an atheist "is not true knowledge (*vera scientia*), since no act of awareness (*cognitio*) that can be rendered doubtful seems fit to be called knowledge (*scientia*)" (AT VII 141: CSM II 101). And yet, as Alanen rightly emphasizes (2003: 261 n. 1), Cartesian *Scientia* involves more than "a system of justified, doubt-proof beliefs," and hence requires more than the knowledge of God that the atheist is lacking. For a different analysis, see Vinci (1998: 19–26).

never go astray. Granted that error is not only a negative absence of perfection but rather an absence of perfection that he somehow *should have* possessed, the fact that God has not endowed him with complete immunity from error requires further explanation.

Before addressing Descartes' explanation of this issue, note that his distinction between privation and negation in the context of the Fourth Meditation differs from the traditional scholastic distinction. In scholastic terminology, a pure negation is a mere absence of perfection, whereas a privation is a lack of perfection a thing ought to possess *by its nature*. For Aquinas, for instance, to be without hands is a privation for a human being because a human being is born to have hands and thus should have possessed them according to her nature. By the same token, lacking wings is not a privation for human beings but only a negation, because wings are not things we are born to have by our nature.[28] But Descartes does not retain the original meaning of these terms when he equates the essence of error with privation in the Fourth Meditation. Since he holds that the human intellect is essentially finite and, as such, lacks a clear and distinct understanding of many things,[29] it is unlikely that he considers error to be a lack of some knowledge (*cognitio*) that he should have possessed *by his very nature*. In viewing error as an absence of knowledge that "somehow should be in [him]," Descartes might appear to be pointing to a lack of some knowledge with which *God* should have endowed him, given God's omnipotence and absolute veracity. Descartes may thus be construed as saying that God *should have endowed his nature* with an intellect that is "perfect of its kind," all of whose perceptions are clear and distinct. Cecilia Wee has recently suggested a reading along these lines (2006a: 118–22). She argues that, for Descartes,

error is not just a negation – it is a *privation* in him, for it is an absence of the perfection of error-freedom that *should* be in him, that *should* have been endowed upon him by God ... A God who "wills what is best" would have given him a faculty of gaining knowledge that was perfect of its kind, so that he would not suffer the privation that is error. (2006a: 119)

This reading has some textual support. Descartes emphatically maintains, as noted, that when he concentrates on the nature of God, "it seems impossible that he should have placed in [him] a faculty which is not

---

[28] "Thus, if a man has no wings, that is not an evil for him, because he was not born to have them ... But it is an evil if he has no hands, for these he is born to and should have – if he is to be perfect. Yet this defect is not an evil for a bird. Every privation, if taken properly and strictly, is of that which one is born to have, and should have" (Aquinas 1975: 3.6.1).

[29] See, e.g., Fourth Meditation (AT vii 56: CSM ii 39; AT vii 60: CSM ii 42); *Principles*, i, 36.

perfect of its kind, or which lacks some perfection which it ought to have" (AT VII 55: CSM II 38). He then goes on to argue:

The more skilled the craftsman the more perfect the works produced by him; if this is so, how can anything produced by the supreme creator of all things not be complete and perfect in all respects? There is, moreover, no doubt that God could have given me a nature such that I was never mistaken; again, there is no doubt that he always wills what is best. Is it then better that I should make mistakes than that I should not do so? (AT VII 55: CSM II 38)

Descartes further contends that were God to grant him an intellect that is perfect of its kind, his freedom would not be impaired in any manner. Quite the opposite, his choices would then be markedly freer: "For if I always saw clearly what was true and good, I should never have to deliberate about the right judgment or choice; in that case, although I should be wholly free, it would be impossible for me ever to be in a state of indifference" (AT VII 58: CSM II 40). Descartes repeats this point toward the end of the Fourth Meditation:

I can see, however, that God could easily have brought it about that without losing my freedom, and despite the limitations in my knowledge, I should nonetheless never make a mistake. He could, for example, have endowed my intellect with a clear and distinct perception of everything about which I was ever likely to deliberate. (AT VII 61: CSM II 42)

A closer look at the Fourth Meditation, however, reveals that Descartes does not take the essence of error to be an absence of the perfection of error-freedom that God should have bestowed on him. Descartes explicitly states, as noted in the previous section, that the privation constituting the essence of error "lies in the operation of the will insofar as it proceeds from [him]" (AT VII 60: CSM II 41), or, again, that the privative essence of error is found "in the incorrect use of free will" (ibid.). In the *Principles*, Descartes asserts even more forcefully that "the fact that we fall into error is a defect in the way we act or in the use we make of our freedom, but not a defect in our nature. For our nature remains the same whether we judge correctly or incorrectly" (I, 38). These remarks clearly indicate that Descartes does not consider the privative essence of error to lie in the finitude of the intellect that God has bestowed on us. What is more, he raises various explicit arguments throughout the Fourth Meditation to show that no reason could prove that God ought to have granted us a faculty of knowledge greater than the one he actually did, even though it was in God's power to do so, thereby ensuring our absolute immunity from error.

In the rest of this section I will argue that Descartes does not consider error to be a lack of some knowledge "which somehow should be in [him]" *according to his nature* (as the scholastic distinction between privation and negation implies), nor does he view it as an absence of knowledge he suffers *because of his nature* (owing to an omission of God) – as Wee's reading proposes. Although both these alternatives enjoy some support in the literature, I find that, for different reasons, neither succeeds in adequately capturing Descartes' idea of error-as-privation. Instead, I suggest that Descartes takes error to be a lack of some knowledge that the agent should have possessed given *her own pretence* to hold a piece of knowledge that she in fact lacks. The absent *cognitio*, in cases of error, should have been possessed by the agent given her own false (unjustified) claim to knowledge, as manifest in her exercise of her power of judgment on matters about which she is to some degree ignorant. Although we are not obliged to attain a clear and distinct apprehension of all the objects of our *awareness*, we are obliged to attain a clear and distinct apprehension of the objects of our *judgments*. Granted the essential limitation of our intellect, we are commanded to refrain from making judgments whenever we lack clear understanding of the matter in question.[30] This implies that the positive element of error (which is the operation of judgment) is the element that ought not to be, given the confusion and obscurity of perception. Gueroult suggests such an understanding when he claims that "error adds to ignorance its affirmation as science . . . . That is the positive thing that constitutes its essence and that *ought not be*" (1984: I, 214).

Unlike mere ignorance, which is purely negative and as such lacks any normative import, error-as-privation involves both negative and positive constituents.[31] Its positive element, which differentiates it from pure ignorance, is the operation of judgment; its negative element is the absence of a clear and distinct perception of the object to which this operation applies.

---

[30] Stephen Menn articulates such a view when claiming: "what distinguishes error from mere ignorance is not that it is an ignorance of something we ought to know, but that it involves my *making a judgment* in ignorance" (1998: 305). Error is not a negation but a privation, since it is "a deviation from the standard God intended us to conform to" (p. 306). For an illuminating discussion of Descartes' debt to Augustine in the theodicy of error of the Fourth Meditation, see Menn (1998: 301–22).

[31] Notice that Descartes' use of the term "privation" in the Fourth Meditation differs significantly from his use of this term in other contexts. For instance, while raising in the Third Meditation (AT VII 44) and in the Fourth Replies (AT VII 234) the possibility that cold is nothing but the privation of heat (*frigus nihil aliud esse quàm privationem caloris*), he clearly does not mean that cold may be a lack of perfection (heat) that a thing *ought to have*. As I pointed out in Chapter 1, n. 72 above, whether Descartes uses privation in the latter context to denote a non-thing, or a non-existing thing or, instead, a negative but still real quality, remains unclear.

This point is worth emphasizing. In claiming that the negative element of the privation that is error is an absence of clarity and distinctness in the perception assented to, I oppose above all the commonly held substantive reading that considers this negative element to be an absence of truth. In particular, I disagree with Gueroult's contention that the negative constituent of the privative essence of error lies in the ideas being representations of nothingness (1984: 1, 214, 221, 223, 225), as well as with Menn's suggestion that "error is not simply the absence of truth, but the absence of truth from the kind of thing (namely, a judgment) which could and should be true" (1998: 305 n. 3). I also challenge the view that, for Descartes, the negative element of error-as-privation is the absence of *the perfection of error-freedom*, one that God ought to have endowed us with given his omnibenevolence (as in Wee 2006a: 118–19). Finally, I take issue with a recent interpretation of Descartes' position in the Fourth Meditation, whereby confusion and obscurity are themselves privations, since ideas *ought* to be clear and distinct (Kaufman 2000: 402; 2003a: 398–99).

3 THE DUAL METAPHYSICAL STATUS OF ERROR

In considering error as a privation rather than a pure negation, Descartes does not withdraw his original claim that error is a pure negation in relation to God. On the contrary, most of his arguments from this point onward in the Fourth Meditation aim to prove that error is a privation with regard to human beings and at the same time a pure negation with respect to God.

To establish the dual metaphysical status of error, Descartes proceeds along two parallel routes which eventually converge into one cohesive solution. The first route consists in a rigorous investigation into the causes of error and into the cognitive mechanism that allows it to occur in the human mind. Through this analysis, Descartes undertakes to show that God is not responsible for our errors. God has no part in their formation in the human cognition, neither directly (by actively participating in the exercise of our power of judgment in any instance of error) nor indirectly (by creating our mental faculties with an original flaw or imperfection that makes error inevitable). Rather, the source of error lies in our own failure to restrict the operations of our will to stay within the limits of our intellect, a failure for which we bear full responsibility. Note that this line of argument takes the opposite course to the one presented earlier, with which Descartes opens his arguments in the Fourth Meditation. There, Descartes claims that God cannot be the cause of our errors since error is a pure negation and God creates only what is positive and real. But after realizing that error contains a positive element as well (which makes it an absence of knowledge *that somehow should be in him*), Descartes must show that error is *not* privative in relation to God as it is in relation to himself. The general rationale for this move appears to be the following: showing that human errors do not require the concurrence of God for their production proves that human errors are not "things" in relation to God, as they are in relation to us, but are *mere negations*.[32] The causal-mechanistic analysis of error, then, has clear normative ramifications for determining whether we bear full responsibility for the occurrence of error in our minds. This normative question, in turn, determines the dual metaphysical status of error, as a positive imperfection with respect to us and as a pure negation with respect to God.

The second route Descartes follows in the Fourth Meditation has a distinctive, straightforward normative character, directly confronting the issue of the can–ought distinction as applied to God. Through a different set of arguments, Descartes undertakes to show that no reason can be brought in order to prove that God *ought to* have granted him a faculty of knowledge greater than the one he did, so as to assure him complete immunity from error, even though it was clearly within God's *power* to do so.

Although Descartes employs a different array of arguments to support the causal and the strictly normative themes, he does not always distinguish between them and at times even binds them together. Consider, for example, the following passage from the *Principles*:

[E]rrors are not things, *requiring the real concurrence of God for their production.* Considered in relation to God they are merely negations [... that is, *he did not bestow on us everything which he was able to bestow, but which equally we can see he was not obliged to give us* (added in French version)], and considered in relation to ourselves they are privations. (I, 31; my emphases)

My concern below is with the two lines of arguments through which Descartes establishes the dual metaphysical status of error, and then with the ways in which these arguments prove the non-substantive privative essence of error with regard to human beings.

4 THE CAUSAL ANALYSIS OF ERROR

Descartes begins his causal analysis in the Fourth Meditation by showing that error does not arise from any original imperfection in the cognitive

---

[32] *Principles*, I, 31; Fourth Meditation (AT VII 60–61: CSM II 42).

faculties with which God has endowed us. The intellect cannot be the source of our errors, as noted, since this faculty only enables us to perceive the ideas that are subjects for possible judgments, without affirming or denying anything (AT VII 56: CSM II 39). The intellect is indeed finite and limited in scope and, as such, lacks clear and distinct ideas of many things. But the finitude of our intellect, which Descartes considers essential to its nature (AT VII 60: CSM II 42), does not by itself constitute the source of our errors, since we can prevent error by holding back assent to ideas insufficiently clear and distinct. Descartes addresses this argument toward the end of the Fourth Meditation, when he writes:

What is more, even if I have no power to avoid error in the first way just mentioned, which requires a clear perception of everything I have to deliberate on, I can avoid error in the second way, which depends merely on my remembering to withhold judgment on any occasion when the truth of the matter is not clear. (AT VII 61–62: CSM II 43)[33]

Descartes proceeds to show that the source of his errors does not lie in the faculty of will that he received from God, for this faculty is "so perfect and so great that the possibility of a further increase in its perfection or greatness is beyond his understanding" (AT VII 57: CSM II 39). For Descartes, the infinitude of the human will consists, in the first place, in its unlimited scope. Among all the things we can conceive of, however confusedly, there is nothing to which our will cannot apply itself (that is, affirm or deny, pursue or avoid). Now, since the human will is perfect of its kind and cannot be restricted in any manner, it cannot be the origin of the positive imperfection that constitutes the essence of error. In Descartes' formulation, "the power of willing which I received from God is not, when considered in itself, the cause of my mistakes; for it is both extremely ample and also perfect of its kind" (AT VII 58: CSM II 40).

In the Fourth Meditation, Descartes alludes to another sense in which the human will may be taken to be infinite and, as such, to bear a likeness to the infinite will of God. He states that the divine will does not appear any greater than the human will when considered as will "in the essential and strict sense" (AT VII 57: CSM II 40). Elaborating on this statement in the next two chapters, I will argue that this other sense of infinitude of the will has to do with the way we experience our freedom. Descartes

---

[33] This argument, as I show below, also allows Descartes to maintain that no reason can prove that God ought to have given him a faculty of knowledge greater than the one he did (AT VII 56: CSM II 39).

writes, accordingly, that it is by virtue of the infinite freedom he experiences within himself that he considers himself to be godlike: "It is only the will, or freedom of choice, which I experience within me to be so great that the idea of any greater faculty is beyond my grasp; so much so that it is above all in virtue of the will that I understand myself to bear in some way the image and likeness of God" (AT VII 57: CSM II 40).

Descartes' next step, and perhaps the linchpin of his position concerning human responsibility, is to show that God does not participate in any manner in the operation of our will, and in particular in any instance of error: "The privation, I say, lies in the operation of the will in so far as it proceeds from me, but not in the faculty of will which I received from God, nor even in its operation, in so far as it depends on him" (AT VII 60: CSM II 41). Several lines later, Descartes expounds on this point:

Finally, I must not complain that the forming of those acts of will or judgments in which I go wrong happens with God's concurrence. For in so far as these acts depend on God, they are wholly true and good; and my ability to perform them means that there is in a sense more perfection in me than would be the case if I lacked this ability. As for the privation involved – which is all that the essential definition of falsity and wrong consists in – this does not in any way require the concurrence of God, since it is not a thing; indeed, when it is referred to God as its cause, it should be called not a privation but simply a negation. For it is surely no imperfection in God that he has given me the freedom to assent or not to assent in those cases where he did not endow my intellect with a clear and distinct perception; but it is undoubtedly an imperfection in me to misuse that freedom and make judgments about matters which I do not fully understand. (AT VII 60–61: CSM II 42)

This passage illuminates two key points. First, since we exercise our power of judgment without God's concurrence, God is not responsible for that which is a fault in the operation of our will – the decision, which is entirely our own, to exert our will without having a clear and distinct understanding of the matter in question. God, therefore, bears no responsibility for our errors, and the operation of our will with respect to him is wholly true and good. Second, God cannot be blamed for giving us the freedom to assent to matters about which we lack clear and distinct apprehension. In slightly different terms, the fact that God has endowed us with the freedom to perform faulty acts of judgment is not to be held against him, nor does it make God responsible for our errors. On the contrary, our ability to perform these acts constitutes one of our most remarkable perfections. As Tierno writes, Descartes associates "our capacity to err with the existence of a perfection in our nature" (1997: 47).

The same infinite power of choice that leads us into erroneous judgments when we misuse it renders us worthy of moral praise when we succeed in using it correctly. Several years later Descartes writes in the *Passions of the Soul*:

> I see only one thing in us which could give us good reason for esteeming ourselves, namely, the exercise of our free will and the control we have over our volitions. For we can reasonably be praised or blamed only for actions that depend upon this free will. It renders us in a certain way like God by making us masters of ourselves, provided we do not lose the rights it gives us through timidity. (art. 152)

For Descartes, our virtuousness and self-esteem both depend on our knowing that nothing truly belongs to us but this freedom to dispose our volitions, and that we ought to praised or blamed for no other reason than our using this freedom well or badly (*Passions*, art. 153). But such knowledge alone is insufficient to merit us moral praise, for which we must also actualize this knowledge while experiencing within ourselves "a firm and constant resolution" to use this freedom well (ibid.).[34]

On several occasions, Descartes addresses the irresolvable tension between our absolute freedom of choice and divine preordination. In a letter to Princess Elizabeth dated November 3, 1645, he contends:

> As for free will, I agree that if we think only of ourselves we cannot help regarding ourselves as independent; but when we think of the infinite power of God, we cannot help believing that all things depend on him, and hence that our free will is not exempt from this dependence. For it involves a contradiction to say that God has created human beings of such a nature that the actions of their will do not depend on his. (AT IV 332: CSMK 277)

Although both doctrines are self-evident,[35] their reconciliation is beyond human grasp: "we can easily get ourselves into great difficulties if we attempt to reconcile this divine preordination with the freedom of our will, or attempt to grasp both these things at once" (*Principles*, I, 40; see also I, 41). Just as "we cannot help regarding ourselves as independent," he writes to Princess Elizabeth, namely, as possessing a boundless free will, so also do we have self-evident knowledge of the dependence of all things on God. Neither of these self-evident doctrines excludes the other, even though the way in which they can be mutually settled is unattainable to us.[36]

And yet, Descartes is convinced that "the independence which we experience and feel in ourselves, and which suffices to make our actions

---

[34] I elaborate on this issue in Chapter 6 below.

[35] *Principles*, I, 39, 40; letter to Princess Elizabeth, November 3, 1645 (AT IV 332: CSMK 277).

[36] In the same letter to Elizabeth, Descartes writes: "But just as the knowledge of the existence of God should not take away our certainty of the free will which we experience and feel in

praiseworthy or blameworthy, is not incompatible with a dependence of quite another kind, whereby all things are subject to God" (AT IV 332–33: CSMK 277). Two points are of special importance in this passage. The first is that the mere fact that we cannot resist perceiving our will as entirely independent of any external coercion, and therefore as absolutely free, is sufficient to render us fully responsible for our choices and make us susceptible to moral praise or blame. The second is that the independence or freedom that we experience within ourselves is "not incompatible" with our ultimate dependence on God, because each of these cases refers to a completely different kind of "dependence." In a strict metaphysical sense, only God may be considered a substance, since anything created depends solely and fully on him – including our exercise of the will. But in a weaker sense of "dependence," which is also metaphysical and yet pertaining to the human sphere, the human mind is also a substance and therefore possesses limitless free will, a power independent of anything external to it – even, in a certain respect, the will of God.

Descartes' emphasis on our inner experience of the boundless freedom of our will does not suggest that he regards this freedom as merely a psychological or phenomenological experience. As the next chapter will show, he insists that our freedom is revealed to us by the natural light of reason,[37] and that the freedom of our will "is so evident that it must be counted among the first and most common notions that are innate in us."[38] Just as the distinction between substance and accident is a real distinction rather than a distinction of reason, so is the distinction between the independence of our will with respect to the human domain and the ultimate dependence of all things on God in a strict metaphysical sense.

By the same token, Descartes' distinction between the privative essence of error with respect to human beings, and its purely negative essence with regard to God, *is not* a distinction between the psychological and the metaphysical planes, respectively, as Gueroult seems to hold.[39] *Pace*

---

ourselves, so also the knowledge of our free will should not make us doubt the existence of God" (AT IV 332–33: CSMK 277).

[37] Third Replies, AT VII 191: CSM II 134.

[38] *Principles*, I, 39. See also *Principles*, I, 41; letter to Mersenne, December 1640 (AT III 259: CSMK 161); letter to Princess Elizabeth, November 3, 1645 (AT IV 332: CSMK 277). See also Campbell (1999: 181); Ragland (2006a: 381).

[39] 1984: I, 220–27. Gueroult suggests that, from a metaphysical perspective, error "has no reality in itself" (p. 224). In his reading, since error "entails no positive imperfection of my nature or of my faculties – given that it is not a reality at all – the psychological phenomenon of error, in spite of the privative character it presents, does not entail any privative character on the metaphysical plane. Because of this fact, it requires no cause, in the metaphysical sense of the case, the psychological explanation concerns not error, but a real operation in my consciousness, namely, the

Gueroult, I think that this distinction is between two metaphysical layers, each pertaining to a different order and approached from a different perspective. As Descartes states in the *Principles*, "our errors, if considered in relation to God, are merely negations; if considered in relation to ourselves they are privations" (I, 31).

With these considerations in mind, we may now return to Descartes' contention in the Fourth Meditation that God does not participate in the operation of the human will. Not only is our God-granted faculty of will not the source of our error, being perfect of its kind and infinite in scope and essence, but God has no part in the use we make of this faculty in any particular instance of error. This brings us to Descartes' positive, concluding account of the source of human error:

> So what then is the source of my mistakes? It must be simply this: the scope of the will is wider than that of the intellect; but instead of restricting it within the same limits, I extend its use to matters which I do not understand. Since the will is indifferent in such cases, it easily turns aside from what is true and good, and this is the source of my error and sin. (AT VII 58: CSM II 40–41)

The source of human error, as this passage indicates, is precisely what constitutes its privative essence: our own misuse of free will, that is, our failure to retain our judgments within the limits of our intellect.

Some scholars have suggested that Descartes considers human error to result from the different scope of the two faculties, the intellect and the will.[40] Occasionally, Descartes does express himself in a manner that may support this reading. In the *Principles*, for instance, he explicitly stipulates that "the scope of the will is wider than that of the intellect, and this is the cause of error" (I, 35). Likewise, in the Fourth Meditation he states: "I notice that [my errors] depend on two concurrent causes, namely on the faculty of knowledge which is in me, and on the faculty of choice" (AT VII 56: CSM II 39). Nevertheless, it is unlikely that Descartes considers the original disparity in scope between the will and the intellect, which arises from the very nature of these faculties (AT VII 60: CSM II 42), to be the source of our errors. Were he to embrace such a view, he could not single out human beings as sole authors of their erroneous judgments as they misuse their freedom of choice, nor could he assert that the privation

---

operation of my faculties, of which error is only epiphenomenal. By allowing the establishing of the nonpositive character from the metaphysical point of view of privation or positive imperfection that characterizes error on the psychological plane, the psychological path leads to the solution of a problem essential to metaphysics, in conformity with the requirements of the latter: to safeguard completely divine veracity" (1984: I, 224).

[40] See, e.g., Kenny (1972: 1); Gibson (1987: 324); Tierno (1997: 32, 35, 43–44).

which is the essence of error lies in our own incorrect use of free will. Rather than being the cause of our errors, the disparity in scope between the two faculties is what makes error possible, allowing us to extend the operations of our will beyond the limits of our intellect. As Lex Newman observes, "limitation in our intellect explains the possibility of judgment error; misuse of our free will explains its actuality" (2008: 339).

Just like this disparity, the indifference of the will with which Descartes concludes the above extract from the Fourth Meditation is not the cause of our errors either, but rather one of the conditions that make error possible. Furthermore, the indifference (or indecisiveness) of our will, which makes it possible for us to err, also enables us to hold back from making ill-considered judgments on matters we do not clearly apprehend. Incurring an error, in Descartes' view, is not only voluntary but also avoidable. When the ideas in our mind are confused or obscure, we have the power to choose whether to assent to them or dissent from them (incurring an error in both cases), or suspend judgment about them (thereby ensuring ourselves against error).

On this issue, a significant difference emerges between the substantive reading of Descartes' concept of error and the non-substantive reading that this chapter suggests. In the substantive reading, the responsibility we bear for our erroneous judgments relies on our alleged power to choose between placing ourselves *at risk of error* (by passing judgment on matters we do not clearly apprehend) or avoiding that risk. In the non-substantive reading, however, our choice of whether to pass judgment on the basis of a confused or obscure perception is a choice between incurring a state of error or avoiding it. This is not to suggest, of course, that we consciously and deliberately wish to err. Descartes emphasizes that "although there is in fact no one who expressly wishes to go wrong, there is scarcely anyone who does not often wish to give his assent to something which, though he does not know it, contains some error" (*Principles*, 1, 42). In distinguishing between expressly wishing to go wrong and expressly wishing to give one's assent to matters *containing some error*, Descartes employs the term "error" in its more standard, substantive sense. Yet I take him to mean that although we willfully give our assent to matters we *actually* do not fully understand, at the moment of choosing we are unaware that we lack a distinct understanding of them. In this sense, we cannot be said to "expressly wish to go wrong." Descartes concludes: "Indeed, precisely because of their eagerness to find the truth, people who do not know the right method of finding it often pass judgment on things of which they lack perception, and this is why they fall into error" (ibid.).

5 THE NORMATIVE QUERY: GOD AND HUMAN PRONENESS TO ERROR

To prove the purely negative metaphysical status of error in reference to God, Descartes does not confine himself to showing that God does not take part in the creation of human error. He also considers the strictly normative question of whether God *ought* to have granted him absolute freedom from error. Descartes aims to prove that God was not obliged to guarantee us complete immunity from error by granting us an intellect all of whose perceptions are clear and distinct, even though God's omnipotence ensured him the power to do so.

On this issue, Descartes employs two different strategies. The first is to disqualify a priori any attempt to comprehend and evaluate the perfection of God's works. Descartes sets forth three main arguments, which I will sketch here briefly.[41] He begins by claiming that, as finite thinkers, we cannot comprehend the impenetrable motives and purposes underlying God's actions.[42] The implication is that even if some of God's works are not wholly perfect, a possibility that Descartes explicitly denies in his replies to Gassendi (AT VII 374: CSM II 257–58), the perfection of God's actions would not be blemished since his ends are impenetrable to us. Descartes then introduces his second argument, which rules out our ability to evaluate the perfection of any of God's particular works. He states that "what would perhaps rightly appear very imperfect if it existed on its own is quite perfect when its function as a part of the universe is considered" (AT VII 55–56: CSM II 39). This argument suggests that the perfection of particular things in the universe can only be evaluated from a global perspective, namely, in relation to the role they play in the universe considered as a whole. Since human beings lack the divine all-encompassing overview of the universe, they are incapable of judging or estimating the role that a particular thing might play in the universal scheme of things.[43] Finally, toward the end of

---

[41] For more extensive discussions of these arguments, see, e.g., Gueroult (1984: I, 214–20, 227–28); Tierno (1997: 35–36, 57–69); Newman (1999: 570–72).

[42] AT VII 55: CSM II 38–39. Descartes observes that this reason alone has brought him to consider the customary search for final causes in physics to be totally useless (AT VII 55: CSM II 39). See also *Principles*, I, 28; III, 2.

[43] AT VII 55–56: CSM II 39. Descartes writes to Gassendi: "When you say that I observe that some of God's works are not wholly perfect, you are plainly inventing something I neither wrote nor thought. I simply said that if certain things are considered not from the point of view of the part they play in the world but as separate wholes, then they can appear to be imperfect" (Fifth Replies, AT VII 374: CSM II 257–58).

the Fourth Meditation Descartes presents another argument that differs from the previous two in addressing the perfection of the universe as a whole rather than the perfection of particular things. Descartes maintains that a universe whose parts are all exactly alike is not as perfect as a universe comprising a great variety of parts, some of them immune to error and others not.[44] The third argument, then, assumes precisely what the previous argument denies: that despite our limited point of view, we are capable of evaluating the perfection of God's works. What is more, this argument asserts exactly what Descartes emphatically denies in the Fifth Replies: that some of Gods works are not wholly perfect, or at least, in Tierno's wording, "that human beings, considered in themselves, would be more perfect if they were 'immune from error'" (1997: 36).[45]

Descartes' second strategy is to show that whatever perfections God has seen fit to bestow upon us were granted not because we had a right to them but as a matter of privilege. Therefore, we cannot consider that any perfection that God has elected not to confer on us, for reasons to remain forever mysterious, is something that God is denying us (as if it were something that human nature was entitled to possess). Rather, we should consider the lack of such perfections to be merely negative. Resting on this reasoning, Descartes indicates that, in relation to God, the finitude of the human intellect is only negative and not privative, since it is not an absence of perfection that our nature is entitled to possess. Descartes writes:

For although countless things may exist without there being any corresponding ideas in me, it should not, strictly speaking, be said that I am deprived of these ideas [... it cannot be said that my understanding is deprived of these ideas, as if they were something to which its nature entitles it (added in French version, AT

---

[44] "Had God made me this way [immune from error], then I can easily understand that considered as a totality, I would have been more perfect than I am now. But I cannot therefore deny that there may in some way be more perfection in the universe as a whole because some of its parts are not immune from error, while others are immune, than there would be if all the parts were exactly alike. And I have no right to complain that the role God wished me to undertake in the world is not the principal one or the most perfect of all" (AT VII 61: CSM II 42–43). For a comparison between the Cartesian and the Augustinian doctrine of the excellence of creation, see Catherine Wilson (2008: 44–48).

[45] As Newman points out, this argument appeals to "the principle of organic unities – a principle that allows that the good of a whole may be enhanced by decreases in the perfection of its parts" (1999: 570–71). Note that Descartes invokes a similar argument in his letter to Mersenne of October 17, 1630, when he writes: "God leads everything to perfection, in one sense, i.e., collectively, but not in another, i.e., in particular. The very fact that particular things perish and that others appear in their place is one of the principal perfections of the universe" (AT I 154: CSMK 26).

IX 45)], but merely that I lack them, in a negative sense. This is because I cannot produce any reason to prove that God ought to have given me a greater faculty of knowledge than he did; and no matter how skilled I understand a craftsman to be, this does not make me think he ought to have put into every one of his works all the perfections which he is able to put into some of them. (AT VII 56: CSM II 39)

Descartes restates this argument a few paragraphs later:

Indeed, I have reason to give thanks to him who has never owed me anything for the great bounty that he has shown me, rather than thinking myself deprived or robbed of any gifts he did not bestow. (AT VII 60: CSM II 42) [... rather than entertaining so unjust a thought as to imagine that he deprived me of, or unjustly withheld, the other perfections which he did not give me. (added in French version, AT IX 48)]

By this argument, as Newman remarks, Descartes aims to show that an omniperfect God would have morally sufficient reason for endowing us with faculties that are imperfect of their kinds. For every imperfection of a kind (as opposed to imperfection of *instances* of a kind) is "a design limitation of the sort to which all creatures are susceptible: every product is essentially limited, even when produced by God" (1999: 563).[46]

This conclusion suggests that the relation between "can" and "ought" applies differently to God and to human beings. Accordingly, Descartes writes in the *Principles* that "when one of us men has the power to prevent some evil, but does not prevent it, we say that he is the cause of the evil; but we must not similarly suppose that because God could have brought it about that we never went wrong, this makes him the cause of our errors" (I, 38). The reason for this difference, Descartes explains, is that "the power which men have over each other was given them so that they might employ it in discouraging others from evil; but the power which God has over all men is both absolute and totally free." Descartes applies the same reasoning to intellectual error. The power of God to grant us complete immunity from error, which he has not actualized for reasons hidden from our sight, does not render God responsible for our errors, nor does it give us the right to demand this of him. By contrast, the power that God has given us to suspend judgment on matters that we do not clearly apprehend was given to us so that we might employ

---

[46] As Newman elucidates, "following in the Aristotelian tradition, Descartes distinguished two varieties of imperfection: *imperfect instances* of a kind, and *imperfect kinds*. Only the former *need* involve intolerable imperfection for which an omniperfect creator would have no morally sufficient reason" (1999: 563).

it to avoid error. This very fact, when combined with our inner awareness of our absolute freedom, is what renders us fully responsible for our errors.[47]

6 ERROR AS PRIVATION: ALTERNATIVE INTERPRETATIONS

In this section, I consider two current interpretations of Descartes' notion of error-as-privation which I addressed briefly earlier in this chapter. Both interpretations, for very different reasons, relate the privative essence of error to the working of our intellect, not to our incorrect use of free will.

Cecilia Wee holds that when Descartes considers error as privation, he means that it is "an absence of the perfection of error-freedom" that should have been endowed upon him by a non-deceiving God (2006a: 119). She thereby suggests that we are deprived of a greater faculty of knowledge, one that God *ought to* have conferred on us given his omnibenevolence. In her reading, when Descartes claims that error is a "lack of some knowledge which somehow should be in [him]," he is referring to an *enduring* lack of perfection which his *nature* suffers by being deprived of the perfection of error-freedom that God could have (and indeed, should have) bestowed on him. By contrast, my reading suggests that Descartes is not referring here to a flaw in our nature (an imperfection of a kind), but to a *particular* piece of knowledge that his *mind* lacks when incurring a state of error, namely, a clear and distinct *cognitio* of the content being judged.

Wee's understanding of Descartes' deviation from the scholastic distinction between negation and privation may be phrased as follows: whereas the scholastic conception takes privation to be an absence of perfection that a creature ought to possess *"according to his nature"*, in Wee's reading, Descartes takes error to be a lack of perfection he suffers *because of his nature*, an absence one's nature ought not to endure given God's benevolence. On these grounds, she further suggests that Descartes might consider privative the material falsity of ideas of sense. To support this claim she turns to the Third Meditation, where Descartes states that these ideas

---

[47] Note that Descartes employs this argument to reject Mersenne's claim that the rashness of judgment depends on the innate or acquired temperament of the body: "I do not agree. That would take away the freedom and scope of our will, which can remedy such rashness. If it does not remedy it, the error which results is a privation in relation to us, but a mere negation in relation to God" (June 11, 1640, AT III 65: CSMK 148).

are in him because of a deficiency or lack of perfection in his nature. In Wee's formulation:

> One result of this definition of privation is that Descartes may be willing to accept that one can suffer a privation *because* of one's nature. For example, he had claimed in the Third Meditation that his false ideas are in him because of a deficiency or lack of perfection in his nature – the perfection in question being that of *not* having only clear and distinct ideas. Descartes, in the light of what has just transpired in the Fourth Meditation, might well accept this absence as a privation. *Qua* finite thinker, God should have endowed him with faculties that are "perfect of their kind" – where this would include an intellect that always perceived clearly and distinctly. (2006a: 119)

Wee's interpretation, in my view, overlooks Descartes' main objective in the Fourth Meditation. In establishing the purely negative essence of error with respect to God, as we have just seen, Descartes makes a significant effort to prove that God ought not to grant him complete immunity from error, although he clearly possesses such power. Had Descartes thought that God should have granted him an intellect such that all his perceptions were clear and distinct, he would have had to accept as well that error was a privation with regard to God and a pure negation with regard to us. Descartes also insists, as noted, that the privation that constitutes the essence of error is found *in the incorrect use of free will* (AT VII 60: CSM II 41). He emphasizes that this privation, rather than consisting in the finitude of his intellect, lies *in the operation of the will* insofar as it proceeds from him (ibid.). What is more, Descartes explicitly stipulates that "the fact that we fall into error is a defect in the way we act or in the use we make of our freedom, but not a defect in our nature" (*Principles*, I, 38). Not only does error result from the misuse of free will, error *is* a misuse of free will, irrespective of the content being judged.

For similar reasons, I disagree with Wee's further remark that the inherent absence of clarity and distinctness in sensory ideas is privative (in the Fourth Meditation's sense)[48] because it results from a deficiency in our nature. On the contrary, Descartes considers any perfection that we lack *according to our nature* to be purely negative, not privative, precisely because it is not a perfection that we should have possessed, either through our own endeavors or by God's gift.[49] When discussing the inherent

---

[48] See above, n. 31.

[49] "And I have no cause for complaint on the grounds that the power of understanding or the natural light which God gave me is no greater than it is; for it is in the nature of a finite intellect to lack understanding of many things, and it is in the nature of a created intellect to be finite" (AT VII 60: CSM II 42). As Tierno indicates, this paragraph implies that the human

obscurity of ideas of sense in the Third Meditation, then, Descartes considers their irremediable lack of clarity as purely negative, *precisely because* it originates in "a deficiency and lack of perfection in [his] nature."[50]

Analyzing Descartes' arguments in the Fourth Meditation, by which he seeks to exempt God from any responsibility for our errors, Wee contends that Descartes himself finds these arguments insufficient. Discussing what she calls "the argument from the freedom of will," she maintains that Descartes himself acknowledges that even though his faculty of will is perfect of its kind, God could and should have granted him a similarly perfect intellect. In her words:

> The "solution" offered here may enable Descartes to avoid making errors in the future. However, it is scarcely effective as an answer to the original difficulty, *as Descartes himself subsequently acknowledges*. This is because the faculty of free will endowed upon him by God may indeed be "perfect of its kind," but the same is by no means true of his intellect, which is "extremely slight" and "very finite" … *Descartes himself points out* that an omnibenevolent God could surely have endowed him with not only a perfect-of-its-kind free will, but a similarly perfect intellect blessed with only clear and distinct perceptions. (2006a: 122; my emphases. See also pp. 128–30)

Wee's interpretation of the Cartesian idea of error-as-privation is, in some respects, reminiscent of Gassendi's critique of Descartes' position on this issue (Fifth Objections, AT VII 313: CSM II 217–18). Gassendi objects to Descartes' analysis regarding the responsibility for error, for he (Gassendi) appears to consider the fault to lie as much in the imperfection of the intellect as in the misuse of the will. But Descartes emphatically rejects his critic's argument, claiming that "we never understand anything in a bad fashion; when we are said to 'understand in a bad fashion,' all that happens is that we judge that our understanding is more extensive than it in fact is" (Fifth Replies, AT VII 377: CSM II 259).

Discussing the Fourth Meditation's account of error-as-privation, Dan Kaufman argues that Descartes considers any idea that is not clear

---

intellect is necessarily finite (1997: 33), that is, that the idea of an infinite, created intellect is self-contradictory. Although God, the creator of all things and of the eternal truths, was free to create essences whose concepts are self-contradictory (letter to Mersenne, May 27, 1630, AT I 152: CSMK 25; letter to Mesland, May 2, 1644, AT VI 118: CSMK 235), by virtue of his infinite benevolence he has chosen to limit his creation to things whose concepts are logically possible, which our minds can perceive clearly and distinctly. I therefore take the above quotation to be part of Descartes' general normative theme, whereby we have no reason to bemoan God's free choices.

[50] Descartes states: "[I]f they are false, that is, represent non-things, I know by the natural light that they arise from nothing – that is, they are in me only because of a deficiency and lack of perfection in my nature" (AT VII 44: CSM II 30).

and distinct to be privative, since "ideas *ought* to be clear and distinct" (2000: 402; see also 2003a: 398–99). Kaufman asserts that in holding that "clarity and distinctness are something our ideas ought to have," Descartes employs the term "privation" in the scholastic sense (2000: 402). In his reading, Descartes even thinks that materially false ideas *ought* to be perceived clearly, and therefore considers the confusion and obscurity of these ideas to be privative.

Kaufman begins by arguing that "Descartes' reasoning concerning the cause of confusion and obscurity in materially false ideas is remarkably similar to Aquinas' limping example" (2000: 401). Just as the act of limping, according to Aquinas, consists of a real component (walking) and a privative component (limping), which is an absence of a perfection that one is born to have and should have, so is the material falsity of ideas in Descartes: "The positive aspect of the idea – the sensation – has a real cause; but the privative aspect – the confusion and obscurity – has a privative cause, namely a defect in my nature" (p. 402). Kaufman then specifies further:

[I]n the Fourth Meditation, Descartes himself distinguishes negations from privations in the scholastic tradition: "For error is not a pure negation [i.e., not simply the defect or lack of some perfection to which I have no proper claim] but rather a privation or lack ... which somehow should be in me" (AT VII 55: CSM II 38). So, if Descartes thinks that confusion and obscurity are privations, then he must say that ideas *ought* to be clear and distinct. Descartes does think that clarity and distinctness are something our ideas ought to have; and they will be clear and distinct, provided we do not abuse the faculties God has given us by making rash judgments. Descartes even thinks that materially false ideas, despite their confusion and obscurity, *ought* to be perceived clearly ... But because of bad habits acquired since childhood, we do not refrain from taking "great care in our judgments," although we ought to. (2000: 402)

In suggesting that Descartes, in the Fourth Meditation, uses "privation" in the scholastic sense, Kaufman appears to refer to the normative import that Descartes assigns to this term, to signify an absence of perfection that one *ought to have*. But except for this rather limited point of similarity, a significant difference prevails between Descartes' usage of "privation" and the scholastic usage of the term, which I addressed above.[51] Kaufman appears to be cognizant of this difference when he holds that the fault for

---

[51] As mentioned earlier, Descartes considers the fact that his intellect lacks clear and distinct ideas of many things, let alone the inherent obscurity of his ideas of sense, to be an absence that he suffers *because of his nature*, not an absence of perfection that he was born to have, or should have, *according to his nature* (as the scholastic usage of the term suggests).

not having clear and distinct ideas lies in our abuse of our faculty of judgment. But he seems to ignore Descartes' doctrine that our intellect is essentially limited in scope and, as such, lacks clear and distinct ideas of many things.[52] Although Descartes usually employs this doctrine to absolve God of any responsibility for the finitude of our intellect, this doctrine also suggests that human beings cannot categorically be blamed for the confusion or obscurity of their perceptions. Hence, the lack of clarity and distinctness in ideas, when considered on its own, is purely negative not only with regard to God but also with regard to us. For this very reason, mere ignorance lacks the normative import that error-as-privation does possess. As I have argued throughout this chapter, the absence of clear and distinct ideas, which is purely negative when considered on its own, becomes privative only in the presence of a voluntary act of judgment by which we manifest our claim to possess a piece of knowledge we in fact lack.

I now turn to Kaufman's further contention that Descartes considers the confusion and obscurity of materially false ideas privative, viewing them as ideas that "ought to be perceived clearly." To support this reading, Kaufman addresses Descartes' statement in the first part of the *Principles* that our sensations "may be clearly perceived provided we take great care in our judgments concerning them to include no more than what is strictly contained in our perception" (I, 66; Kaufman 2000: 402). But in speaking of judgments in this oft-cited statement, Descartes does not mean to signify the acts of affirmation and denial elicited by the will. The word "judgments" in this context signifies, rather, unnoticed and unconscious judgments that our intellect is habituated to make about things outside us (the third grade of sensory response).[53] Since our intellect makes these habitual and unnoticed judgments at great speed, Descartes clarifies, we do not distinguish them from simple sense perceptions (AT VII 438: CSM II 295). Hence it seems implausible that in equating the essence of error with privation, Descartes is pointing to our failure to eliminate the unnoticed judgments that render our sense perceptions confused. Again, Descartes insists that "the fact that we fall into error is a defect in the way we act or in the use we make of our freedom, but not a defect in our nature. For our nature remains the same whether we judge correctly

---

[52] Descartes argues that "it is in the nature of a finite intellect to lack understanding of many things," and that "it is in the nature of a created intellect to be finite" (Fourth Meditation, AT VII 60: CSM II 42. See also *Principles*, I, 36).

[53] Recall that in the Sixth Replies, Descartes writes: "The third grade includes all the judgments about things outside us which we have been accustomed to make from our earliest years – judgments which are occasioned by the movements of these bodily organs" (AT VII 437: CSM II 295). See Chapter 1, section 5 above.

or incorrectly" (*Principles*, I, 38). And since he does consider the inherent obscurity and confusion of sensory ideas to arise from the union of body and mind,[54] he cannot think that these ideas "*ought* to be perceived clearly" and that the fault for not perceiving them clearly and distinctly resides in us.

In suggesting that Descartes does not take lack of clarity and distinctness in ideas to be privative, I surely do not mean to deny the positive role he assigns to the will in the search for truth, a role that allows him to call upon us to do our utmost to expand the sphere of objects we perceive clearly and distinctly by enhancing our natural light of reason. As Alanen observes, "the inner light does not ... shine all by itself, automatically, and it takes more than opening one's eye and turning it inward for it to work properly" (2003: 106). This task requires us to actively and voluntarily exert intellectual effort; voluntary cognitive activity is required to put our thoughts in order and to resist the effects of "external" disruptions of all kinds, including the senses, the passions, and the unnoticed judgments that our intellect is accustomed to making since childhood.[55] Nevertheless, Descartes acknowledges the essential limitation of our intellect. As he writes to Queen Christina, while knowledge is often beyond our powers, "there remains only our will, which is absolutely within our disposal" (November 20, 1647, AT v 83: CSMK 325). On these grounds, he holds that every person "ought to be praised or blamed for no other reason than his using [the freedom of his will] well or badly."[56] Not only are many of our thoughts not subject to the control of our will, and not only are there countless objects that our mind cannot perceive clearly, but also, the mind is incapable of keeping its attention fixed on what it *does* clearly and distinctly perceive.[57] Therefore, the only obligation to which we are subject categorically and unconditionally is to avoid misusing our power of judgment. Only by limiting our judgments to clear and distinct

---

[54] See, e.g., Sixth Meditation (AT VII 81: CSM II 56); letter to Hyperaspistes, August 1641 (AT III 424: CSMK 190); *Principles*, IV, 200.

[55] Cottingham places special emphasis on the active role of the will in the search for truth, as well as in determining the duration of time that the mind may remain focused on clear and distinct ideas. He thus writes: "the true role of the will in the search for truth lies ... in what Descartes called the *directio ingenii* – the voluntary and autonomous decision to direct the mind in ways which will allow its natural rational powers to operate properly and productively" (2002: 352). It is in this sense, according to Cottingham, that the irresistibility of the natural light may depend on the free choice of human beings, "as to how far they keep the light focused" (p. 354). I refer to Cottingham's interpretation of this important issue in the next chapter.

[56] *Passions*, art. 153; see also art. 152; *Principles*, I, 37; letter to Princess Elizabeth, November 3, 1645 (AT IV 332–33: CSMK 277).

[57] Fourth Meditation (AT VII 62: CSM II 43); Fifth Meditation (AT VII 69: CSM II 48); letter to Mesland, May 2, 1644 (AT IV 116: CSMK 233–34).

perceptions can we ensure ourselves against "intellectual sin," to use Garber's wording (2001: 105), which is error in judgment.

7 ERROR AND RATIONALITY

In identifying error with any assent to confused or obscure ideas, *qua* a misuse of free will, Descartes implies that the right use of the will, and in particular, the obligation to avoid misusing the will, constitutes for him a self-justified end and not only a means for other ends, however valuable. The border between the irrational and the rational, the wrong and the right, lies exactly between cases where we misuse our free will and cases where we refrain from doing so. Far from being static and consequentialist, Descartes' underlying conception of rationality is thoroughly dynamic, placing the pragmatic concepts of "use" and "misuse" of free will at its very center. Its deontological and non-consequentialist feature lies in the constitutive role it assigns to our epistemic duty to always refrain from misusing our power of choice. Descartes accordingly concludes the Fourth Meditation with the statement that acquiring the habit of avoiding error is "man's greatest and most important perfection" (Fourth Meditation, AT VII 62: CSM II 43).

Reflecting on Descartes' project in the *Meditations*, scholars disagree on the extent to which he succeeds in establishing the validation of human reason, owing to an alleged problem of circularity in his metaphysical arguments. The first to make this charge was Antoine Arnauld. In the Fourth Objections, he writes:

I have one further worry, namely how the author avoids reasoning in a circle when he says that we are sure that what we clearly and distinctly perceive is true only because God exists.

But we can be sure that God exists only because we clearly and distinctly perceive this. Hence, before we can be sure that God exists, we ought to be able to be sure that whatever we perceive clearly and evidently is true. (AT VII 214: CSM II 150)

The problem of circularity may be formulated as follows: Descartes intended his proof of the existence of God to demonstrate that clarity and distinctness are reliable marks of the truth. But neither the premises nor the conclusion of this proof can be counted as true unless we assume that whatever we perceive clearly and distinctly is true. This way of begging the question led to Descartes being charged with circular reasoning.

This problem raises many questions regarding the validity of reason and the possibility of knowledge in Descartes' system. I will not enter here into a discussion of this problem's various aspects or of the innumerable solutions offered in the literature. Instead, I argue that Descartes' deontological conception of rationality invites us to reconsider the destructive potential that the problem of circularity implies for his entire philosophical edifice.

To be sure, I believe that Descartes' consistent interest was to attain the truth and not merely to reach psychological certainty or unshakable conviction, as some scholars have claimed.[58] We also have reasons to think that Descartes believed his *Meditations* revealed the true essence of things and established firm and stable foundations in the sciences, as he expected it would.[59] Granted this, the question of whether Descartes can be exonerated of the charge of circularity is indeed pivotal to our assessment of his success in attaining the goals he had set himself. And recalling his insistence that "nothing can ever be perfectly known" without knowledge of God, we may realize that what is at stake here is the possibility of knowledge (*scientia*).[60]

And yet, I suggest that even if Descartes cannot be acquitted of the charge of circularity, and even if our clear and distinct ideas might indeed be false, we would not be considered irrational for assenting to them. On the contrary, in so doing, we would deserve moral praise for using our free will correctly, despite the possibility that we are holding false beliefs.

In the Second Replies, Descartes faces the objection that God might frequently deceive human beings and still be considered omnibenevolent.

---

[58] See, e.g., Rubin (1977); Larmore (1984: 68–71); Loeb (1992). That the search for truth was Descartes' aim, or at least important among his aims, is evidenced by, e.g., *Rules*, Rule 4 (AT x 371: CSM I 15); *Discourse*, Part Four (AT VI 31: CSM I 126); Second Replies (AT VII 142: CSM II 102); *Principles*, I, 4. See also the discussion in Williams (1978, esp. pp. 34–36, 198–200).

[59] First Meditation (AT VII 17: CSM II 17). On January 28, 1641, Descartes writes to Mersenne: "I may tell you, between ourselves, that these six Meditations contain all the foundations of my physics. But please do not tell people, for that might make it harder for supporters of Aristotle to approve them. I hope that readers will gradually get used to my principles, and recognize their truth, before they notice that they destroy the principles of Aristotle" (AT III 297–98: CSMK 173). In a similar vein, Descartes was reported to have argued in the *Conversation with Burman* that "one should not devote so much effort to the *Meditations* and to metaphysical questions, or give them elaborate treatment in commentaries and the like. Still less should one do what some try to do, and dig more deeply into these questions than the author did; he has dealt with them quite deeply enough. It is sufficient to have grasped them once in a general way, and then to remember the conclusion …. The author did follow up metaphysical questions fairly thoroughly in the *Meditations*, and established their certainty against the sceptics, and so on" (CB 48 = AT v 165: CSMK 346–47). As I show elsewhere, moreover, Descartes' antagonism toward anyone attempting to criticize or correct his original doctrines in the *Meditations* indicates, among other things, his conviction of their truthfulness (Naaman-Zauderer 2004; 2007: 218–46; 2008: 321–25). See also Mullin (2000: 7–8).

[60] Fifth Meditation (AT VII 69: CSM II 48). See also Third Meditation (AT VII 36: CSM II 25); letter to Mersenne, April 15, 1630 (AT I 144: CSMK 22).

The objector states that just as a doctor may deceive his patients or a father his children upon finding that the knowledge of pure truth would be unendurable to them, so might God frequently and intentionally deceive us for whatever justifiable reason (as the biblical story of Nineveh exemplifies; AT VII 125–26: CSM II 89–90). Deception is possible, moreover, even without assuming divine deceit. As the objection runs, the mere limitation of our nature might cause us to be constantly or at least very frequently deceived about matters that we think we perceive clearly and distinctly (AT VII 126: CSM II 90). I will not dwell on Descartes' full response to this objection but only on one of his arguments, which is particularly relevant to our discussion:

First of all, as soon as we think that we correctly perceive something, we are spontaneously convinced that it is true. Now if this conviction is so firm that it is impossible for us ever to have any reason for doubting what we are convinced of, then there are no further questions for us to ask: we have everything that we could reasonably want. What is it to us that someone may make out that the perception whose truth we are so firmly convinced of may appear false to God or an angel, so that it is, absolutely speaking, false? Why should this alleged "absolute falsity" bother us, since we neither believe in it nor have even the smallest suspicion of it? For the supposition which we are making here is of a conviction so firm that it is quite incapable of being destroyed; and such a conviction is clearly the same as the most perfect certainty. (AT VII 144–45: CSM II 103)

Interpreting this passage, scholars have read into it a variety of views regarding the goals of Descartes' inquiry in the *Meditations*. Some scholars consider it evidence of their view that this goal was perfect certainty (the unshakability of convictions), rather than absolute truth (e.g., Loeb 1992: 203). Frankfurt holds that, in this passage, "Descartes explicitly acknowledges the possibility that what is certain may not be true 'speaking absolutely,'" and that "he makes it clear that certainty takes priority over absolute truth in his conception of the goals of inquiry" (1978: 37). Yet others have suggested various arguments to show that Descartes does not really admit the possibility that our clear and distinct perceptions are, absolutely speaking, false.[61]

---

[61] Kenny, for example, argues that far from admitting this possibility in this passage, Descartes states only that we need not be troubled by someone "feigning" the occurrence of such a possibility, "because we are certain that what he supposes is only a fiction" (1968: 195). Were Descartes to admit the possibility of such a discrepancy between the perfectly certain and the true, he would have been obliged to accept that God is a deceiver (pp. 195–96). Williams also thinks that the reference to absolute falsehood in this passage is not to be taken seriously. In his view, "we cannot understand Descartes if we break the connection between the search for certainty and the search for truth, or the connection between knowledge and the correspondence of ideas to

My view is that Descartes does not take seriously the possibility that a perfectly certain conviction is in fact absolutely false, neither in this passage nor anywhere else. But what is striking about his response in the above quotation is that he is not rejecting this possibility outright by invoking divine veracity, as we might expect him to do. Rather, he argues that this possibility need not bother us, "since we neither believe in it nor have even the smallest suspicion of it." Insofar as we attain such perfect certainty, Descartes states, "there are no further questions for us to ask: we have everything that we could reasonably want."

The key to our understanding of this passage, I believe, is Descartes' non-consequentialist conception of error and rationality. Even if it were true that our most certain perceptions might be absolutely false, we would not be counted as misusing our free will by assenting to them. In such cases, moreover, we would not only escape blame for sin and error but also deserve praise for using our free will correctly – irrespective of the results. Again, insofar as we fulfill our rational duty to limit our judgments to clear and distinct perceptions "there are no further questions for us to ask: we have everything that we could reasonably want." Human rationality, in a significant respect, does not hinge on our prospects to attain the truth. The principal achievement of this conception is that it frees human rationality from objective standards of falsity and truth, without thereby abandoning its full commitment to the search for absolute truth.

In a recent paper, Della Rocca has pointed to a new problem of circularity internal to the Fourth Meditation. In his reading, until Descartes can point to a relevant difference between ideas that are clear and distinct and those that are not, he cannot explain why we should not assent to non-clear ideas and, correlatively, why in assenting to clear and distinct ideas, we are behaving properly (2006: 156). Descartes' circular reasoning in the Fourth Meditation is thus apparent: "To suppose or assert that clear and distinct ideas are true in the course of trying to remove doubts about clear and distinct ideas is to argue in a circle" (p. 158).

Della Rocca's way of approaching this problem rests on his substantive reading of Descartes' notion of error. Earlier in this paper, he writes: "Error

---

reality." According to Williams, Descartes only presents here "in a particularly emphatic and indeed rhetorical form the idea that for a person actually presented with clear and distinct perception, no question can possibly arise of his being mistaken" (1978: 199–200). See also Wilson (1978: 236 n. 42). As Frankfurt rightly maintains, however, Descartes does not deny, rather surprisingly, that the possibility of "feigning" is quite genuine and only states we need not be worried by it (1978: 38).

occurs only when the mind gives its assent to a representational content that is false, and true belief occurs only when assent is given to a true idea" (2006: 146). In this reading, Della Rocca may reasonably hold that Descartes regards the right use of free will as a *mere* means to attain the truth: "*Why*, for Descartes, should we assent only to clear and distinct ideas? ... The reason Descartes offers seems to be: we should assent to clear and distinct ideas and should not assent to non-clear and distinct because clear and distinct ideas are guaranteed to be true and non-clear and distinct are not" (p. 157).[62] He then concludes: "This latest challenge is, I believe, the most serious one facing Descartes' strategy in Meditation IV. A defender of Descartes would need to show that, contrary to what I have just suggested, there is a plausible truth-independent basis for the claim that we should assent only to such-and-such an idea" (p. 159).

I will try to take up Della Rocca's gauntlet by highlighting the truth-independent merit that Descartes assigns to the enhancement of our freedom of will. Whereas our knowledge depends on the truthfulness of our clear and distinct perceptions, attaining the highest grade of freedom requires us only to render our perceptions clear and distinct. The will's irresistible inclination toward clear and distinct ideas is indeed no guarantee of their veracity before the Fourth Meditation is complete. But even then, it does ensure the fullest actualization of our freedom, since, in this state, the operation of our will is wholly spontaneous and free. Whenever the intellect actualizes its nature to the fullest extent, the will also fulfills its true essence, acting spontaneously and freely to the highest possible degree. Therefore, although Descartes cannot assume before the end of the Fourth Meditation that all his clear and distinct ideas are true, he can nevertheless be sure that rendering his ideas clear and distinct will

---

[62] Among the textual evidence that Della Rocca adduces in support of his reading is the following from the Fourth Meditation, where Descartes explains why the pure intellect cannot be the source of his errors: "Nor is my power to understand to blame; for since my understanding comes from God, everything that I understand I undoubtedly understand correctly, and any error here is impossible" (AT VII 58: CSM II 40). Della Rocca reads the word "correctly" in this passage to mean "truly." He therefore takes this passage to show that "at this stage of his argument Descartes presupposes that clear and distinct ideas are guaranteed to be true" (2006: 157). My reading is different. In claiming that "everything that I understand I undoubtedly understand *correctly*," I think Descartes need not be taken to mean that whatever the *pure* intellect perceives is undoubtedly *true*, but rather that all its perceptions are *clear and distinct*. Granted that the content of an erroneous judgment may be true (yet not known as such to the agent eliciting it), in order to show that the pure intellect is not the source of his errors, *it is not enough* for Descartes to establish the truthfulness of all that the pure intellect perceives. For this purpose, he must show that everything that the pure intellect perceives cannot but be *clear and distinct*, and I hold that this is precisely what he means when he says that "everything that I understand I undoubtedly understand correctly, and any error here is impossible."

enhance his freedom of will and allow him to attain the highest level of freedom of which he is immediately conscious.

The truth-independent merit of limiting our judgment only to clear and distinct ideas is thus the merit of self-mastery: judging and acting in accordance with internal standards rather than being activated from the outside. By eliminating the distracting forces of the senses, the passions, and prejudice, we become transparent to ourselves as far as possible, fully attentive to our ideas as well as to the interconnections between them, and thereby capable of basing our judgments and actions on such self-understanding. Indeed, in such cases, the will cannot resist assenting to the ideas (affirming them as true). But even if we are misled and our clear and distinct ideas are in fact false, this does not undermine the brute fact that our will, in this condition, determines itself entirely from within, moving on the basis of the mind's complete understanding of its mental contents. Limiting our judgments only to clear and distinct ideas thus ensures our rational activity, independently of the truthfulness of our clear and distinct ideas.

I elaborate on this theme in the chapters to follow. In Chapters 3 and 4, I show that the proper use of free will has an independent merit because it allows us to experience, in the fullest and most significant manner, our similitude to God. And in Chapter 6, I show that Descartes defines virtue in pragmatic terms rather than in terms of consequences, identifying it with the right use of the will. Descartes also states that the exercise of virtue is itself our supreme good and, as such, constitutes the ultimate end for which we *ought* to strive in all our actions, and not simply a means for attaining other ends. To act virtuously is precisely to act firmly and resolutely on the basis of our best judgment, in accordance with the recommendation of reason. We are regarded as complying with our duty to exercise virtue even when it becomes apparent that our choice was intrinsically bad, provided we have striven to use our reason as best we could and acted resolutely on our best judgment. The kind of knowledge required for the exercise of virtue is not just that of a particular concrete good but knowledge of ourselves as possessing free will, which is precisely the knowledge of the supreme good. By the same token, in pure inquiry, even if we cannot rule out the possibility that our clear and distinct ideas are in fact absolutely false, we can be assured of acting rationally by basing our judgments on them alone. So long as we keep complying with this duty "there are no further questions for us to ask: we have everything that we could reasonably want."

CHAPTER 3

Free will

> The Lord has made three marvels: something out of nothing; free
> will; and God in Man.
>
> (Descartes, *Early Writings*, AT x 218: CSM 1 5)

The previous chapter presented Descartes' notion of error as a misuse of
free will in the context of his deontological perspective. My concern in
this chapter is to analyze his position on the essence of human free will,
as a basis for the next chapter's discussion of Descartes' doctrine that it
is in virtue of the will rather than the intellect, that we understand ourselves to be godlike.[1] This doctrine, which dominates Descartes' writings from the *Meditations* onward, appears in its most radical form in
the Fourth Meditation, where he states that the will of God "does not
seem any greater" than the human will "when considered as will in the
essential and strict sense" (AT vii 57: CSM ii 40). A close examination
of Descartes' position on the essence of freedom is thus the key to our
understanding of the superiority of our will as the most remarkable manifestation of our similitude to God.

I FREE WILL IN THE FOURTH MEDITATION

A fundamental theme in Descartes' discussion of error in the Fourth
Meditation is that God has endowed him with an infinite power of
will that "is both extremely ample and also perfect of its kind" (AT vii
58: CSM ii 40). "It is above all in virtue of the will," he states, "that I
understand myself to bear in some way the image and likeness of God"
(AT vii 57: CSM ii 40). When speaking of the infinite scope of the will in

---

[1] See, for example, letter to Mersenne, December 25, 1639 (AT ii 628: CSMK 141–42); Fourth
Meditation (AT vii 57: CSM ii 40); letter to Queen Christina, November 20, 1647 (AT v 83,
85: CSMK 325, 326); *Conversation with Burman* (CB 31 = AT v 159: CSMK 342); *Passions*, art. 152.

the *Principles*, Descartes writes that it "extends to anything that can possibly be an object of any other will – even the immeasurable will of God"
(1, 35). But in the Fourth Meditation we find a more qualified formulation
of this doctrine, resting on an epistemic point of view:

Besides, I cannot complain that the will or freedom of choice which I received
from God is not sufficiently extensive or perfect, *since I know by experience that
it is not restricted in any way.* Indeed, I think it is very noteworthy that there is
nothing else in me which is so perfect and so great that the possibility of a further increase in its perfection or greatness is *beyond my understanding.* (AT VII
56–57: CSM II 39; my emphases)

It is only the will, or freedom of choice, *which I experience within me to be so
great that the idea of any greater faculty is beyond my grasp*; so much so that it is
above all in virtue of the will that I understand myself to bear in some way the
image and likeness of God. (AT VII 57: CSM II 40; my emphasis)[2]

In these passages, Descartes is not committing himself to the view that
the human will may indeed extend to every possible object, including
all the objects of the divine will. Rather, he argues that he *cannot think*
of any greater faculty of choice than the one he experiences within himself. Descartes appears to be suggesting that, among all the things he can
conceive of, however confusedly, there is nothing to which his will cannot apply itself (that is, affirm or deny, pursue or avoid). This reading is
confirmed by Descartes' statement several lines later that God's will is
incomparably greater than the human will, not only regarding the knowledge accompanying it but also with respect to the number of objects over
which it extends:

For although God's will is incomparably greater than mine, both in virtue of the
knowledge and power that accompany it and make it more firm and efficacious,
and also in virtue of its object, in that it ranges over a greater number of items,
nevertheless it does not seem any greater than mine when considered as will in
the essential and strict sense. (AT VII 57: CSM II 40)

Although God's will is incomparably greater than the human will with
respect to its objects, it still *does not seem* any greater than the human
will when considered as will "in the essential and strict sense" (*in se for-
maliter et praecise spectata*, which is, in a more literal rendering, "when
it is viewed formally and precisely in itself"). This statement suggests an
essential similitude between human and divine free will that, as noted,
Descartes articulates on other occasions as well.

---

[2] See also letter to Mersenne, December 25, 1639 (AT II 628: CSMK 141–42).

Descartes considers the will, both human and divine, a faculty of choice that is free by its very nature or essence. He not only uses "freedom of choice" (*arbitrii libertas*) and "will" (*voluntas*) interchangeably,[3] but also explicitly affirms that freedom is the essence of will.[4] Moreover, Descartes claims that we have inner consciousness of our freedom,[5] and that our freedom of will is so evident "that it must be counted among the first and most common notions that are innate in us" (*Principles*, I, 39). Postulating that freedom is the essence of will, Descartes explains the sense in which divine will may not seem any greater than human will by addressing the essence of human *freedom*:

> This is because the will simply consists in our ability to do or not to do something (that is, to affirm or deny, to pursue or avoid); or rather, it consists simply in the fact that when the intellect puts something forward for affirmation or denial or for pursuit or avoidance, our inclinations are such that we do not feel we are determined by any external force. (AT VII 57: CSM II 40)

As the opening phrase ("this is because" [*quia*]) indicates, Descartes intends his definition of human freedom to explain in what sense our will can seem essentially similar to the will of God. But because of an apparent tension between the two clauses of this definition, separated by the phrase "or rather" (*vel potius*), the full paragraph poses a serious challenge to the understanding of Descartes' position on the issue. Whereas the first clause takes free will to consist simply in our positive power to do or not to do something (namely, to do or to choose otherwise), the second clause takes human free will to consist in spontaneity or self-determination: the will's inclination toward what the intellect puts forward for affirmation or denial, without being determined by any external force.[6]

How should we regard the relationship between the two clauses of this paragraph? Does Descartes mean that both spontaneity and the positive power to do otherwise are essential to our free will? Or is his use of "or rather" meant to qualify the statement in the first clause whereby freedom

---

[3] See, for example, Fourth Meditation (AT VII 56: CSM II 39; AT VII 57: CSM II 40); cf. *Passions*, art. 153.

[4] Second Replies (AT VII 166: CSM II 117); *Passions*, art. 41.

[5] *Conversation with Burman* (CB 32 = AT V 159: CSMK 342); Third Replies (AT VII 191: CSM II 134); *Principles*, I, 41.

[6] As some scholars rightly emphasize, when saying that our freedom requires that "we do not feel [*sentiamus*] we are determined by any external force," Descartes does not mean that our freedom demands only that we feel ourselves undetermined by external coercion but also that we *be* so undetermined. See, for instance, Campbell (1999: 185); Ragland (2006a: 381). An action is spontaneous, to use Chappell's formulation, "if it is performed by its agent entirely on his own, without being forced or helped or affected by any external factor" (1994: 180).

requires the two-way power of the will, thus showing that only spontaneity is essential to our free will? Endorsing the latter alternative, Kenny reads the full paragraph to suggest that "free will often does consist in liberty of indifference, but that sometimes it consists only in liberty of spontaneity, and that is all that is essential to it" (1972: 18). According to Kenny, we have the liberty to assent or not to assent only to things of which our intellect lacks clear and distinct perception (p. 20), but whenever the ideas that come before the mind are clear and distinct, at the very moment of perceiving them, we cannot but judge them to be true (p. 29). Defending the rival alternative, Alanen holds that it would be mistaken to read the above paragraph as suggesting that freedom of spontaneity excludes the ability to do otherwise. This ability, she writes, "is mentioned as the very essence of will in itself, which is infinite or unrestricted and by which we are images of God" (2003: 227). Accordingly, Alanen reads this paragraph as admitting that we are free not to embrace the truth, even when perceiving it clearly and distinctly (p. 242).

To determine which of these two options captures Descartes' position on the essence of freedom, so as to specify in what sense our will may appear similar to God's, we need to relate to subsequent passages in the Fourth Meditation and to additional textual sources. In the two sections that follow, I seek to refine the distinction between the positive two-way power of the will and the indifference of the will in Descartes' usage, and elaborate on the exact meaning he assigns to each of them. Although my reading is that neither the positive two-way power of the will nor its indifference is essential to our freedom, the evidence is different for each case and must be examined separately.

2 CARTESIAN INDIFFERENCE

The term "indifference," as is well known, was used by Descartes' Jesuit contemporaries to signify the positive power of the will to choose one or the other of two opposing alternatives. As Chappell points out, an action is indifferent in the scholastic–Jesuit sense, "if its agent is able, on the point of performing it, not to perform it, or to perform some other action instead" (1994: 181). Descartes, as noted, does assign the human will such positive power. Writing to Mesland that the will has this two-way positive power, he portrays it as "a positive faculty of determining oneself to one or other of two contraries, that is to say, to pursue or avoid, to affirm or deny."[7] Descartes, however, does not call this power

7 February 9, 1645 (AT IV 173: CSMK 245).

of the will "indifference," a term for which he reserves quite another meaning. In the letter to Mesland cited above he introduces his own sense of "indifference," which he characterizes in negative terms as "that state of the will when it is not impelled [*impellitur*] one way rather than another by any perception of truth or goodness" (AT IV 173: CSMK 245). Following Kaufman's abbreviations, I hereafter use "S-indifference" for the scholastic–Jesuit sense of this term, and "C-indifference" for the Cartesian one.

Some scholars have suggested that Descartes reserves his own sense of "indifference" for a state in which the will is equally inclined in two opposite directions, a situation where the reasons for each alternative are *perfectly balanced*. In his introduction to *Descartes' Conversation with Burman*, Cottingham writes that Descartes uses the word "indifference" "to refer to the situation where one has no particular reason for taking either of two alternative courses of action ... This is like the situation of Buridan's ass, equidistant from two equally lush meadows" (Cottingham 1976: xxxvii). Chappell also writes that, according to Descartes' sense of the term, "an action is indifferent *only if* its agent has no reason to perform it, or the reasons for and against it are evenly balanced" (1994: 181; my emphasis). Endorsing Chappell's reading, Kaufman suggests that C-indifference "is the state that Buridan's famous ass was in with respect to the equally appealing equidistant bales of hay" (2003a: 395).

But Descartes clearly does not limit the indifference of the will (in his sense of the term) to a state of a perfect balancing of reasons. On the contrary: the "negative" definition he offers in the letter to Mesland cited above appears to exclude only a situation where the will is *impelled* to act by reasons invoked by the intellect. It does include, however, all other states of the will: those wherein the weight of the evidence for and against a given alternative is perfectly balanced (hereafter referred to as "complete indifference"), and the more prevalent situations where the will inclines, though not decisively, to one side or another (which I call "incomplete indifference"). Textual evidence definitely indicates that C-indifference admits of degrees and, therefore, cannot be confined to a perfect balancing of reasons. To take just three examples:

I did not say that a person was indifferent only if he lacked knowledge, but rather, that he is more indifferent the fewer reasons he knows which impel him to choose one side rather than another. (Letter to Mesland, May 2, 1644, AT IV 115: CSMK 233)

I did not write that grace entirely prevents indifference, but simply that it makes us incline to one side rather than to another, and so diminishes indifference without diminishing freedom; from which it follows, in my view, that this free-dom does not consist in indifference. (AT iv 117–18: CSMK 234)

I am making the further supposition that my intellect has not yet come upon any persuasive reason in favour of one alternative rather than the other. This obviously implies that I am indifferent as to whether I should assert or deny either alternative, or indeed refrain from making any judgment on the matter.

What is more, this indifference does not merely apply to cases where the intel-lect is wholly ignorant, but extends in general to every case where the intellect does not have sufficiently clear knowledge at the time when the will deliberates. (Fourth Meditation, AT vii 59: CSM ii 41)

Each of these paragraphs unequivocally suggests that Descartes does not limit indifference of the will to cases of perfect balance but applies it, in different degrees, to all situations where the will is not impelled to action by the intellect's clear and distinct ideas.[8] The lesser the weight of reasons that incline the will in one direction, the greater its degree of indifference that, in turn, is in inverse proportion to the will's degree of spontaneity and freedom.[9] When the will is completely undetermined (when it is indifferent to the highest degree) it does not incline in either direction and is thus at the lowest grade of spontaneity and freedom (AT vii 58: CSM ii 40).

The relationship between C-indifference and S-indifference is thus not a relationship between two different *states* of the will, let alone two mutu-ally exclusive states, but rather one between two distinct *meanings* of this term, intensionally different and yet sharing a certain extensional overlap. Indifference in the scholastic sense is a power, not a state, of the will (as C-indifference is).[10] As Michelle Beyssade points out, Cartesian indiffer-ence is "the state of hesitation or wavering because of ignorance or insuf-ficient knowledge" (1994: 193). Descartes' implicit distinction between complete and incomplete C-indifference is thus a distinction between

<hr>

[8] Kenny appears to acknowledge this when he claims: "Where there is no such clarity [in the ideas], however, indifference remains and this is true not only where there are no reasons, or equal reasons, in either side, but wherever the reasons on one side fall short of certainty" (1972: 20). Ragland also observes that indifference, as Descartes normally uses the term, "denotes a motiv-ational state that comes in degrees" (2006a: 381). Thus, he writes: "In a state of perfect indif-ference, the motivations for and against a given act of will are perfectly balanced. We become progressively less indifferent as the motivations on one side outweigh those on the other, and we lose indifference altogether when we are motivated in only one direction" (2006a: 381). See also Ragland (2006b: 384); Wee (2006b: 392).
[9] Fourth Meditation (AT vii 58–59: CSM ii 41). For Descartes' identification of freedom with spontaneity see also Sixth Replies (AT vii 433: CSM ii 292); letter to Mesland, February 9, 1645 (AT iv 175: CSMK 246).
[10] This point was emphasized by Michelle Beyssade (1994: 193–94); see also Kaufman (2003a: 395).

two different motivational states of the will, differing from one another in degree (in the will's extent of indecisiveness).

Scholars tend to pin the difficulty of construing Descartes' position on human freedom on his alleged tendency to employ the word "indifference" as alternately signifying C-indifference or S-indifference.[11] Contrary to this reading, I argue that Descartes consistently uses the term "indifference" in his own sense. The ambiguity usually associated with his use of this term stems from his failure to consistently specify whether he is referring to complete or incomplete C-indifference in particular instances.[12] On some occasions, he employs "indifference" to signify both complete and incomplete indifference, as in the three passages quoted above. On other occasions, however, Descartes appears to be addressing only one of the two modes of indifference, though he often does not specify which. One such case is the following passage from the Fourth Meditation, where Descartes sums up his conclusions regarding the source of his errors:

> So what then is the source of my mistakes? It must be simply this: the scope of the will is wider than that of the intellect; but instead of restricting it within the same limits, I extend its use to matters which I do not understand. *Since the will is indifferent in such cases, it easily turns aside from what is true and good, and this is the source of my error and sin.* (AT VII 58: CSM II 40–41; my emphasis)

Most probably, Descartes is not referring to complete indifference in this passage when claiming that incurring a state of error is accompanied by indifference of the will. After all, complete indifference is supposed to ensure us against error by determining us to suspend judgment about things we do not clearly and distinctly perceive.[13] In this passage, then, Descartes appears to be referring to a state of partial (incomplete)

---

[11] See, e.g., Kenny (1972: 28); Imlay (1982: 88); Chappell (1994: 181); Kaufman (2003a: 393ff.); Alanen (2003: 228–29, 240).

[12] Note that Descartes remains faithful to his sense of "indifference" even in his letters to Mesland, while attempting to persuade his Jesuit correspondent that the difference between them is only a matter of words. A good example is the following passage from his 1644 letter: "And so, since you regard freedom not simply as indifference but rather as a real and positive power to determine oneself, the difference between us is a merely verbal one – for I agree that the will has such a power" (May 2, 1644, AT IV 116: CSMK 234).

[13] "I think it will be a good plan to turn my will in completely the opposite direction and deceive myself, by pretending for a time that these former opinions are utterly false and imaginary. I shall do this until the weight of preconceived opinion is counter-balanced and the distorting influence of habit no longer prevents my judgment from perceiving things correctly" (First Meditation, AT VII 22: CSM II 15). This view reappears in the Seventh Replies: "When in the First Meditation I said that I wanted for a time to try to convince myself of the opposite of the views which I had rashly held before, I immediately added that my reasons for wanting to do this was as it were to counter-balance the weight of preconceived opinion so that I should not incline to one side more than the other" (AT VII 465: CSM II 312–13).

indifference, the only state of the will wherein the occurrence of error is at all possible. Less certain, however, is whether Descartes is addressing only incomplete C-indifference when he writes to Mesland that "wherever there is an occasion for sinning, there is indifference" (May 2, 1644, AT iv 117: CSM ii 234). This uncertainty is due to Descartes' distinction between suspending judgment in pure theoretical contexts and suspending judgment in the moral and religious domains. When dealing with intellectual judgments, he insists that acquiring "the habit of avoiding error" by suspending judgment whenever a distinct perception is lacking is where "man's greatest and most important perfection is to be found" (AT vii 62: CSM ii 43). In discussing the religious and moral spheres, however, Descartes holds that the suspension of assent (and the complete indifference of the will that determines it) is itself a form of sin, from which we are obliged to refrain. In the *Conversation with Burman*, he is reported to have made this view patently clear:

[W]e have inner consciousness of our freedom, and we know that we can withhold our assent when we wish. In the pursuit of good and evil, however, when the will is indifferent with respect to each of the two, it is already at fault, since it ought to seek after the good alone without any indifference, in contrast to the situation in theoretical subjects. (CB 32 = AT v 159: CSMK 342)

Descartes holds a similar position with respect to matters of faith. "With regard to supernatural matters," he continues, "the theologians teach that this is an area where we are corrupted through original sin: we need grace to enable us to recognize and pursue the good in this sphere" (ibid.).[14] On matters of faith, we need grace in order to avoid a state of complete indifference (and the ensuing suspension of judgment), which is already a fault. As Descartes explains to Mesland, grace does not "entirely prevent[s] indifference" but does diminish it by making us incline to one side rather than to another (May 2, 1644, AT iv 117–18: CSMK 234).

I say more about this issue in Chapter 5 below, and my present aim is only to illustrate Descartes' ambiguous use of "indifference" in the extra-theoretical domain. In contending that indifference of the will with regard to good and evil is already a sin, Descartes is probably referring to (what I called) complete indifference, a state consisting in a perfect balancing of reasons that determines the will to withhold judgment. But when Descartes writes to Mesland that indifference gives "occasion for

---

[14] As noted, Descartes also writes to Mesland that on matters of faith we need grace to make us incline to one side rather than another, thereby diminishing our indifference without diminishing our freedom (AT iv 117–18: CSMK 234).

sinning," he seems to be referring to the partial (incomplete) indifference that accompanies most of our practical decisions.

3 THE TWO-WAY POWER OF THE WILL

Does Descartes indeed hold that, of the two modes of C-indifference, only partial (incomplete) indifference is accompanied by the will's positive power to determine itself "to one or other of two contraries"? Exploring this question requires preliminary consideration of what precisely Descartes means when he speaks of the will's positive two-way power.[15] This question hinges, *inter alia*, on the kind of control Descartes presumably ascribes to the will over the formation and suspension of beliefs. To assume that, in endorsing this power, Descartes credits the human will with direct control over beliefs would mean that whenever our will enjoys this positive power, we can simply decide regardless of the weight of the evidence whether to assent to a given proposition, to dissent from it, or to suspend judgment about it. By contrast, to assume that the will's control over assent can only be indirect, would mean that the will's positive power to act or to judge against the weight of evidence is not exercised immediately or directly over beliefs but only through the mediation of another voluntary activity – attending to contrasting reasons that incline the will in the opposite direction. Deciding which of these two views Descartes embraces is not an easy task, since both can muster persuasive evidence in their support. The present discussion will focus on whether Descartes holds that our will enjoys direct control over beliefs in the face of confused or obscure ideas, postponing the question of the will's ability to resist assenting to clear and distinct perceptions to a later section.

At times, Descartes appears to be holding that suspension of assent is merely a matter of decision. Toward the end of the Fourth Meditation, for example, he claims that avoiding error by suspending judgment "depends merely on [his] remembering to withhold judgment on any occasion when the truth of the matter is not clear" (AT VII 61–62: CSM II 43). In his letter to Clerselier, Descartes similarly maintains that "in order to get rid of every kind of preconceived opinion, all we need to do is resolve not to affirm or deny anything which we have previously affirmed or denied until we have examined it afresh."[16] In the same letter, however, Descartes

---

[15] Fourth Meditation (AT VII 57: CSM II 40); letter to Mesland, February 9, 1645 (AT IV 173: CSMK 245); letter to Mesland, May 2, 1644 (AT IV 116: CSMK 234).

[16] Appendix to Fifth Replies (AT IXA 204: CSM II 270). This reference is given by Della Rocca (2006: 148).

acknowledges the difficulty of renouncing his preconceived opinions, and therefore insists on invoking reasons for doubt: "Nevertheless, I did say that there was some difficulty in expelling from our belief everything we have previously accepted. One reason for this is that before we can decide to doubt, we need some reason for doubting; and that is why in my First Meditation I put forward the principal reasons for doubt" (AT IXA 204: CSM II 270).[17]

The First Meditation's method of universal doubt clearly indicates that doubting, far from being an arbitrary enterprise, requires us to attend to reasons, even such that we may later find questionable or false.[18] Moreover, as Janet Broughton has shown (2002: 97ff.), aside from the universal doubt of the First Meditation, Descartes employs the method of doubt in the positive, constructive phase of his project "to help us identify and establish what we can know with absolute certainty."[19] The positive use of the method of doubt, which requires attending to "local" reasons for doubting particular propositions, is constitutive of the meditator's persistent endeavour to avoid error in the search for truth. Descartes refers to this issue, for example, when he writes to Mesland that "as soon as our attention turns from the reasons which show us that the thing is good for us ... we can call up before our mind some other reasons to make us doubt it, and so suspend our judgment, and perhaps even form a contrary judgment" (May 2, 1644, AT IV 117: CSMK 233–34).

While it is thus agreed that Descartes spells out the need to attend to reasons for doubt, it is less clear and indeed disputable whether he thinks that attending to reasons is necessary for the suspension and formation of beliefs and, if so, how weighty these reasons must be. Whereas some scholars read Descartes as acknowledging, at least under certain conditions, our ability to exercise direct control over beliefs in the face of confused or obscure perceptions, Lex Newman appears to hold that the Cartesian will never has direct control over its doxastic states (2008). In Newman's interpretation, the alleged power of the will to act against the weight of evidence can only be exercised indirectly, through the representation of countervailing reasons. Newman characterizes the "Indirect Voluntarism" he assigns to Descartes as follows: "Our assent cannot be

---

[17] In the Fifth Objections, Gassendi observes that to free his mind from preconceived opinions in the First Meditation all Descartes needed to do was "make a simple and brief statement" that he was regarding his previous knowledge as uncertain (AT VII 257: CSM II 180). Descartes replies: "Is it really so easy to free ourselves from all the errors which we have soaked up since our infancy?" (AT VII 348: CSM II 242).

[18] See also Seventh Replies (AT VII 465: CSM II 312–13).

[19] See, e.g., AT X 522: CSM II 415–16; AT II 38–39; CSMK 99.

directly aroused or suppressed by the action of our will, but only indirectly
... via the representation of reasons for belief (broadly construed): assent
to a proposition is determined by perceptual attention to supporting reasons; dissent is determined by attention to refuting reasons; suspension,
or doubt, is determined by attention to undermining reasons" (2008: 343).
In Newman's reading, insofar as the weight of evidence favors a certain
proposition, we cannot arbitrarily decide whether to believe or disbelieve
this proposition. We can only direct our mind's attention to rebutting reasons so as to change the inclination of our intellect and will. As Newman
concludes, "the will's freedom of alternate possibility arises in connection
with this power to help direct attention, not with a power of direct control over assent" (p. 349).

If we accept Newman's interpretation, nothing appears to bar us from
inferring, as Newman indeed does, that the will in all its states always
enjoys this positive power (p. 350). The will always has the ability to direct
the mind's attention to countervailing reasons, not only where it indeci-
sively inclines to one side but also when the weight of the evidence is
evenly balanced and, indeed, even when the reasons for choosing are all
on one side. Understanding the positive two-way power of the will as a
power that can be exercised over beliefs only indirectly may provide us
with a plausible sense of Descartes' perplexing statement in his 1645 letter to Mesland, whereby the will has this positive power "not only with
respect to those actions to which it is not pushed by any evident reason
on one side rather than on the other, but also with respect to all other
actions" (AT IV 173: CSMK 245).[20]

Yet other reasons suggest that, in certain circumstances, Descartes
must have allowed the human will to exercise direct control over beliefs.
As Della Rocca points out (2006: 148–52), to assume that the voluntary
control of the will over assent is always indirect, would be incompatible
with the doctrine that judgments are acts of the will. Had Descartes
assumed that whenever the weight of evidence favors a given proposition,
however slightly, the will irresistibly inclines to assent to it (unless the

---

[20] When Descartes says the will possesses the positive power to do otherwise with respect to all of
its *actions*, he might not be committing himself to the claim that the will enjoys this power even
when in a state of complete indifference, since it is not clear he considers a suspension of judgment an *action* of will. Some of the evidence, however, does support this latter perception. In the
Appendix to Fifth Replies, Descartes states that "making or not making a judgment is an act
of will" (AT VII 204: CSM II 270). See also Rosenthal (1986: 429–30); Broughton (2002: 45–46,
58). But even if we accept that the suspension of judgment, just like affirmation and denial, is an
act of the will, we must recall that this act does not constitute an act of judgment but an act of
choosing between making an act of judgment and avoiding it.

mind attends to countervailing reasons that reverse its inclination), he would have cut the ground from under his doctrine that belief requires something over and above the mere consideration of evidence by the intellect (Della Rocca 2006: 150).[21] In assessing Descartes' conception of voluntary control, then, this consideration must be taken into account. Otherwise, holding that the will can act against the weight of evidence only by directing the mind's attention to countervailing reasons commits Descartes to the view held by Spinoza that "when we say that someone suspends judgment, we are saying nothing but that he sees that he does not perceive the thing adequately" (*Ethics*, Part II, Proposition 49 Scholium, see Gebhardt 1925: II, 134).[22]

But how can we simply decide to believe a certain proposition, *p*, while attending to reasons that favor not-*p*? Apart from being phenomenologically implausible, as some scholars have noted,[23] this view appears to be at odds with Descartes' principle that our will has a natural tendency to truth and goodness, in proportion to the clarity and distinctness of the intellect's perceptions.[24] It would be more plausible, I think, to view Descartes as admitting the ability of the will to exercise direct control over the *suspension* of beliefs toward which it is undecidedly inclined (when the perceptions of the intellect are not clear and distinct). After all, as he clarifies in the *Comments on a Certain Broadsheet*, his main reason for holding that judgments are operations

---

[21] According to Della Rocca, though it is implausible that Descartes endorses direct control of the will over belief *in the absence of any evidence either way*, he does appear to admit the will's direct control over the formation and suspension of beliefs in another sense. In holding that a separate act of assent is still needed after examining the relevant evidence, Descartes implies that *after examining the relevant evidence*, belief formation and suspense are under the direct control of the will (2006: 149).

[22] English translations of the *Ethics* are Edwin Curley's. See Curley 1985, vol. I.

[23] Emphasizing the *conceptual* implausibility of this view, Bernard Williams writes: "one's incapacity to believe or disbelieve at will is not a contingent limitation, as one's incapacity to blush at will is" (1978: 177). In an earlier work, he writes that our inability to believe or disbelieve something at will has its origins in the very characteristic of beliefs, namely, that they aim at truth (1973: 148). As he goes on to explain, "If I could acquire a belief at will, I could acquire it whether it was true or not ... If in full consciousness I could will to acquire a 'belief' irrespective of its truth, it is unclear that before the event I could seriously think of it as a belief, i.e. as something purporting to represent reality" (p. 148). Curley also criticizes the view that one can decide to believe at will. But what he takes to be phenomenologically implausible is the view that one can decide whether to believe or disbelieve a proposition for which one has *no evidence at all* one way or the other, rather than the view that we can decide whether to believe something while attending to reasons that *undecidedly* favor it (Curley 1975: 178; see also Wilson 1978: 145). As I show below, Curley rightly criticizes the former view, which is *not* the one held by Descartes. See also Della Rocca (2006: 149).

[24] Letter to Mersenne, May 1637 (AT I 366: CSMK 56); Second Replies (AT VII 166: CSM II 117); Sixth Replies (AT VII 432: CSM II 292); *Passions*, art. 177.

of will was to account for our freedom to withhold assent (AT VIIIB 363: CSM I 307) in order to avoid error. Some support for this reading is found in Descartes' rejection of the view presented by Gassendi: "when the intellect's perception is obscure, then the will in this case will make a judgment that is doubtful and tentative" (AT VII 317: CSM II 220). The alleged dependence of the will on the intellect entails, according to Gassendi, "that we do not have the power so much to guard against error as to guard against persisting in error" (AT VII 317: CSM II 220). Descartes emphatically rejects this view and states that if the will could not be directed to anything not determined by the intellect, we could not guard against persisting in error (an ability Gassendi does admit we have). Descartes concludes:

[T]his would be quite impossible unless the will had the freedom to direct itself, without the determination of the intellect, towards one side or the other; and this you have just denied. If the intellect has already determined the will to put forward some false judgment, then what is it, may I ask, that determines the will when first it began to guard against persisting in error? (AT VII 378: CSM II 260)

Had Descartes held that the will cannot withhold assent despite the inclination of the intellect when its perceptions are obscure or confused, he would have had to accept Gassendi's contention that at best we can guard against persisting in error, not against incurring it. In rejecting this view, Descartes seems to allow for situations where the will moves against the inclination of the intellect, and thus exercises direct control over the suspension of beliefs.

Notice, however, that Descartes admits to situations where the will is indifferent and yet does not enjoy direct control over the suspension of beliefs. He appears to be suggesting that when the weight of reasons strongly favors a given belief we consider highly probable, we lack the power to withhold judgment about it merely by a decision of our will.[25] The textual evidence that supports this reading also shows that when the weight of evidence is evenly balanced, the will is determined to withhold judgment about the propositions at stake and thus lacks the two-

---

[25] Curley thinks Descartes acknowledges our ability not only to suspend assent at will, even when the weight of evidence favors one of the sides, but also to judge not-*p* when the evidence favors *p* (1975: 174). But as his analysis proceeds, Curley reads Descartes as denying the will's direct control over the suspension of beliefs that we find highly probable, insisting on having reasonable grounds for doubting them (p. 176). Curley concludes: "We cannot just decide not to believe something we find highly probable, but we can bring it about that we no longer find it probable by attending to arguments which cut against the belief or against the grounds on which we hold it" (p. 176).

way power to assent or not assent to them.[26] Toward the end of the First Meditation, Descartes writes that although he has just found all his former opinions worthy of doubt, these habitual opinions keep coming back and capturing his belief despite his wishes, since he has more reasons in favor of them than against them (AT VII 22: CSM II 15).[27] Descartes realizes that to stop believing these highly probable opinions and suspend judgment about them he must *balance* the weight of the evidence for and against them:

I shall never get out of the habit of confidently assenting to these opinions, so long as I suppose them to be what in fact they are, namely highly probable opinions – opinions which, despite the fact that they are in a sense doubtful, as has just been shown, it is still much more reasonable to believe than to deny. In view of this, I think it will be a good plan to turn my will in completely the opposite direction and deceive myself, by pretending for a time that these former opinions are utterly false and imaginary. *I shall do this until the weight of preconceived opinion is counter-balanced and the distorting influence of habit no longer prevents my judgment from perceiving things correctly.* In the meantime, I know that no danger or error will result from my plan. (AT VII 22: CSM II 15; my emphasis)

Descartes repeats this point in the Seventh Replies:

When in the First Meditation I said that I wanted for a time to try to convince myself of the opposite of the views which I had rashly held before, I immediately added that my reason for wanting to do this was *as it were to counter-balance the weight of preconceived opinion so that I should not incline to one side more than the other.* (AT VII 465: CSM II 312–13; my emphasis)

These passages suggest that, regarding highly probable opinions, withholding assent by a mere decision of the will is unfeasible.[28] Moreover,

---

[26] Kenny alludes to this view when marking off a state of indifference (in the sense of a balance of reasons) from what he calls "the liberty of perversion," which consists in the possibility of acting against the weight of reasons (1972: 28, 30). Compare Davies (2001: 118, 122), who holds that even in a situation of balanced evidence, we can decide whether to believe or disbelieve.

[27] At the beginning of the First Meditation, Descartes states that for a proposition to be found *worthy of doubt* (and thus be treated for a time "as if" it were false), finding it not completely certain on even the minutest grounds for doubt is enough (AT VII 18: CSM II 12). Similarly, in the Second Meditation he asserts: "Anything which admits of the slightest doubt I will set aside just as if I had found it to be wholly false" (AT VII 24: CSM II 16). But Descartes distinguishes between the rigorous conditions for an opinion to be *worthy of doubt* (what Broughton calls "the strong maxim for assent" [2002: 44–45]) and those required for *the implementation of the doubt*, namely, the conditions in which a suspension of judgment is *attainable*. Whereas the slightest reason is indeed sufficient for a proposition to be considered metaphysically uncertain and thus *eligible for being doubted*, this reason is insufficient to allow us to suspend judgment about it or to render our assent to it *unreasonable* (Broughton 2002: 47–49; Perin 2008: 61).

[28] Compare Broughton, for example, who takes Descartes' position in the First Meditation about suspending judgment to be clear: "it is here and now within my power to suspend judgment

Descartes' prescription to balance the evidence for and against these highly probable opinions indicates that he takes a situation of perfect indifference, wherein we have no reason to prefer one of two opposing propositions, to be an efficient remedy against error. Since the will cannot incline toward an object unless the mind, however confusedly, conceives the object to be true or good, it cannot arbitrarily choose to believe a proposition in the absence of any reason that makes it appear worthy of belief.

We see, then, that the decision on whether Descartes regards the two-way power of the will as essential to human freedom requires preliminary consideration of whether, and in what circumstances, he approaches this power as exercised directly or indirectly over the formation and suspension of beliefs. The decision on this issue may thus change according to how we construe Descartes' position on the ability of the will to act against the weight of the evidence.

4 DESCARTES' CONCEPTION OF HUMAN FREEDOM

Granted that C-indifference is not identified with the positive power of the will to choose otherwise, we need to distinguish between the n following two questions, which are often intermingled: (1) Is C-indifference essential to our freedom of will? (2) Is the will's positive power to choose otherwise essential to freedom of will?

Descartes answers the first question in the negative, explicitly stating that the indifference of the will is indicative of a defect in knowledge, namely, of a certain degree of ignorance:

But the indifference I feel when there is no reason pushing me in one direction rather than another is the lowest grade of freedom; it is evidence not of any perfection or freedom, but rather of a defect in knowledge or a kind of negation. For if I always saw clearly what was true and good, I should never have to deliberate about the right judgment or choice; in that case, although I should be wholly free, it would be impossible for me ever to be in a state of indifference. (Fourth Meditation, AT VII 58: CSM II 40)

---

about the truth of anything I have believed" (2002: 58). Unless our grasp of a given proposition *p* is very simple and very clear and distinct, she states, Descartes "must be read as saying that for any *p*, I can suspend judgment whether *p* by deciding to suspend judgment whether *p*" (p. 46 n. 8; see also p. 58). Frankfurt also thinks that suspension of judgment, for Descartes, results directly from a decision or an act of will, so that "a person suspends judgment merely by resolving that his judgments are suspended" (Frankfurt 1970: 18). But Frankfurt does acknowledge the essential role that Descartes ascribes to his skeptical arguments in the overthrow of his beliefs: "Even if he can empty his mind by making a decision, Descartes needs to do more than this in order to keep his judgments effectively suspended" (p. 21), (that is, to develop arguments that justify this decision and reinforce his resolution).

Complete indifference, then, is the lowest level of freedom, but when the will enjoys the highest grade of spontaneity and freedom, that is, when it is irresistibly inclined toward the distinct perceptions of the intellect, it is impossible for it to be indifferent. A few paragraphs later in the Fourth Meditation, Descartes indicates that the will is indifferent whenever the intellect lacks sufficient knowledge:

> I am making the further supposition that my intellect has not yet come upon any persuasive reason in favour of one alternative rather than the other. This obviously implies that I am indifferent as to whether I should assert or deny either alternative, or indeed refrain from making any judgment on the matter.
>
> What is more, this indifference does not merely apply to cases where the intellect is wholly ignorant, but extends in general to every case where the intellect does not have sufficiently clear knowledge at the time when the will deliberates. (AT VII 59: CSM II 41)[29]

In the Sixth Replies, Descartes explicitly states that "indifference does not belong to the essence of human freedom, since not only are we free when ignorance of what is right makes us indifferent, but we are also free – indeed at our freest – when a clear perception impels us to pursue some object" (AT VII 433: CSM II 292).[30] In holding that indifference is not essential to human freedom, however, Descartes is not answering the second question, that is, he is not denying that the positive two-way power of the will is essential to our freedom. The second question is indeed harder to answer, and I take it up now in greater detail.

In the Fourth Meditation, immediately after expounding his twofold definition of freedom, Descartes writes:

> In order to be free, there is no need for me to be inclined both ways [*in utramque partem ferri posse*]; on the contrary, the more I incline in one direction – either because I clearly understand that reasons of truth and goodness point that way, or because of a divinely produced disposition of my inmost thoughts – the freer is my choice. Neither divine grace nor natural knowledge ever diminishes freedom; on the contrary, they increase and strengthen it. (AT VII 57–58: CSM II 40)

Although Descartes had intended this passage to explicate his preceding definition of freedom, the passage appears too ambiguous to help us decide whether he considers the positive two-way power of the will essential to our freedom. As Kenny points out, the words "*in utramque partem ferri posse*" can be read either as "to be able to go both ways" or as "to

---

[29] Likewise, he writes to Mesland that a person "is more indifferent the fewer reasons he knows which impel him to choose one side rather than another" (May 2, 1644, AT IV 115: CSMK 233).
[30] See also letter to Mesland, May 2, 1644 (AT IV 117–18: CSMK 234).

be inclined both ways."[31] According to the former option, this passage presents the positive two-way power to choose either way as inessential to freedom; according to the latter, what is said to be inessential to our freedom is the state of complete indifference, that is, a state where the will does not incline in one direction more than the other.

Cottingham appears to embrace the former option when he writes: "Descartes explicitly denies the need for human freedom to be grounded in some supposed contra-causal power. 'In order for me to be free,' he asserts in the Fourth Meditation, 'there is no need for me to be capable of moving in each of two directions'" (Cottingham 2002: 350). Kenny supports the latter option. In this particular passage, he argues, what is said to be inessential to human free will is the indifference consisting in the balancing of reasons, not the power to act either way (what Kenny calls "liberty of indifference").[32] Kenny relies on the French version of the text, which contains the word "indifferent": *Car, afin que je sois libre, il n'est pas nécessaire que je sois indifférent à choisir l'un ou l'autre des deux contraires* ("in order to be free, there is no need for me to be indifferent as to the choice of one or the other of two contraries" AT IX 46).

Michelle Beyssade discerns a discrepancy between the Latin text of the Fourth Meditation (1641) and its later French version of 1647, taking it to mark a change in Descartes' original conception of free will. Her translation of the Latin phrase "*in utramque partem ferri posse*" gives the verb "*ferri*" an active denotation, meaning "to be able to go both ways." She therefore thinks that, in the Latin text, Descartes regards the positive power of choosing between two contraries as unnecessary for human free will. The French version, however, makes "the state of indifference or wavering or balance due to ignorance" unnecessary for human freedom (1994: 194). The French text of 1647, concludes Beyssade, leaves open the question that the original Latin had resolved in the negative, namely, whether the two-way power is necessary for human freedom (1994: 194–95).

I hold with Kenny that both the Latin and the French texts claim that what is inessential to our freedom is the indifference of the will, not its two-way positive power. But unlike Kenny, I hold that while the Latin text asserts that *complete* indifference is inessential to our freedom, the

---

[31] The latter alternative is the one adopted in the translation of Cottingham, Stoothoff, and Murdoch of the 1641 Latin text.

[32] See Kenny (1972: 18–19). Imlay (1982: 90); Campbell (1999: 186); Alanen (2003: 228); Kaufman (2003a: 394); and Ragland (2006b: 395–96), each on different grounds, also hold that, in this passage, Descartes denies that indifference (in the sense of perfect balance) is essential to human freedom.

French version widens the scope of this claim to include all grades of C-indifference, either complete or incomplete. Note that this passage follows the second clause of Descartes' definition of freedom, stating that free will consists in the will's inclination toward the perceptions of the intellect. To explain this second clause, Descartes proceeds to clarify that our freedom of will does not require release from internal inclinations; on the contrary, our freedom is enhanced in proportion to our intellectual assurance. The greater our inclination in one direction, either by virtue of the natural light of our reason or – in matters of faith – the supernatural light of divine grace, the freer our choice. The rival interpretation of the Latin text, therefore, which reads this passage as asserting that the positive two-way power of the will is inessential to our freedom, is less compatible with the full passage. If my reading of the Latin original is correct, the French text could represent an attempt to remove possible misunderstandings by replacing complete indifference (as in the Latin original) with any state of indifference, in whatever degree. Rather than marking a change in Descartes' position on this issue, the French text makes the original Latin more precise in asserting that "in order to be free, there is no need for me to be indifferent" (i.e., internally undetermined) "as to the choice of one or the other of two contraries." In all states of indeterminacy (either complete or incomplete), the will is indifferent as to the choice of one or the other of two opposites. According to this reading, the French text paves the way for the announcement that follows, whereby the indifference of our will, in whatever degree, is not essential to our freedom: "For if I always saw clearly what was true and good, I should never have to deliberate about the right judgment or choice; in that case, although I should be wholly free, it would be impossible for me ever to be in a state of indifference" (AT VII 58: CSM II 40).

Several lines later in the Fourth Meditation, however, we find evidence indicating that, for Descartes, the positive power of the will to choose otherwise is *not* essential to human freedom. Reflecting on the Cogito, he asserts: "I could not but judge that something which I understood so clearly was true" (AT VII 58: CSM II 41). Descartes then proceeds to shed light on his experience of intellectual necessity: "but this was not because I was compelled so to judge by any external force, but because a great light in the intellect was followed by a great inclination in the will, and thus the spontaneity and freedom of my belief was all the greater in proportion to my lack of indifference" (AT VII 58–59: CSM II 41).

In this paragraph, Descartes identifies human freedom with spontaneity in keeping with the second clause of his definition of freedom: a great inclination in the will to embrace the perceptions of the intellect, without any external coercion. Moreover, Descartes explicitly denies that the will's positive power to do or choose otherwise is essential to human freedom: "I could not but judge that something which I understood so clearly was true." When the will is spontaneous and free to the highest possible degree, then, it lacks this positive two-way power. Insofar as the ideas occurring in the mind are clear and distinct, the will cannot but accept them as true; it can neither reject them as false nor suspend judgment about them. Only when we are no longer attending to the reasons that led us to assent to these objects can we call up other reasons that might make us doubt them or undermine our judgment about them.[33] Descartes asserts this view in subsequent Meditations and in his replies to the objections raised against his arguments in this work.[34] In a letter to Regius of May 24, 1640, he likewise maintains that "our mind is of such a nature that it cannot help assenting to what it clearly understands" (AT III 64: CSMK 147). Descartes remains faithful to this position in later writings as well. In the *Principles*, for instance, he unequivocally states that "the minds of all of us have been so moulded by nature that whenever we perceive something clearly, we spontaneously give our assent to it and are quite unable to doubt its truth" (I, 43). And in a letter to his Jesuit correspondent Denis Mesland of May 2, 1644, Descartes writes:

And I agree with you when you say that we can suspend our judgment; but I tried to explain in what manner this can be done. For it seems to me certain that "a great light in the intellect is followed by a great inclination in the will"; *so that if we see very clearly that a thing is good for us, it is very difficult – and, on my view, impossible, as long as one continues in the same thought – to stop the course of our desire.* But the nature of the soul is such that it hardly attends for more than a moment to a single thing; hence, as soon as our attention turns from the reasons which show us that the thing is good for us, and we merely keep in our memory the thought that it appeared desirable to us, we can call up before our mind some other reason to make us doubt it, and so suspend our judgment, and perhaps even form a contrary judgment. (AT IV 115–16: CSMK 233–34; my emphasis)

Descartes expressly argues here that suspension of judgment is quite impossible so long as our mind is attending to a clearly and distinctly perceived good. Only when the attention of the mind is deflected from the

---

[33] Letter to Mesland, May 2, 1644 (AT IV 116: CSMK 233–34).
[34] See, for example, Fifth Meditation (AT VII 65: CSM II 45; AT VII 69–70: CSM II 48); Second Replies (AT VII 145–46: CSM II 104; AT VII 166: CSM II 117); Sixth Replies (AT VII 433: CSM II 292); Seventh Replies (AT VII 460: CSM II 309).

reasons that have led us to believe that this thing is good for us can we suspend our judgment, or even form a contrary judgment by citing other, contrasting reasons that incline our will to the opposite side.[35]

Two notable passages, however, might appear inconsistent with Descartes' declared position on this issue. Descartes seems to assert in these passages that we *do* have the power to resist a clearly and distinctly perceived truth or goodness at the very moment of perceiving it. The first is from article 37 of the *Principles*, and the second is from Descartes' letter to Mesland of February 9, 1645. I cite them in turn:

> [I]t is a supreme perfection in man that he acts voluntarily, that is, freely; this makes him in a special way the author of his actions and deserving of praise for what he does. We do not praise automatons for accurately producing all the movements they were designed to perform, because the production of these movements occurs necessarily. It is the designer who is praised for constructing such carefully-made devices; for in constructing them he acted not out of necessity but freely. By the same principle, when we embrace the truth, our doing so voluntarily is much more to our credit than would be the case if we could not do otherwise. (*Principles*, I, 37)

> But perhaps others mean by "indifference" a positive faculty of determining oneself to one or other of two contraries, that is to say, to pursue or avoid, to affirm or deny. I do not deny that the will has this positive faculty. Indeed, I think it has it not only with respect to those actions to which it is not pushed by any evident reasons on one side rather than on the other, but also with respect to all other actions; so that when a very evident reason moves us in one direction, although morally speaking we can hardly move in the contrary direction, absolutely speaking we can. For it is always open to us to hold back from pursuing a clearly known good or from admitting a clearly perceived truth, provided we consider it a good thing to demonstrate the freedom of our will by so doing. (Letter to Mesland, February 9, 1645, AT IV 173: CSMK 245)

In the letter to Mesland, Descartes explicitly states that the will possesses the positive power of determining itself on one or other of two opposites with respect to all its actions – not only when it is indifferent (not pushed by a very evident reason in one side) but, apparently, also in the face of clearly and distinctly perceived reasons. In the passage from the *Principles*, Descartes appears to present the reason for holding this view – "we do not praise automatons for accurately producing all the movements they were designed to perform" by necessity, nor do we deserve praise for actions we perform under duress. Descartes thus concludes that when we

---

[35] See also *Conversation with Burman* (April 16, 1648) (CB 6 = AT v 148: CSMK 334; CB 81 = AT v 178: CSMK 353).

embrace the truth, our action is indeed voluntary and therefore praise-worthy only because we could have done otherwise (either by dissenting from the truth or by suspending judgment in its regard). For an action to be voluntary and praiseworthy, then, it must be free not only from external duress but also from internal, intellectual compulsion (the coercive force of the intellect's distinct perceptions).

Scholars disagree on how we should construe Descartes' position in these passages. Some approach them as pointing to a change in Descartes' position which occurred at some point between 1641 and 1645,[36] whereas others hold they need not be read as indicating that Descartes retracted from his previous stance.[37] Yet others claim that throughout his career Descartes consistently held that the two-way power of the will is essential to human freedom, even though he only explicitly stated so in these later sources.[38]

Despite the serious challenge posed by the 1645 letter to Mesland and by article 37 of the *Principles*, I believe these textual sources are insufficient to indicate a genuine change in Descartes' position on such a crucial and persistent facet of his thinking. Moreover, I will argue that these sources can be reconciled with Descartes' explicit compatibilistic approach. But before proceeding to analyze them, let me introduce several preliminary considerations that need to be taken into account.

The suggestion that Descartes changed his original position on this matter does not seem plausible in the face of clear indications that he maintained it in writings published after 1644.[39] In article 43 of the

---

[36] See, e.g., Gilson (1913: 310–19); Alquié (1950, ch. 14, esp. pp. 288ff.); Michelle Beyssade (1994); Schmaltz (1994: 13); Williston (1997: 436ff.).

[37] See, for example, Kenny (1972: 28ff.); Williams (1978: 178, 181–83); Larmore (1984: 66–68); Schmaltz (1994: 11–12); Nelson (1997: 171–72); Cottingham (2002: 352–55, 2008b: 197–98); Hoffman (2003: 266; 2009: 213–15); Kaufman (2003a: 393, 397); Gilbert (2005: 212ff.); Wee (2006b: 395–98); Newman (2008: 349–50). On Newman's interpretation, as noted, the alleged two-way power of our will is an ability to help control the intellect's perceptual attention, which means that only by diverting our attention away from what is clear and distinct can we "hold back" from assenting to it.

[38] See, for instance, Imlay (1982: 90ff.); Campbell (1999: 179ff., esp. pp. 187–89); Davies (2001: 19, 114, 128–34); Alanen (2003: 226–33, 237, 240–46). Ragland's position on this issue may also be placed in this category. He contends that Descartes embraces the principle of alternative possibilities "throughout his career in a way that coheres with his other main claims about freedom" (2006a: 377–78). But Ragland reads the Fourth Meditation as suggesting a distinction between two different senses of the phrase "I could have done otherwise." In one of its senses, this phrase means "I had a reason or motive for doing otherwise" (Ragland calls it "alternative of indifference"). But in its other sense, this phrase means "external forces did not determine me to do what I did" (what he calls "alternatives of self-determination": 2006a: 386). He concludes that although we lack alternatives of indifference in the face of evident reasons, we still enjoy alternatives of self-determination (2006a: 386, 392–94; see also 2006b).

[39] See also Newman (2008: 348–49); Kaufman (2003a: 393); Hoffman (2003: 264, 266–67).

Principles, as noted, he asserts that "the minds of all of us have been so moulded by nature that whenever we perceive something clearly we spontaneously give our assent to it and are quite unable to doubt its truth." Note that this claim appears not only in the 1644 Latin original but also in the French translation published in 1647, which Descartes endorsed unequivocally.[40] Moreover, as Kaufman observes (2003a: 393), had Descartes changed his view on such a critical issue between 1641 and 1645, he could have made appropriate changes not only in the French edition of the *Principles* but also in the 1647 French translation of the *Meditations*, which he sanctioned as well. In the *Conversation with Burman* of April 16, 1648, Descartes claims that so long as someone pays attention to clear and distinct ideas, "he is compelled to give his assent to them" (CB 6 = AT v 148: CSMK 334), and that otherwise "we could not prove that God exists" (CB 81 = AT v 178: CSMK 353). Further textual evidence appears in the *Passions of the Soul*, published in 1649. In this work, Descartes emphatically asserts that we cannot pursue evil while we are entirely certain that what we are doing is evil: "if we were wholly certain that what we are doing is bad, we would refrain from doing it, since the will tends only towards objects that have some semblance of goodness" (art. 177). Given this assertion, as Hoffman points out, Descartes could hardly have intended in his 1645 letter to Mesland that we can pursue evil as evil, namely, that we have a positive power to follow the worst while we clearly and distinctly perceive the better (2003: 264).[41]

But even aside from this direct textual evidence, Descartes could not have abandoned his view that clear and distinct perceptions compel assent without undertaking a fundamental revision of his most basic epistemological doctrines. One is his conception of error that I discussed in the previous chapter. Had Descartes believed we can dissent from a clearly and distinctly perceived truth, he could not have argued that "it is quite impossible" for us to go wrong so long as we restrict the operations of the will to the clear and distinct perceptions of the intellect. Toward the end

---

[40] See Preface-Letter to the French edition of the *Principles* (AT ixb 1: CSM 1 179). The French edition, published in 1647, renders article 43 as follows: "*nous sommes naturellement si enclins à donner nostre consentement aux choses que nous appercevons manifestement, que nous n'en sçaurions douter pendant que nous les appercevons de la sorte*" (AT ixb 43).

[41] Byron Williston argues that the view sketched in the 1645 letter to Mesland becomes the dominant position in the *Passions of the Soul*, a work that transfers the focus from the need to act in truth to the need to act determinately (1997: 438ff.). But the rules of action that Descartes sets out in his correspondence with Princess Elizabeth, in the *Passions of the Soul*, and also in Part Three of the *Discourse*, as I show in Chapters 5 and 6 below, apply only to practical decision-making on matters of which clear and distinct apprehension is often unattainable.

of the Fourth Meditation, he writes: "if, whenever I have to make a judgment, I restrain my will so that it extends to what the intellect clearly and distinctly reveals, and no further, then it is quite impossible for me to go wrong" (AT VII 62: CSM II 43). Significantly, Descartes is not making in this passage the more obvious claim that he cannot possibly err insofar as he *assents* to clear and distinct perceptions of the intellect. Rather, he is committing himself to the more revealing statement that he cannot go wrong insofar as he *applies his power of judgment* only to clear and distinct perceptions of the intellect. This claim definitely indicates that we can never misuse our free will so long as we keep its operations within the limits of our intellect.

Furthermore, in view of Descartes' non-consequentialist conception of error, the status of a judgment that denies a clearly and distinctly perceived truth is by no means clear. Evidently, such a judgment cannot be considered erroneous since it is based on a clear and distinct perception of the intellect. But neither can it be considered free of error (one that renders its agent praiseworthy) since it denies a clearly and distinctly perceived truth, judging it to be false. One objection could argue that reading Descartes as a radical voluntarist may offer a new understanding of his fundamental distinction between "right use" and "misuse" of free will, on which his definition of error rests. Assuming that a clear and distinct perception is not necessarily followed by an affirmation of the will, such an interpretation may suggest that only when we succeed in assenting to our clear and distinct perceptions *despite the fact that we could have done otherwise*, do we deserve credit for using our free will correctly. Alanen's interpretation (2003) alludes to this line of thought:

Only because she is free to pursue or not pursue the good can an agent make the pursuit of the true and the good … truly her own end. Without this freedom, she can be determined by the true and the good, but not because of her own will and commitment … We cannot be moral beings and not pursue the good, and we cannot be rational and not accept the true. But having the power to control the inclinations of our will leaves room for choice between good and evil, between rationality and irrationality, and it is only to the extent we can make that choice and freely commit ourselves to the true or the good that we can pursue them as autonomous agents. (2003: 245)

Alanen's interpretation seems to be resting on a substantive reading of Descartes' notion of error, according to which we may be blamed for incurring an error only when we affirm what is false or deny what is true. Read in this way, Descartes would consider any dissent from a clear and distinct perception of the intellect erroneous precisely because it denies what is true. But this reading may also imply that whenever we dissent from a clearly perceived truth or goodness, we should be blamed for not using our free will correctly on the grounds that we have acted against the strong (though not compelling) inclination of our will to follow the perceptions of the intellect. On this alternative account, which I am not sure Alanen actually endorses, Descartes would count any dissent from a clearly and distinctly perceived truth as an instance of error – *qua* a mis-use of free will. Unless we succeed in assenting to our clear and distinct perceptions by controlling our ability to dissent from them, we shall not escape the blame for error due to our incorrect use of the will.

This account, however appealing, might encounter serious difficulties in explaining Descartes' insistence in the Fourth Meditation that inso-far as we restrain the will "so that it extends to what the intellect clearly and distinctly reveals, and no further, then it is quite impossible for me to go wrong" (AT vii 62: CSM ii 43). Considering the centrality of this view for Descartes' theodicy and theory of error, to which he devotes his arguments in the Fourth Meditation, I adhere to Kenny's contention that "to abandon the theory that clear and distinct perception necessitates the will is to call in question the whole validation of reason in which the *Meditations* culminates" (1972: 29).

With these preliminary considerations in place, we may now proceed to a more detailed analysis of the quotations from article 37 of the *Principles* and of the 1645 letter to Mesland.

5 ARTICLE 37 OF THE *PRINCIPLES*

[I]t is a supreme perfection in man that he acts voluntarily, that is, freely; this makes him in a special way the author of his actions and deserving of praise for what he does. We do not praise automatons for accurately producing all the movements they were designed to perform, because the production of these movements occurs necessarily. It is the designer who is praised for constructing such carefully-made-devices; for in constructing them he acted not out of neces-sity but freely. By the same principle, when we embrace the truth, our doing so voluntarily is much more to our credit than would be the case if we could not do otherwise. (*Principles*, i, 37)

This passage indicates that an action is considered voluntary and, as such, morally praiseworthy, only if we do not perform it out of necessity, that is, only if we could have avoided acting or could have performed another action instead. Descartes seems to be suggesting, then, that we deserve praise for embracing a clearly and distinctly perceived truth by virtue of our ability to resist embracing it, that is, to do otherwise. To read Descartes in this way, however, will render his position in this treatise inconsistent, given his explicit assertion to the contrary in article 43 (cited earlier). This difficulty invites us to look for another interpretation of his view in the above quotation from the *Principles*. Reflecting on this passage, Hoffman suggests that even if we are compelled to assent to a clear and distinct idea of something as true, we still deserve praise for doing so because we could have failed to render our ideas clear and distinct and to focus our attention on them (2003: 267). Hoffman emphasizes further that "it is only a contingent truth that we acquire and continue to pay attention to our clear and distinct ideas," and that "it is something we might easily fail to do or even fail to attempt to do" (2003: 267; 2009: 214. See also Kenny 1972: 23).

This interpretation, which I wish to pursue, calls for some comment on the essential role that the two-way power of the will plays in our attaining the highest level of freedom. Even though this positive power is not essential to our freedom in a strict sense (since we do not enjoy it while attaining the highest degree of freedom), it is still essential to our freedom in an indirect sense. The reason is that our prospects to intensify our freedom hinge on our ability to control our judgments while avoiding error, as well as on our ability to render our ideas clear and distinct by "purifying" our intellectual activity and directing our attention to them. And even after we acquire a clear and distinct perception of the truth, and thereby reach the highest grade of freedom, we still need this power to keep our attention fixed on it rather than letting it slip out of focus. Since focusing attention is an act of the will, as Cottingham emphasizes,

it emerges that human beings are more than doxastic robots, led by the nose, or determined by the architecture of their divinely-structured intellect. They are truly in control of the circumstances of their search for the truth, since the irresistibility of the natural light will always be contingent on their own free choice as to how far they keep the light focused. (2002: 354)[42]

The two-way power of the will is thus essential to our ability to attain the highest degree of spontaneity and freedom although, in this particular state, this positive power is lacking! Gibson excels at making this point (notice that Gibson uses "liberty of indifference" to signify the two-way power of the will – which I called "S-indifference" – rather than to denote Cartesian "indifference"):

It is only at the moment of conviction, when all the reasons for doubt are at length removed, that Descartes denies the liberty of indifference. As long as there

---

[42] See also Newman (2008, esp. pp. 349–51).

is uncertainty he lays great stress on it, as the only force standing between us and chaos … It would thus be unfair to accuse Descartes of Jansenism because he admits a freedom which is not that of indifference. It is only because the freedom which is indifference has once been exercised that the freedom which is not indifference can ultimately be enjoyed. (1987: 335–36)

These considerations might help us explain why Descartes opens his definition of freedom in the Fourth Meditation by stating it consists in the ability of the will to do or not to do something.[43] In view of the indispensable role played by the two-way power of the will in enhancing our degree of freedom, we may plausibly assume that rather than seeking to withdraw from the first clause through the second, which defines freedom as spontaneous self-determination, Descartes was seeking only to formulate his view more precisely. Given that Descartes often speaks of the two-way power of the will as the power *to determine oneself* on one or other of two contraries,[44] the second clause may be seen as a rectification of the first. The full definition can thus be paraphrased as follows: free will consists in the positive power to determine oneself without a feeling of external coercion, either on one or other of two contraries (when the perceptions of the mind are confused or obscure) or on one side (when the natural light of reason or the supernatural light of grace illuminates them). The following article from the *Principles* reinforces this reading: "That there is freedom in our will, and that we have power *in many cases* to give or withhold our assent at will, is so evident that it must be counted among the first and most common notions that are innate in us" (1, 39; my emphasis).

I turn now to consider Descartes' position in the passage from the 1645 letter to Mesland. This challenging quotation will play a significant role in the next chapter's discussion of the alleged essential similarity between human and divine free will.

6 THE 1645 LETTER TO MESLAND

I do not deny that the will has this positive faculty. Indeed, I think it has it not only with respect to those actions to which it is not pushed by any evident reasons on one side rather than on the other, but also with respect to all other actions; so that when a very evident reason moves us in one direction, although

---

[43] Some scholars have objected that had Descartes thought that the first clause of this definition misidentified the essence of human freedom, he would have deleted it. See, e.g., Ragland (2006b: 388); Imlay (1982: 91).

[44] See, for instance, Fifth Replies (AT VII 378: CSM II 260); letter to Mesland, May 2, 1644, (AT IV 116: CSMK 234); letter to Mesland, February 9, 1645 (AT IV 173–74: CSMK 244–45).

morally speaking we can hardly move in the contrary direction, absolutely speaking we can. For it is always open to us to hold back from pursuing a clearly known good or from admitting a clearly perceived truth, provided we consider it a good thing to demonstrate the freedom of our will by so doing. (Letter to Mesland, February 9, 1645, AT IV 173: CSMK 244–45)[45]

In this passage, Descartes appears to affirm that we enjoy the power to do or choose otherwise, even in the face of clear and distinct ideas. He states that our will, in all its actions, enjoys the positive power to determine itself on one or other of two contraries, and that we may always hold back from pursuing a clearly known good or from admitting a clearly perceived truth. This statement, however, is subject to two main qualifications, which I now consider in turn. The first is that holding back from this assent or from this pursuit is open to us "provided we consider it a good thing to demonstrate the freedom of our will by so doing." The second qualification is that we can resist a clearly and distinctly perceived truth only "absolutely speaking," but not "morally speaking."

Focusing on the first qualification, Kenny argues that the full passage need not be read to mean that we can resist assenting to a clearly perceived goodness or truth while our attention is focused on them. Rather, we can only resist by distracting our attention from these objects by, for instance, dwelling on the thought "that it would be a good thing to demonstrate our freedom by perversity. This would provide a reason in the contrary sense, without which the will could not act; and *eo ipso* this would render the perception of truth and goodness unclear" (1972: 29).[46] According to Kenny, whereas the 1644 letter to Mesland states we can resist a clearly and distinctly perceived good as soon as our attention turns away from the reasons showing that this is good for us (AT IV 115–16: CSMK 233–34), the 1645 letter suggests a reason one could use for doing so (1972: 29).[47]

---

[45] As some scholars have pointed out, both the date and the addressee of this letter are uncertain (see, e. g., Kenny 1972: 26; Williams 1978: 181 n. 4).

[46] But note that in most cases we divert attention from our clear and distinct ideas because of the weakness of our minds. As Hoffman rightly emphasizes, Descartes usually "conceives of the initial diversion of attention from our clear and distinct idea not as brought about by our will, but rather as something that we undergo" (2003: 266). This view appears not only in the 1644 letter to Mesland (AT IV 116: CSMK 233) but also in the *Meditations*. See, e.g., Third Meditation (AT VII 36: CSM II 25); Fifth Meditation (AT VII 69–70: CSM II 48); Second Replies (AT VII 146: CSM II 104); Seventh Replies (AT VII 460: CSM II 309).

[47] Various scholars have endorsed Kenny's reading of this passage, or at least some version of it. Among them are Cottingham (1976: 89; 2002: 352–55); Schmaltz (1994: 11–12); Nelson (1997: 171–72); Hoffman (2003: 266; 2009 213–14); Gilbert (2005: 215, 223 n. 13); and Newman (2008: 349–50).

In line with this interpretation, I find it implausible that we can simultaneously concentrate on the overwhelming reasons put forward by the intellect, and on our conscious desire to demonstrate the freedom of our will from subservience to reason. Apparently, one is either fully committed to the search for truth or driven by some other, extra-theoretical countervailing motive of the kind just introduced. Moreover, had Descartes intended in this letter to overturn his original doctrine, he would not have confined himself to an incidental remark without indicating how it might fit into his declared position on the issue. A more plausible explanation is, I think, that seeking to conciliate his Jesuit correspondent, Descartes downplayed the significant differences between their views by showing they were mainly terminological.

Descartes' second qualification reinforces this reading: "when a very evident reason moves us in one direction, although morally speaking we can hardly move in the contrary direction, absolutely speaking we can." While Kenny does not address Descartes' distinction between moral and absolute possibility, some scholars find his interpretation of the first qualification applicable to this distinction as well. Alan Nelson, for instance, suggests: "When Descartes writes that absolutely speaking we can hold back from admitting a clearly perceived truth, he is simply restating that the will can be diverted from a clear and distinct perception" (1997: 172).[48] Nelson's interpretation, I think, does not fit well with Descartes' suggestion that it is with regard to *the same situation of choice* that, "morally speaking," we cannot act or judge against the weight of the evidence, whereas "absolutely speaking" we can. This point was made by Ragland: "the 'two senses' passage maintains that, with respect to one and the same act of will, and at the same time, we can be both morally *unable* to hold back and absolutely *able* to hold back" (2006a: 392).[49]

Alanen proposes a different interpretation of the moral–absolute distinction. In her reading, when Descartes states that moving in the

---

[48] See also Davies (2001: 131).

[49] Despite the temptation to invoke here Descartes' distinction between moral and absolute (or metaphysical) certainty, such an analogy appears to have no basis. In discussing the moral impossibility of choosing otherwise in the 1645 letter to Mesland, Descartes refers to cases where all the reasons are on one side rather than to cases where there are more reasons in favor of a certain belief than against it, as moral certainty implies. Descartes' most explicit discussion of moral versus absolute (or metaphysical) certainty is found in the *Principles* (IV, 205–06). As the French version of this text runs, "moral certainty is certainty which is sufficient to regulate our behaviour, or which measures up to the certainty we have on matters relating to the conduct of life which we never normally doubt, though we know that it is possible, absolutely speaking, that they may be false" (AT IXB 323). See Curley (1993, esp. pp. 18–20).

contrary direction would be morally impossible for us, he means only that it would be non-rational or morally unjustified ("not conceivable for a moral, rational agent") to do so. And when he states that "absolutely speaking," we can always resist assenting to a clearly perceived truth or good, he is acknowledging we have a real possibility of doing so: "it is conceivable absolutely and is a real possibility" (2003: 245). Alanen's normative interpretation of the moral impossibility (or necessity) is in line with the radical voluntarism she assigns to Descartes. By the same token, she suggests a normative reading of the experience of intellectual necessity to which Descartes appeals while discussing the certainty of the "I exist" (Fourth Meditation, AT vii 58–59: CSM ii 41). Alanen argues that the experience of necessity appealed to in this passage "is not a matter of natural, psychological necessity, but of normative necessity: a recognition of a rational obligation to assent to what cannot be denied without contradiction and to the truth of what can be deduced from self-evident propositions" (2003: 104. See also Moyal 1987).

I think it would be wrong to read Descartes' insistence on our experience of intellectual necessity when confronting clear and distinct perceptions as a kind of *deontic* necessity, to use Ragland's phrase, namely, as something which is *morally obligatory*. In Descartes' deontological thinking, as I suggested in Chapter 2 above, rationality hinges on the (negatively formulated) duty to avoid assenting to matters we apprehend confusedly or obscurely. Unsurprisingly, therefore, Descartes does not explicitly prescribe consistent assent to our clear and distinct perceptions while attending to them. Such a prescription is not required because of the brute fact that psychologically or phenomenologically we cannot possibly do otherwise. So long as our attention is focused on clearly perceived reasons, we can be wholly assured that we shall always assent to them. It is only when discussing the practical domain, where clear and distinct apprehension might be unattainable, that Descartes defines the right use of the will in terms of resolution – prescribing us to resolutely judge and act in accordance with the *recommendations* of reason.[50]

In my understanding, moral necessity or impossibility, in this context, denotes a kind of practical or psychological impossibility, whereas absolute possibility signifies what is possible from an absolute, metaphysical point of view, irrespective of our inner experience.[51] In saying that

---

[50] See, for instance, letter to Princess Elizabeth, August 4, 1645 (AT iv 265: CSMK 257). I discuss this issue in Chapter 6 below.

[51] Descartes uses the phrase "absolutely speaking" (*absolute loquendo*) or equivalents on other occasions as well, usually to signify the consideration of things from God's absolute point of view, as

choosing otherwise when a very evident reason moves us in one direction is morally impossible for us, therefore, Descartes may mean that for us to do so is psychologically or practically impossible. From an absolute, purely metaphysical perspective, however, it is always possible for our will to act independently of our intellect, even in the face of clear and distinct ideas. The reason is that, metaphysically speaking, our intellect and will remain distinct from one another even when the intellect's perceptions are clear and distinct. Although we experience our intellect and our will as unified at the very moment of illumination – an experience that makes us morally (psychologically) incapable of acting against the intellect's overwhelming reasons – metaphysically or absolutely speaking we are capable of doing so.

In the next chapter I show that this understanding of the moral–absolute distinction has broad implications for the coherence of Descartes' assertion that divine and human freedom *may seem* essentially similar. More specifically, I suggest that this understanding may enable us to meet one of the most perplexing challenges posed by Descartes' conception of freedom: how to reconcile his assertion that it is through the will that we understand ourselves to be godlike with his doctrine of the divine creation of the eternal truths.

it were, independently of any actual limitation of our minds. See, e.g., letter to Clerselier, April 23, 1649 (AT v 355–56: CSMK 377); Second Replies (AT vII 145: CSM II 103).

CHAPTER 4

Free will and the likeness to God

I IN THE IMAGE AND LIKENESS OF GOD

Continuing the task I embarked on in the preceding chapter, I now turn to investigate the Cartesian doctrine stating that, from among all our mental capacities, it is by virtue of the will that we understand ourselves to be godlike. In the *Conversation with Burman*, Descartes argues that "the will is greater and more godlike than the intellect" (CB 31 = AT v 159: CSMK 342). As he explains to Queen Christina, although the goods of the soul include both the power of knowledge and the power of the will, "knowledge is often beyond our power; and so there remains only our will, which is absolutely within our disposal" (November 20, 1647, AT v 83: CSMK 325). He then concludes: "free will is in itself the noblest thing we can have, since it makes us in a way equal to God and seems to exempt us from being his subjects; and so its correct use is the greatest of all the goods we possess" (AT v 85: CSMK 326). This theme is also prominent in the *Passions of the Soul*, where Descartes asserts that our free will "renders us in a certain way like God by making us masters of ourselves" (art. 152). And in the Fourth Meditation, as noted, he states that "it is above all in virtue of the will that I understand myself to bear in some way the image and likeness of God" (AT vii 57: CSM ii 40).[1] Descartes then goes even further, claiming that the will of God "does not seem any greater" than ours "when considered as will in the essential and strict sense" (AT vii 57: CSM ii 40).

To account for the essential similarity between divine and human free will suggested in this statement, Descartes sets forth his position on the essence of human freedom, as discussed in the previous chapter. But this

---

[1] Note that as early as the end of 1639, Descartes had written to Mersenne that the human desire to possess all the perfections we believe to be in God "is due to the fact that God has given us a will which has no limits. It is principally because of this infinite will within us that we can say we are created in his image" (December 25, 1639, AT iii 628: CSMK 141–42).

strategy seems rather perplexing, in view of the well-known Cartesian theory of the creation of the eternal truths. The latter entails an essential *dis*similarity between God's will and our own: whereas human intellect and will are metaphysically distinct from one another, God's intellect and will are one and the same, neither one prior to the other. Descartes explicitly remarks, moreover, that "no essence can belong univocally to both God and his creatures" (Sixth Replies, AT VII 433: CSM II 292). "As for the freedom of the will," he says, "the way in which it exists in God is quite different from the way in which it exists in us" (AT VII 431: CSM II 291). If neither the positive two-way power of the human will nor its spontaneous self-determination can be claimed to bear an essential similitude to God's freedom, why did Descartes intend his definition of human freedom to explain the sense in which our will can seem essentially similar to the divine?

My concern in this chapter is to offer a coherent account of Descartes' outlook on the relationship between divine and human free will, which will dispel the tension between the two doctrines. Relying on the account developed in the previous chapter, I seek to explain the privileged stance allocated in the Cartesian scheme to the human will as the most significant mark of our rational essence and our similitude to God. By dint of the incomprehensibility of God, I will argue, Descartes is able to ascribe normative status to our *experience* of freedom as an independent source of moral agency and responsibility. Despite the essential difference between human and divine free will, I conclude, when our will functions in full keeping with its nature as free and spontaneous to the highest degree, we experience it as *unified* with our intellect, akin to the way we understand the unity of God's intellect and will.

2 THE *DISSIMILARITY* THESIS

In the Sixth Replies, Descartes begins his discussion of the essential *dis*-similarity between divine and human freedom by remarking on the relation between intellect and will in God:

It is self-contradictory to suppose that the will of God was not indifferent from eternity with respect to everything which has happened or will ever happen; for it is impossible to imagine that anything is thought of in the divine intellect as good or true, or worthy of belief or action or omission, prior to the decision of the divine will to make it so. I am not speaking here of temporal priority: I mean that there is not even any priority of order, or nature, or of "rationally determined reason" as they call it, such that God's idea of the good impelled him to choose one thing rather than another. (AT VII 431–32: CSM II 291)

Descartes makes two fundamental and closely related statements here regarding divine freedom. The first is that indifference is essential to the will of God: "it is self-contradictory to suppose that the will of God was not indifferent from eternity with respect to everything which has happened or will ever happen." The second statement, which sheds light on the first, is that God's absolute indifference consists in the lack of any priority between divine intellect and will. To suppose that God was not indifferent from eternity is self-contradictory, for the very reason that it is impossible to imagine that the divine intellect thinks of anything as good or true prior to the decision of the divine will to make it so. Descartes emphasizes that he is not speaking of temporal priority but of "any priority of order, or nature, or of 'rationally determined reason.'" The reason for things being true or good is the very fact that God has willed them to be so. Otherwise, Descartes continues, "God would not have been completely indifferent with respect to the creation of what he did in fact create. If some reason for something's being good had existed prior to his preordination, this would have determined God to prefer those things which it was best to do" (AT VII 435: CSM II 294).

Descartes is echoing here his doctrine of divine creation of the eternal truths and its underlying conception of the simplicity and inseparability of God's nature, which he first announced in his 1630 correspondence with Mersenne: "The mathematical truths which you call eternal have been laid down by God and depend on him entirely no less than the rest of his creatures" (April 15, 1630, AT I 145: CSMK 23). Descartes asks his correspondent to "proclaim everywhere that it is God who has laid down these laws in nature just as a king lays down laws in his kingdom" (ibid.). Underlying this doctrine is the view that "in God willing and knowing are a single thing in such a way that by the very fact of willing something he knows it and it is only for this reason that such a thing is true" (May 6, 1630, AT I 149: CSMK 24). There is no real distinction between God's knowing, willing, and creating the eternal truths, precisely because "in God, willing, understanding and creating are all the same thing without one being prior to the other even conceptually" (May 27, 1630, AT I 153: CSMK 25–26).[2] The lack of real or conceptual priority between

---

[2] In the *Principles* (I, 60–62), Descartes presents three sorts of distinctions: A *real* distinction exists only between substances, namely, between mutually separable things (capable of existing independently). A *modal* distinction exists between two things that are separable but not mutually separable (as one can exist apart from the other but not vice-versa). Descartes writes that such a distinction exists between a mode and the substance of which it is a mode, or between two modes of the same substance (since neither can exist apart from the substance of which they are modes). Finally, a *conceptual* distinction exists between two things that can be thought apart but are mutually inseparable in reality, such as that between a substance and its attributes (i.e.,

God's intellect and will means that God was not necessitated to will and accomplish whatever he in fact did. This entails not only God's complete freedom of indifference but also God's power to have done otherwise.[3] Descartes repeatedly asserts that God was free not to create the eternal truths, and just as free not to create anything else. As he famously writes to Mersenne, God "was free to make it not true that all the radii of the circle are equal – just as free as he was not to create the world" (May 27, 1630, AT I 152: CSMK 25). Likewise, in his letter to Mesland of May 2, 1644, Descartes writes that "God cannot have been determined to make it true that contradictories cannot be true together, and therefore that he could have done the opposite."[4] He adds that "even if God has willed that some truths should be necessary, this does not mean that he willed them necessarily; for it is one thing to will that they be necessary, and quite another to will this necessarily, or to be necessitated to will it" (AT IV 118: CSMK 235). As some scholars have observed, this implies that the

essential properties, without which the substance is unintelligible) or between two attributes of a single substance. Accordingly, Descartes indicates that we can recognize such a distinction "by our inability to form a clear and distinct idea of the substance if we exclude from it the attribute in question, or, alternatively, by our inability to perceive clearly the idea of one of the two attributes if we separate it from the other" (I, 62). Granted this, I think Dan Kaufman is entirely correct when he claims that by ruling out any conceptual *priority* between God's intellect and will, Descartes does not commit himself to the stronger assertion that there are no conceptual *distinctions* in God (2003b: 572; 2005: 4). To support this reading, we may also invoke Descartes' *Conversation with Burman*, where he states that "although we may conceive that the decrees could have been separated from God, this is merely a token procedure of our own reasoning: the distinction thus introduced between God himself and his decrees is a mental not a real one" (CB 50 = AT V 166: CSMK 348).

[3] "If some reason for something's being good had existed prior to his preordination, this would have determined God to prefer those things which it was best to do" (AT VII 435: CSM II 294). Yet, as Kaufman accurately points out (2003a: 397, 400ff.), in claiming that indifference is essential to God's freedom Descartes uses "indifference" in his own sense, to signify a motivational state of the will free from any internal compulsion or necessitation. Descartes, as noted, characterizes God's indifference in terms of a lack of any prior reason for something being true or good, a reason thought of by God's intellect that could have restricted God in willing and creating something (Sixth Replies, AT VII 431–32: CSM II 291; AT VII 435: CSM II 294).

[4] See also letter to Arnauld, July 29, 1648 (AT V 224: CSMK 358–59); letter to More, February 5, 1649 (AT V 272: CSMK 363). Frankfurt reads this doctrine to imply that "the eternal truths are inherently as contingent as any other proposition" (1977: 42). I will not dwell here on the intriguing problems raised by Descartes' doctrine of the eternal truths in connection with the modal status of the necessary and the possible. Generally, however, I tend to side with Alanen's contention that "it would be a mistake to assume some notion of modality in terms of which Descartes's concept of divine power could be explicated" (2008: 364). Since Descartes denies any modal order prior to God's act of knowing, willing, and creating something, as Alanen points out, to understand God's power through "our" modal concepts would be an illegitimate attempt, in Descartes' own view (p. 364). Moreover, discussing the issue in a letter to Mersenne, Descartes invokes the incomprehensibility of God's power, a topic I address below (April 15, 1639, AT I 145–46: CSMK 23).

eternal truths are necessary precisely because God has freely and absolutely indifferently willed them to be so: God has willed some propositions to be not only true but also necessarily true.[5]

In the Third Meditation, Descartes further maintains that God's nature
is simple and indivisible. All the divine attributes are mutually inseparable: "the unity, the simplicity, or the inseparability of all the attributes of
God is one of the most important of the perfections which I understand
him to have."[6] The simplicity and indivisibility of God's nature entails the
simplicity and indivisibility of the divine act. As Descartes writes in the
Principles, it is by one and the same perfectly simple act that God simultaneously understands, wills, and creates: "Even [God's] understanding
and willing does not happen, as in our case, by means of operations that
are in a certain sense distinct one from another; we must rather suppose
that there is always a single identical and perfectly simple act by means of
which he simultaneously understands, wills and accomplishes everything"
(1, 23).[7]

Consider now Descartes' discussion of the essential dissimilar-
ity between God's freedom of indifference and our own in the Sixth
Replies. While our freedom of indifference consists in ignorance and is
therefore not essential to our freedom, God's freedom of indifference "is
the supreme indication of his omnipotence" (AT VII 432: CSM II 292).
Descartes continues:

[Man] is never indifferent except when he does not know which of the two alternatives is the better or truer, or at least when he does not see this clearly enough
to rule out any possibility of doubt. Hence the indifference which belongs to
human freedom is very different from that which belongs to divine freedom.
The fact that the essences of things are said to be indivisible is not relevant here.
For, firstly, no essence can belong univocally to both God and his creatures; and,
secondly, indifference does not belong to the essence of human freedom, since
not only are we free when ignorance of what is right makes us indifferent, but we

[5] Della Rocca (2005: 23); Kaufman (2005: 16ff.). In the Sixth Replies, Descartes explicitly states
that God did not will "that the three angles of a triangle should be equal to two right angles
because he recognized that it could not be otherwise," but on the contrary: "it is because he
willed that the three angles of a triangle should necessarily equal two right angles that this is true
and cannot be otherwise; and so on in other cases" (AT VII 432: CSM II 291). Further evidence
appears in the Fifth Replies: "I do not think that the essences of things, and the mathematical
truths which we can know concerning them, are independent of God. Nevertheless I do think
that they are immutable and eternal, since the will and decree of God willed and decreed that
they should be so" (AT VII 380: CSM II 261).
[6] AT VII 50: CSM II 34. See also Second Replies (AT VII 137: CSM II 98).
[7] Descartes reiterates this point in his 1644 letter to Mesland, claiming that "the idea which we
have of God teaches us that there is in him only a single activity, entirely simple and entirely
pure" (AT IV 119: CSMK 235).

are also free – indeed at our freest – when a clear perception impels us to pursue some object. (AT VII 433: CSM II 292)[8]

How, then, can we make sense of Descartes' insistent assertion that we bear the likeness and image of God by virtue of our will? The doctrine of divine simplicity and its underlying theory of the creation of the eternal truths appear to distance us even further from accomplishing this task. The indivisibility of intellect and will in God makes God's absolute freedom of indifference essentially different from our own. While divine indifference stems from the lack of any prior reason that could have possibly restricted God's act of knowing, willing, and creating something, human indifference rests on a certain degree of ignorance – on our failure to grasp the reasons that make something true or good.

It has been suggested that the point of similarity between human and divine free will lies in the lack of any external constraint.[9] But the human will's ability to determine itself without being forced or affected by external coercion, which is precisely what constitutes human spontaneity, is inseparably linked to the will's irresistible inclination toward the reasons put forward by the intellect. By contrast, God's freedom from external constraint lies in the fact that "there can be nothing whatsoever which does not depend on him" (AT VII 435: CSM II 293), and is thus inseparably connected to his absolute indifference. As Ragland aptly observes, the second clause of Descartes' definition of freedom identifies human freedom not simply with being undetermined by external forces but with being carried toward what the intellect put forward in an undetermined way (2006a: 384).[10] Spontaneity, therefore, which constitutes the essence of our freedom, cannot be the

[8] Similarly, Descartes writes to Mersenne that "indifference in our case is rather a defect than a perfection of freedom" (AT III 360: CSMK 179).

[9] While acknowledging the complexity of offering a satisfactory rejoinder to this question, Charles Larmore thinks that the best solution would be to say that the common feature is only the absence of external constraint, which is precisely how Descartes characterizes human free will (1984: 68). Stephen Menn suggests a similar line of thought, claiming that the freedom that reflects the *imago dei* is "specifically freedom from irrational constraint," which is the freedom *not* to assent to irrational impulses. "Because I am, by my essence, potential *nous*, nothing compels me to deviate from the divine standard" (1998: 321).

[10] Ragland, however, appears to identify "self-determination" with "freedom from outside constraint." According to him, self-determination is the first of the two distinctive elements that constitute human spontaneity – being undetermined by external forces and doing what we want to do (2006a: 384). My understanding is slightly different. Self-determination, as I read Descartes, is the positive element of the will's spontaneity (that of being motivated or determined to act from within the human mind), while freedom from external coercion is its negative, complementary element (that of not being induced or forced by any factor other than the human mind). Self-determination (what Kenny depicts as "doing something because we want to do it," 1972: 17) and freedom from external constraint are thus two sides of the same coin, both constituting human spontaneity.

point of similarity to God's will, since human will is spontaneous insofar as nothing except prior reasons invoked by the intellect determines it to act. Finally, and for exactly the same reasons, God's two-way power is also essentially different from our own. Both require indifference, but of different kinds. In requiring indifference, God's two-way power stems from the inseparability of divine intellect and will and is therefore essential to God's freedom. The human ability to choose otherwise, by contrast, involves a certain degree of ignorance, given that when we perceive something clearly and distinctly, we cannot resist assenting to it as true or good.[11]

Some scholars have relied on these considerations to hold that Descartes' theory of the creation of the eternal truths rules out any analogy between divine and human free will. Tad Schmaltz, for example, has rightly argued that "the fact that God is the cause of the eternal truths seems connected to a significant *dis*analogy between our will, which is distinct from our intellect, and God's will, which is identical to His intellect" (2000: 94).[12] And yet, the doctrine that it is the will that makes us godlike is of major importance in Descartes' later thinking and thus hard to abandon.

To resolve this dilemma, we need to pay attention to the normative standing that Descartes ascribes to the manner in which we experience our freedom of will. Descartes does not merely tend to "focus" on the epistemic viewpoint when discussing the infinite freedom of our will.[13] Rather, my claim is that Descartes' epistemic focus is inherent in his view that self-evident awareness of our freedom is the source of our moral agency, entitling us to moral praise or blame.

3 THE HUMAN EXPERIENCE OF FREEDOM AND THE INCOMPREHENSIBILITY OF GOD

Discussing the infinite scope of our will in the Fourth Meditation, Descartes does not endorse the view that our will extends to every possible object, including all the objects of the divine will. Rather, he argues that he cannot think of a faculty of choice greater than the one he experiences within himself: "It is only the will, or freedom of choice, which I

[11] For different interpretations, see Alanen (2003: 227, 256) and Ragland (2006a: 384ff.). Both, though on different grounds, think that Descartes regards the two-way power of the will as essential to our freedom and, as such, as marking the similitude to God's freedom.

[12] Following J.-L. Marion (1991: 23), Schmaltz's general thesis is that "Descartes' view on the eternal truths leads to 'the disappearance of analogy,' and especially to the disappearance of the scholastic view that there is an analogical resemblance between God's mind and our own" (2000: 86; see also pp. 88–96).

[13] See Chapter 3, section 1, above.

experience within me to be so great that the idea of any greater faculty is beyond my grasp; so much so that it is above all in virtue of the will that I understand myself to bear in some way the image and likeness of God" (AT VII 57: CSM II 40).[14] Descartes' epistemic perspective functions here at three levels. He claims that his *inability to grasp* a faculty of will greater than the one he *experiences within himself* is what makes him *understand himself* as being created in the image of God. Since among all the things we can conceive of, however confusedly, there is nothing to which our will cannot apply itself (namely, affirm or deny, pursue or avoid), we experience our will as infinite in scope and, in this respect, as created in God's image. But Descartes goes on to indicate that we understand ourselves to be godlike not only through experiencing our will's infinite scope but also through the manner in which we experience its essence: the will of God *does not seem* any greater than our own when considered in the essential and strict sense (AT VII 57: CSM II 40). Here, too, Descartes does not endorse the view that the will of God, when considered in the essential and strict sense, is in fact not greater than his own. He explicitly affirms that God's will is incomparably greater than his, not only in scope ("in virtue of its object, in that it ranges over a greater number of items)" but also in kind ("in virtue of the knowledge and power that accompany it") (AT VII 57: CSM II 40). Descartes might thus be willing to argue that although the will of God is in fact incomparably greater than his own, he *experiences* his free will as essentially similar to the will of God. This understanding of the similarity doctrine requires us to reformulate our initial question. Instead of asking what the essential point of similarity between divine and human freedom is, we should ask what the point of similarity between God's freedom (as we understand it) and the way we *experience* our freedom of choice is.

Descartes, as noted, repeatedly states that we are immediately conscious of our freedom, and that our freedom of will is so evident "that it must be counted among the first and most common notions that are innate in us" (*Principles*, I, 39).[15] As he ironically replies to Gassendi: "You

---

[14] To take another example: "Besides, I cannot complain that the will or freedom of choice which I received from God is not sufficiently extensive or perfect, *since I know by experience that it is not restricted in any way.* Indeed, I think it is very noteworthy that there is nothing else in me which is so perfect and so great *that the possibility of a further increase in its perfection or greatness is beyond my understanding*" (AT VII 56–57: CSM II 39; my emphases).

[15] Descartes states that "we have such close awareness of the freedom and indifference which is in us, that there is nothing we can grasp more evidently or more perfectly" (*Principles*, I, 41). Similarly, he writes to Mersenne: "you are right to say that we are as sure of our free will as of any other primary notion; for this is certainly one of them" (December 1640, AT III 259: CSMK 161).

may be unfree, if you wish; but I am certainly very pleased with my freedom since I *experience it within myself*" (AT VII 377: CSM II 259; my emphasis). In the *Conversation with Burman*, Descartes goes so far as to claim that we experience our will as perfect and absolute and that, in this respect, "the will is greater and more godlike than the intellect."[16] In the Third Replies, Descartes significantly indicates that when discussing our freedom of will, he makes no assumptions beyond our evident experience of freedom:

> On the question of our freedom, I made no assumptions beyond what we all experience within ourselves. Our freedom is very evident by the natural light ...
> There may indeed be many people who, when they consider the fact that God pre-ordains all things, cannot grasp how this is consistent with our freedom. But if we simply consider ourselves, we will all realize in the light of our own experience that voluntariness and freedom are one and the same thing. (Third Replies, AT VII 191: CSM II 134)

In this passage, Descartes clearly does not mean that he treats our inner experience of freedom as merely a psychological feeling. As revealed by the natural light of reason, our inner sense of freedom is indicative of our absolute freedom, which Descartes identifies with absolute independence: the will's spontaneous self-determination unbounded by any external constraint.[17] Yet Descartes is aware of the absolute dependence of all things on God. He regards both the absolute freedom of human will and divine preordination as self-evident,[18] as noted in Chapter 2 above, and holds that their reconciliation is beyond our grasp.[19] Moreover, Descartes holds that we can experience ourselves as absolutely independent provided we do not dwell on our absolute dependence on God. As he explains to Princess Elizabeth, so long as we think of the infinite power of God, we just cannot help believing that everything depends on him, *including our will*:

As for free will, I agree that if we think only of ourselves we cannot help regarding ourselves as independent; but when we think of the infinite power of God,

---

[16] "Let everyone just go down deep into himself and find out whether or not he has a perfect and absolute will, and whether he can conceive of anything which surpasses him in freedom of the will. I am sure everyone will find that it is as I say. It is in this, then, that the will is greater and more godlike than the intellect" (CB 31 = AT V 159: CSMK 342). See also CB 32 = AT V 159: CSMK 342.

[17] "As for free will, I agree that if we think only of ourselves we cannot help regarding ourselves as independent" (letter to Princess Elizabeth, November 3, 1645, AT IV 332: CSMK 277).

[18] *Principles*, I, 39, 40; letter to Princess Elizabeth, November 3, 1645 (AT IV 332: CSMK 277).

[19] "We can easily get ourselves into great difficulties if we attempt to reconcile this divine preordination with the freedom of our will, or attempt to grasp both these things at once" (*Principles*, I, 40; see also *Principles*, I, 41).

we cannot help believing that all things depend on him, and hence that our free will is not exempt from this dependence. For it involves a contradiction to say that God has created human beings of such a nature that the actions of their will do not depend on his. (November 3, 1645, AT IV 332: CSMK 277)

Yet Descartes insists that the independence we feel in ourselves "is not incompatible" with our ultimate dependence on God: "The independence which we experience and feel in ourselves, and which suffices to make our actions praiseworthy or blameworthy, is not incompatible with a dependence of quite another kind, whereby all things are subject to God" (AT IV 332–33: CSMK 277). What is striking about this statement is that our inner awareness of freedom, the mere fact that "we cannot help regarding ourselves as independent," is said to be not only *necessary* for our moral responsibility but also *sufficient* for it. This self-knowledge, namely, our understanding of ourselves as possessing free will, is thus intimately connected to our awareness of our rational duty to use this freedom well. Otherwise, our inner awareness of freedom would not have been sufficient to render us blameworthy for misusing our freedom of choice. But to feel ourselves *committed* to the duty to use free will correctly, we must also understand the value of our free will and the manner in which it determines our moral evaluation. This theme becomes explicit in the *Passions of the Soul* and, in particular, in the virtue of generosity, which Descartes reckons as the highest of all virtues and "the general remedy for every disorder of the passions" (art. 161). True generosity, he writes, has two components: "The first consists in [one's] knowing that nothing truly belongs to him but this freedom to dispose his volitions, and that he ought to be praised or blamed for no other reason than his using this freedom well or badly. The second consists in his feeling within himself a firm and constant resolution to use it well" (*Passions*, art. 153). As we shall see in Chapter 6 below, our experience of freedom, when accompanied by this self-understanding, produces in us a *feeling* of a firm resolve to use free will well. This approach makes us, human beings, an independent source of moral responsibility. By virtue of our self-evident experience of freedom, revealed to us by the natural light of reason, we establish our own standing as moral agents despite our ultimate dependence on God.

When Descartes asserts that we are immediately aware of the absolute independence of our will and that this awareness is sufficient to make our actions praiseworthy or blameworthy, he is referring not only to situations where we attain the highest degree of freedom but also to the more frequent situations where our will is indifferent and thus enjoys the two-way power to do or not do something.[20] As noted, awareness of the positive two-way power of our will in the face of non-distinct perceptions is both necessary and sufficient to render us morally accountable for our erroneous judgments or, alternatively, to make us praiseworthy for avoiding them. And since Descartes maintains that adopting the habit of avoiding error is "man's greatest and most important perfection" (AT VII 62: CSM II 43), the right exercise of this power in avoiding error may appear as the most prominent source of our "sense of godlikeness." Moreover, in claiming that we experience ourselves to bear the likeness of God in virtue of the will, Descartes appears to suggest that we have this experience on account of our very possession of this infinite power and not only on account of the right exercise we make of it. This means that we feel ourselves godlike whenever we exercise this power, even while incurring error. Recall that only as a result of the fact that we err freely while conscious of our freedom do we bear responsibility for our errors.[21] And yet our experience of godlikeness is most prominent not when we consciously enjoy the two-way power of our will, as a consequence of ignorance, but rather in the less frequent situation where we lack this power: whenever our will actualizes its essential spontaneity and freedom to the highest possible extent. *Prima facie*, this suggestion might seem odd: whereas God's will, as we understand it, is absolutely and essentially indifferent, our experience of our highest degree of freedom is one of internal necessity. So how can our inner experience of freedom make us "understand [ourselves] to bear in some way the image and likeness of God"?

A closer look at Descartes' conception of divine freedom reveals an interesting affinity between our experience of the highest degree of freedom and our understanding of God's freedom. In the *Conversation with*

---

[20] This is his formulation in the *Principles*: "That there is freedom in our will, and that we have power in many cases to give or withhold our assent at will, is so evident that it must be counted among the first and most common notions that are innate in us. This was obvious earlier on when, in our attempt to doubt everything, we went so far as to make the supposition of some supremely powerful author of our being who was attempting to deceive us in every possible way. For in spite of that supposition, the freedom which we experienced within us was nonetheless so great as to enable us to abstain from believing whatever was not quite certain or fully examined" (*Principles*, I, 39). In a later article, Descartes writes that "we have such close awareness of the freedom and indifference which is in us, that there is nothing we can grasp more evidently or more perfectly" (*Principles*, I, 41).

[21] Descartes holds, accordingly, that his ability to make erroneous judgment "means that there is in a sense more perfection in [him] than would be the case if [he] lacked this ability" (Fourth Meditation, AT VII 60: CSM II 42).

Burman, Descartes clarifies that God's indifference is not opposed to necessity. Although God's actions were completely indifferent, they were also completely necessary, since God *necessarily willed* what is best:

For although God is completely indifferent with respect to all things, he necessarily made the decrees he did, since he necessarily willed what was best, even though it was of his own will that he did what was best. We should not make a separation here between the necessity and the indifference that apply to God's decrees; although his actions were completely indifferent, they were also completely necessary. Then again, although we may conceive that the decrees could have been separated from God, this is merely a token procedure of our own reasoning: the distinction thus introduced between God himself and his decrees is a mental, not a real one. (CB 50 = AT v 166: CSMK 348)

At first glance, this passage might seem incompatible with Descartes' insistence that God was free to have done otherwise than he did. In particular, it appears to run contrary to his statement in the 1644 letter to Mesland that even if God has willed some truths to be necessary, this does not mean that he willed them necessarily (AT iv 118–19: CSMK 235). In the passage just quoted, what is claimed to be necessary are not the *products* of God's understanding, willing, and creating, but rather God's very act of willing and making his decrees. This initial impression, however, could benefit from more careful scrutiny. In stating that God "necessarily made the decrees he did, since he necessarily willed what was best," Descartes does not mean that God could *not* have made his creations other than they are, or that God was necessitated to will and create what is best for reasons that might have preceded and determined his knowing and willing. Rather, Descartes means that the claim that God necessarily willed the decrees that he enacted does not conflict with the claim that God was completely free and indifferent in enacting them. Given that God's intellect and will are inseparable, the necessity and the indifference that apply to his action cannot be split. Barring any real distinction between God's understanding, willing, and acting, God's action must be entirely necessary and at the same time completely indifferent and free. Any attempt to differentiate between the necessity and the indifference of God's action, as well as between God's intellect and will or between God and his decrees, is but an illegitimate projection (a "token procedure") of our own reasoning, a mental (conceptual) distinction without any foundation in reality.

In the *Conversation with Burman*, significantly, Descartes invokes in this context the incomprehensibility of God's nature and working. He thus concludes: "So it is clear enough how God accomplishes all things in a single act. But these matters are not to be grasped by our powers of reasoning, and we must never allow ourselves the indulgence of trying to subject the nature and operations of God to our reasoning" (CB 50 = AT v 166: CSMK 348). Descartes refers to this point at the very beginning of this section (CB 50), when he claims that we cannot *conceive* "how it happens" that God's action is always single, identical, and perfectly simple, but can only *understand* it.[22] Likewise, he writes to Mersenne that the greatness of God "is something which we cannot grasp even though we know it."[23]

Descartes' distinction between conceiving (or grasping) the nature of God and merely understanding (or knowing) it is by no means obvious. In his letter to Mersenne of May 27, 1630, he explains it in terms of the distinction between merely touching a tangible object and wrapping our arms around it:

I do not conceive [the eternal truths] as emanating from God like rays from the sun; but I know that God is the author of everything and that these truths are something and consequently that he is their author. I say that I know this, not that I conceive it or grasp it; because it is possible to know that God is infinite and all powerful although our soul, being finite, cannot grasp or conceive him. In the same way we can touch a mountain with our hands but we cannot put our arms around it as we could put them around a tree or something else not too large for them. To grasp something is to embrace it in one's thought; to know something, it is sufficient to touch it with one's thought. (AT I 152: CSMK 25)

Our finite mind cannot *grasp* or *conceive* the infinity of God precisely because we cannot *embrace* or *encompass* it in our thought. To *comprehend* God, apparently, is to attain an adequate idea of God's nature, namely, to attend to all his attributes and hold them at once in one thought.[24] As Descartes writes to Clerselier, "Since the word 'grasp' implies some limitation, a finite mind cannot grasp God, who is infinite" (AT VII 210: CSM II 273). But we can still understand the nature of God, meaning we can attain a clear and distinct idea of him. Descartes famously states that the idea we have of God is "the truest and most clear and distinct" of all our

---

[22] CB 50 = AT v 165: CSMK 347. The passage which is at issue in CB 50 is art. 23 of the *Principles*, which states that "there is always a single identical and perfectly simple act by means of which [God] simultaneously understands, wills, and accomplishes everything."

[23] April 15, 1630 (AT I 145: CSMK 23). Descartes repeats this point in the Sixth Replies: "Again, there is no need to ask how God could have brought it about from eternity that it was not true that twice four make eight, and so on; for I admit this is unintelligible to us. Yet on the other hand I do understand, quite correctly, that there cannot be any class of entity that does not depend on God" (AT VII 436: CSM II 294).

[24] AT VII 220: CSM II 155. For Descartes' distinction between clear and distinct ideas and adequate ideas, see Chapter I, section 5, above.

ideas,[25] and that without knowledge of God "nothing can ever be perfectly known."[26] To attain a clear and distinct idea of God, as Descartes explains to Gassendi, is not to represent only part of it but to represent the infinite in its entirety, though in a manner "appropriate to a human idea" (AT VII 368: CSM II 253). Descartes further indicates that "the impossibility of being grasped is contained in the formal definition of the infinite" (AT VII 368: CSM II 253). This implies that our awareness of God's incomprehensibility is an essential part of our understanding of God's nature. Descartes thus writes to Clerselier: "It is sufficient for me to understand the fact that God is not grasped by me in order to understand God in his very truth and as he is, provided I judge also that there are in him all perfections which I clearly understand, and also many more which I cannot grasp."[27] As Beyssade points out, "incomprehensibility is not an obstacle or a limit to our intellectual understanding of God; on the contrary, it reveals God in his truth, in his real and positive transcendence" (1993: 89). Clearly and distinctly perceiving a certain number of God's perfections, then, is not enough for us to understand God, and we must also understand that God is "bounded by no limits" (AT VII 368: CSM II 254) and, as such, must contain an infinitely greater number of perfections of which we are completely ignorant. Such an understanding of God, however valuable, does not allow us to encompass God's *unity* or *simplicity* in our thought, nor even, as Beyssade emphasizes, to comprehend any of God's intelligible perfections, since they are all united in him (1993: 90). For this very reason, we fall short of understanding exactly "how it happens" that God's action is perfectly simple and, as such, both completely indifferent and necessary.

4 THE LIKENESS TO GOD REVISITED

In a recent paper, Della Rocca offers the intriguing suggestion that the doctrine of divine incomprehensibility allows Descartes to take crucial first steps toward a view that disentangles epistemology from God, a view that will become apparent in various ways in Hume, Kant, and in much of the later epistemology (Della Rocca 2005: 29ff. See also 2008: 249). In line with this perspective, though for different reasons, I hold that this doctrine allows Descartes to prepare the way for a God-detached

---

[25] Third Meditation (AT VII 46: CSM II 32); First Replies (AT VII 113–14: CSM II 81–82).
[26] Fifth Meditation (AT VII 69: CSM II 48). See also Third Meditation (AT VII 36: CSM II 25); letter to Mersenne, April 15, 1630 (AT I 144: CSMK 22).
[27] April 23, 1649, (AT V 356: CSMK 378). See also Third Meditation (AT VII 46: CSM II 32); Fifth Replies (AT VII 368: CSM II 253).

conception of human morality, rationality, autonomy, and responsibility, considering our self-evident experience of freedom an independent, both necessary and *sufficient*, source of our moral agency.

Descartes insists, as noted, that we cannot comprehend God's unity and simplicity and that we therefore fall short of understanding exactly "how it happens" that God's action, in being perfectly simple, is both completely necessary and free. But while we cannot "exactly understand" this riddle, we can feel or experience something analogous to it. The manner in which we understand God's freedom emerges as strikingly similar to our own experience of freedom when our will, in perfect accordance with its nature, operates at optimal levels of freedom and spontaneity.

In the closing section of the previous chapter, I offered my interpretation of Descartes' distinction between moral and absolute possibility, which he discusses in the letter to Mesland of 1645 (AT IV 173: CSMK 244–45). I suggested that moral impossibility, in this context, signifies whatever is psychologically impossible, whereas absolute possibility coincides with whatever is possible for us from a metaphysical point of view, regardless of our inner experience. Now, whenever the perceptions of our intellect are clear and distinct, we experience our will as *unified* with our intellect, in a way resembling our understanding of the unity between divine intellect and will. Metaphysically or absolutely speaking, then, our intellect and our will do remain distinct from one another and, in this respect, we can always resist a clearly perceived truth or goodness while attending to it. Morally speaking, however, meaning practically or phenomenologically, it is just impossible for us to resist it. What lies behind this psychological inability is our sense of unification between our intellect and our will, which is a sense of the simplicity and unity of our mind.

In the remainder of this section, I will examine more closely this inner experience of unification and simplicity, which makes us understand ourselves as being godlike and, in particular, will explain how it is that at the moment of illumination, we experience our will as unified with our intellect rather than as subject to it.

A good place to start is the debate between Hobbes and Descartes about the voluntariness of assent. According to Hobbes, free choice concerns only one's actions, not one's volitions, desires, and inclinations. Although we can *act* freely (according to our will), we cannot freely choose *what to will* since our will is subject to necessity.[28] It is against this background

---

[28] According to Hobbes, the question is not "whether a man be a *free agent*, that is to say, whether he can write or forbear, speak or be silent, according to his *will*; but, whether the *will* to write,

that we should read Hobbes' objection to Descartes' claim, in the Fourth Meditation, that the privative essence of error is to be found in the "incorrect use of free will" (AT VII 60: CSM II 41):

> Further, it is not only knowing something to be true that is independent of the will, but also believing it or giving assent to it. If something is proved by valid arguments, or is reported as credible, we believe it whether we want to or not. It is true that affirmation and denial, defending and refuting propositions, are acts of will; but it does not follow that our inner assent depends on the will. (AT VII 192: CSM II 134)

Hobbes concedes that affirmation and denial, defending and refuting propositions, are operations of the will; but he distinguishes between these willful acts of affirmation or denial of propositions and the mind's inner assent to these propositions, an assent that precedes their affirmation or denial and does not in itself depend on the will.

In his reply, Descartes emphatically rejects Hobbes' assertion that "if something is proved by valid arguments, or is reported as credible, we believe it whether we want to or not." He claims that "the qualification 'or not' is inappropriate in such contexts, since it implies that we both will and do not will the same thing" (AT VII 192: CSM II 135). Descartes' reply strongly suggests that he takes assent (or judgment) to be voluntary in two distinct senses. Apart from being in itself an act of the will (a mode of willing), assent is also voluntary in being dependent on the will (in being the result of a prior act of willing that is not in itself an operation of judgment). Descartes therefore assumes that when we voluntarily assent to a clearly and distinctly perceived truth or goodness, we not only voluntarily choose this truth or this goodness but we also will to assent to them.

This observation has important implications for our discussion. Were we not experiencing our will as unified with our intellect at the moment of illumination, we might at that moment want (will) to resist the prior commands of our intellect even though we are unable to do so. Clearly, however, this is not what we feel at that moment. Recall that in the second clause of his definition of freedom, Descartes writes that "when the intellect puts something forward for affirmation or denial ... our inclinations are such that we do not feel we are determined by any external force"

---

and the *will* to forbear, come upon him according to his *will*, or according to anything else in his own power" (1840: 240). Hobbes' causal necessitation thesis provides him with an unequivocal reply: "When first a man hath an *appetite* or *will* to something, to which immediately before he had no appetite nor will, the *cause* of his *will*, is not the *will* itself, but *something* else not in his own disposing" (p. 273).

(AT VII 57: CSM II 40). When the light of the intellect shines in its full intensity, we do not feel that anything at all determines our will from the outside – not only from outside the mind but also from within. Rather than experiencing our intellect as prior to our will and thus as compelling it to action, we feel that we do not will to choose anything except what the intellect clearly and distinctly understands to be worthy of our choice. Morally speaking, then, we *cannot* resist assenting to the clear perceptions of our intellect precisely because *we do not will* to resist them, and we *do not will* to resist them because we *cannot*. On account of this mechanism, we experience our intellect and our will as mutually inseparable, akin to the manner in which we understand the unity between intellect and will in God. Rather than experiencing our will as subject to (and thus as compelled by) the perceptions of our intellect, we experience our will at this valuable moment as self-propelled, wholly independent and free from any kind of restraint – either from within or outside the mind.

Through the experience of our mind as simple and united, our feeling of internal necessity is not only compatible with our experience of ultimate freedom but also manifests and intensifies it. This experience of godlike unification eliminates the tension between freedom and necessity and, as such, is constitutive of Descartes' compatibilism, which asserts that freedom and necessity can coexist.

In an important respect, the valuable experience of the unity and simplicity of our mind is not metaphysically groundless. Descartes insists that the human mind is indeed one and indivisible. Rejecting the Aristotelian distinction between different parts of the soul, he holds that the human mind, in being a substance, is undivided, "single and complete" (Sixth Replies, AT VII 86: CSM II 59). And yet, just as the term "substance" does not apply to God and to us univocally but only analogically (AT VII 86: CSM II 59), so does the unity or simplicity that the human mind shares with God. Divine unity or simplicity entails the unity or simplicity of God's action, but the unity of our mind allows for different faculties and functions. Willing, understanding, sensory perception, and so forth, are not parts of the mind but rather different faculties of the same unified thinking substance (AT VII 86: CSM II 59). In the *Passions of the Soul*, Descartes writes: "For there is within us but one soul, and this soul has within it no diversity of parts" (art. 47). The conflicts usually supposed to occur between rational and irrational parts or forces of the soul itself are conflicts between bodily movements and rational volitions originating in the soul, each pushing the pineal gland in contrary directions: "It is to the body alone that we should attribute everything that can be observed in us to oppose our reason. So there is no conflict here except in so far as the little gland in the middle of the brain can be pushed to one side by the soul and to the other side by the animal spirits" (art. 47). Descartes then concludes: "This makes the soul feel itself impelled, almost at one and the same time, to desire and not to desire one and the same thing; and that is why it has been thought that the soul has within it two conflicting powers" (art. 47).

These passages entail two significant implications for the current discussion. The first is that no conflict is possible between the different faculties of the mind so long as the mind's focus is directed to a clearly and distinctly perceived truth or goodness. Given that the body is the only source of irrational forces that might generate conflicts within the mind, no strife may be presumed between contrary volitions, not even between the faculty of knowledge and the faculty of will, so long as the mind's attention is focused on clear and distinct perceptions and all bodily effects are neutralized. The second implication is that the experience of our will as unified with our intellect is not without foundation in reality. The unity or simplicity of our mind indeed allows for a differentiation between its distinct faculties, such as the faculty of will and the faculty of knowledge. But when both faculties function in full keeping with their nature, we experience them as unified in a manner similar or analogical to the way we understand the absolute unity and simplicity of God. Even though none of the attributes pertaining to God applies univocally to us, the manner we experience our freedom allows us to "recognize some trace" of the individual attributes of God in ourselves (Second Replies, AT VII 137: CSM II 98).

CHAPTER 5

From intellectual to practical reason

In recent years, scholars have become increasingly interested in the writings on ethics and human psychology that occupied Descartes in the last years of his life. Contrary to the earlier, traditional view expressing doubts as to whether these writings could at all be regarded as providing a conception of ethics, the perception now generally accepted is that this is a narrow and inadequate view of Descartes' philosophical project.[1] Scholars engaged in the study of Descartes' ethical thinking, however, disagree about its tenets and its relationship with the rest of his philosophy. Relying on the interpretation suggested so far, my main concern in this and the next chapter is to offer a new understanding of the close kinship between Descartes' views on practical and speculative reason, thereby shedding new light on his assertion that intellectual error and moral wrong share the same privative essence – the misuse of free will.

The present chapter traces Descartes' initial steps toward developing his mature conception of practical reason, pointing to the non-consequentialist features of his views. I begin with a preliminary account of Descartes' general attitude toward the discussion of moral issues within his philosophy, then proceed to examine his view of judgments concerning matters of faith in writings from around 1641. Finally, I discuss Descartes' presentation of his early moral outlook in the Third Part of the *Discourse on the Method* – the *morale par provision*.

I DESCARTES' APPARENT AMBIVALENCE

Descartes' non-substantive conception of intellectual error, as noted in Chapter 2, may appear inapplicable to practical matters where absolute

---

[1] See, for example, Rodis-Lewis (1989: xxv); Morgan (1994: 1–6); Cottingham (1996: 194–95; 1998: 75; 2008a; 2008b, esp. chs. 12–15); Marshall (1998: 1–2); Alanen (2003, esp. chs. 6, 7); Brown (2006); Shapiro (2008: 445, 459ff.).

certainty is often unattainable. This category includes judgments on matters of faith and various practical decisions we make in the pursuit of good and evil as well as in the conduct of everyday life. In such "extra-theoretical" issues, strict application of the duty to restrict our will solely to what we perceive clearly and distinctly is either impossible, or, in other cases, far from recommended. Not only does life often demand that we decide and act although lacking a clear and distinct understanding of the object of our choices, but, even more acutely, withholding judgment or action in moral and religious matters is itself a form of sin.[2] Aware of these considerations, Descartes repeatedly emphasizes the distinction between the intellectual and the practical spheres.[3] In the Synopsis of the *Meditations*, he cautions his readers against a sweeping application of his account of intellectual error in the Fourth Meditation to the practical arena:

(But here it should be noted in passing that I do not deal at all with sin, i.e. the error which is committed in pursuing good and evil, but only with the error that occurs in distinguishing truth from falsehood. And there is no discussion of matters pertaining to faith or the conduct of life, but simply of speculative truths which are known solely by means of the natural light.) (AT VII 15: CSM II 11)

Note that this comment was not included in the original version of the Synopsis but was added to it following Arnauld's recommendation. Arnauld had expressed a concern that Descartes' ideas in the Fourth Meditation would be misunderstood, leading, at best, to unnecessary dispute and criticism and, at worst, to exploitation by heretics.[4] Arnauld

---

[2] "Now we have inner consciousness of our freedom, and we know that we can withhold our assent when we wish. In the pursuit of good and evil, however, when the will is indifferent with respect to each of the two, it is already at fault, since it ought to seek after the good alone without any indifference, in contrast to the situation in theoretical subjects. With regard to supernatural matters, the theologians teach that this is an area where we are corrupted through original sin: we need grace to enable us to recognize and pursue the good in this sphere" (CB 32=AT V 159: CSMK 342).

[3] Descartes emphasizes the distinction between the contemplation of the truth and the conduct of life in a variety of contexts, including those outside his discussion of error. For example, toward the end of the First Meditation he evokes this distinction in connection with his method of doubt: "In the meantime, I know that no danger or error will result from my plan, and that I cannot possibly go too far in my distrustful attitude. This is because that task now in hand does not involve action but merely the acquisition of knowledge" (AT VII 22: CSM II 15). Descartes also raises this distinction in the third part of the *Discourse*, while presenting his *morale par provision* (AT VI 24–25: CSM I 123). See also Second Replies (AT VII 149: CSM II 106); Fourth Replies (AT VII 247–48: CSM II 172); Fifth Replies (AT VII 350–51: CSM II 243).

[4] Fourth Objections (AT VII 215–17: CSM II 151–52).

advised Descartes "to make two things clear, either in the Meditation itself or in the Synopsis":

The first is that when the author is inquiring into the cause of error, he is dealing above all with the mistake we commit in distinguishing between the true and the false, and not those that occur in our pursuit of good and evil ...

The second point I should like our author to stress is that, where he asserts that we should assent only to what we clearly and distinctly know, he is dealing solely with matters concerned with the sciences and intellectual contemplation, and not with matters belonging to faith and the conduct of life... (AT vii 215–16: CSM ii 151–52)

Descartes accepted Arnauld's recommendation for the above considerations of "prudence",[5] but still asked Mersenne to put these qualifying words in parentheses "so that it can be seen that they have been added" (letter of March 18, 1641, AT iii 334–35: CSMK 175). Descartes' wish that his readers should understand that this comment was not included in the original text indicates his ambivalence toward its contents as well as his expressed desire that this ambivalence be noticed by his readers. Indeed, despite this caution, he does assert in the Fourth Meditation that the privation which lies in the misuse of free will "is all that the essential definition of falsity and wrong consists in" (AT vii 60–61: CSM ii 42).

This expressed ambivalence is typical of Descartes' general attitude toward treating moral issues as part of his philosophy. On the one hand, he is characteristically cautious in dealing with moral problems, expressing worries that his views might be misconceived and provoke malicious opposition. In a letter to Chanut dated November 20, 1647, he spells out his main objection to the discussion of ethical matters:

It is true that normally I refuse to write down my thoughts concerning morality. I have two reasons for this. One is that there is no other subject in which malicious people can so readily find pretexts for vilifying me; and the other is that I believe only sovereigns, or those authorized by them, have the right to concern themselves with regulating the morals of other people. (AT v 86–87: CSMK 326)

Similarly, when asked by Burman about the *morale par provision* that he sets out in the *Discourse*, Descartes is reported to have replied: "The author does not like writing on ethics, but he was compelled to include these

---

[5] Descartes confirms this explicitly in a letter to Mesland of May 2, 1644: "The only thing which prevented me from speaking of the freedom which we have to follow good or evil was the fact that I wanted to avoid as far as possible all theological controversies and stay within the limits of natural philosophy. But I agree with you that wherever there is an occasion for sinning, there is indifference" (AT iv 117: CSMK 234).

rules because of people like the Schoolmen."[6] On the other hand, evidence clearly indicates that Descartes' theoretical reasoning was invested with a deep ethical interest, such as, for example, his famous image of the "tree of philosophy" presented in the Preface to the French edition of the *Principles* (1647):

> Thus the whole of philosophy is like a tree. The roots are metaphysics, the trunk is physics, and the branches emerging from the trunk are all the other sciences, which may be reduced to three principal ones, namely medicine, mechanics and morals. By "morals" I understand the highest and most perfect moral system, which presupposes a complete knowledge of the other sciences and is the ultimate level of wisdom.
>
> Now just as it is not the roots or the trunk of a tree from which one gathers the fruit, but only the ends of the branches, so the principal benefit of philosophy depends on those parts of it which can only be learnt last of all. (AT ixb 14–15: CSM i 186)

This passage clarifies that Descartes intended his new science to culminate in the "highest and most perfect moral system," which he takes to be the most beneficial fruits of his philosophy and "the ultimate level of wisdom" (AT ixb 14: CSM i 186). And since these ethical fruits must spring from the trunk of physics, which in turn grows out of metaphysical roots, Descartes' preoccupation with metaphysics, epistemology, and physics emerges as interlaced with, and motivated by, his ethical concern.

From his earliest writings, Descartes expresses genuine interest in the conduct of life, presenting it as the main motive of his pure intellectual enterprise. Early in the *Rules for the Direction of the Mind*, he states that one should consider how to increase the natural light of one's reason "not with a view to solve this or that scholastic problem, but in order that his intellect should show his will what decisions it ought to make in each of life's contingencies" (Rule 1, AT x 361: CSM i 10). He makes a similar point in the *Discourse*: "And it was always my most earnest desire to learn to distinguish the true from the false in order to see clearly into my own actions and proceed with confidence in this life" (AT vi 10: CSM i 115).

The privileged place that Descartes accords to ethics in his philosophy and his genuine concern with the practical ramifications of his pure inquiry are also apparent in his definition of "philosophy," found in the Preface to the French edition of the *Principles* mentioned above: "the

---

[6] CB 80 = AT v 178: CSMK 352. See also letter to Chanut, November 1, 1646 (AT iv 536: CSMK 299).

word 'philosophy' means the study of wisdom, and by 'wisdom' is meant not only prudence in our everyday affairs but also a perfect knowledge of all things that mankind is capable of knowing, both for the conduct of life and for the preservation of health and the discovery of all manner of skills" (AT ıxв 2: CSM ı 179). Given Descartes' doctrine of the unity of science and of human wisdom, which he persistently maintained from the earliest stages of his philosophical career,[7] his refraining from drawing a sharp distinction between intellectual error and moral wrong comes as no surprise. Indeed, in the rest of this book I seek to make the case for the broader thesis that Descartes asserts a close affinity between intellectual error and the various kinds of errors we commit in our moral, religious, and everyday lives. Since absolute certainty might be unattainable in these practical domains, as noted in Chapter 2 above, Descartes "softens" the duty to make right use of free will by redrawing the boundaries of our responsibility and guilt. He does not, however, abandon his pragmatic and non-consequentialist conception of error as a misuse of free will. More specifically, I will show that to judge and act well in extra-theoretical issues, we are not obliged to apprehend clearly and distinctly the *objects* of our judgments, but rather to judge and act on the basis of the right *reasons*. In matters of faith, which are inherently confused and obscure, we are required to possess a clear understanding of the *formal reason* that induces our will to assent to them, for which we need to be supernaturally illuminated by divine grace. In moral issues that fall within the scope of our natural reason, we are instructed to act resolutely in accordance with our best judgment, an instruction that Descartes will later reckon as a moral imperative in his account of virtue. Cartesian morality is defined in terms of the reasons that lead us to make our choices as well as of our attitude toward them and toward ourselves, and not in terms of consequences. In the morality of the *Discourse*, where Descartes has not yet crystallized his metaphysical conception of free will, this reasoning takes the form of second-order moral guidelines or values, which we are prescribed to follow when making our first-order decisions under uncertainty. In his later morality, where he equates virtue with the good use of the will, human virtuousness and happiness both depend on the extent to which we fulfill our *obligation* to practice virtue, namely, to carry out firmly and resolutely whatever reason *recommends*, irrespective of the consequences of our choices.[8]

---

[7] See, for example, *Rules*, Rule ı (AT x 359–61: CSM ı 9–10).
[8] See, e.g., letter to Princess Elizabeth, August 4, 1645 (AT ıv 265: CSMK 257).

2 JUDGMENTS CONCERNING MATTERS OF FAITH

Descartes tends to avoid discussion of theological issues, commonly expressing his wish to leave these matters to the Church.[9] As he explains in the *Conversation with Burman*, "Theology must not be subjected to our human reasoning, which we use for Mathematics and for other truths, since it is something we cannot fully grasp" (CB 78 = AT v 176: CSMK 350). Descartes' reservations about discussing theological issues within his philosophy are motivated by reasons different from those he voices regarding morals. As this section will show, Descartes insists that matters of faith do not fall under the regime of our natural reason and, moreover, that whoever embraces the articles of faith for "incorrect reasons" (pertaining to one's natural reason), will incur a sin no less grave than those who refuse to embrace the articles of faith.

In the Second Replies, Descartes faces the charge that adherence to his principal rule of reason – to avoid assenting to matters we do not clearly and distinctly understand – might lead to the absurdity of a general and strict prohibition to believe in the principles of Christian faith. Since matters of faith are by their very nature not susceptible to clear and distinct perception, adherence to this precept will lead to the assertion that those who uphold the tenets of Christian faith are effectively sinners, while those who reject them are evading sin:

[I]f the will never goes astray or falls into sin so long as it is guided by the mind's clear and distinct knowledge, and if it exposes itself to danger by following a conception of the intellect which is wholly lacking in clarity and distinctness, then note what follows from this. A Turk, or any other unbeliever, not only does not sin in refusing to embrace the Christian religion, but what is more, he sins if he does embrace it, since he does not possess clear and distinct knowledge of its truth. (AT VII 126: CSM II 90)

Rejecting this charge, Descartes maintains that in matters of faith that are inherently confused and obscure, we must distinguish between the subject-matter or the thing itself to which we assent, and the *formal reason* inducing the will to assent to it. Since attaining a clear and distinct perception of the subject-matter is impossible in these issues, we are only

---

[9] See, e.g., *Conversation with Burman* (CB 32 = AT v 159: CSMK 342). In a letter to Mesland of May 2, 1644, Descartes similarly contends: "The only thing which prevented me from speaking of the freedom which we have to follow good or evil was the fact that I wanted to avoid as far as possible all theological controversies and stay within the limits of natural philosophy. But I agree with you that wherever there is an occasion for sinning, there is indifference" (AT IV 117: CSMK 234). See also Gibson (1987: 329–30); Menn (1998: 322–23).

required to possess a clear understanding of the *formal reason* inducing our will to assent:

For although it is said that our faith concerns matters which are obscure, the reasons for embracing the faith are not obscure but on the contrary are clearer than any natural light. We must distinguish between the subject-matter, or the thing itself which we assent to, and the formal reason which induces the will to give its assent: it is only in respect of the reason that transparent clarity is required. As for the subject-matter, no one has ever denied that it may be obscure – indeed obscurity itself. (AT VII 147: CSM II 105)[10]

Descartes writes, accordingly, that "those who make a judgment *when they are ignorant of the grounds* on which it is based are the ones who go astray" (AT VII 147: CSM II 105; my emphasis).

But what is this "formal reason" that when clearly understood is supposed to induce our will to embrace faith? Descartes explains that "the clarity or transparency which can induce our will to give its assent is of two kinds: the first comes from the natural light, while the second comes from divine grace" (AT VII 148: CSM II 105). While "natural knowledge" is guided by the natural light of reason, faith is a matter of revelation and thus supernaturally instructed by the divine light of grace.[11] Descartes then proceeds to explain the nature of this formal reason for embracing faith:

[T]his formal reason consists in a certain inner light which comes from God, and when we are supernaturally illumined by it we are confident that what is put forward for us to believe has been revealed by God himself. And it is quite impossible for him to lie; this is more certain than any natural light, and is often even more evident because of the light of grace. (AT VII 148: CSM II 105)

The formal reason that should underpin our faith, then, is our complete confidence that these principles have been revealed by God, a confidence arising from the supernatural illumination of divine grace. Several years later, in the *Conversation with Burman*, Descartes reaffirms that "with regard to supernatural matters, the theologians teach that this is an area where we are corrupted through original sin: we need grace to enable us to

---

[10] Descartes repeats this point several lines later: "Now although it is commonly said that faith concerns matters which are obscure, this refers solely to the thing or subject-matter to which our faith relates; it does not imply that the formal reason which leads us to assent to matters of faith is obscure" (AT VII 148: CSM II 105).

[11] In a letter to Mersenne, Descartes differentiates between "well doing" in a theological sense, where grace comes into play, and "well doing" in the sense of moral and natural philosophy, where no account is taken of grace. What is only probable according to our natural reason (for example, the premise that the world was created just as it should be), may be absolutely certain by faith (end of May 1637, AT I 366: CSMK 56).

recognize and pursue the good in this sphere" (CB 32 = AT v 159: CSMK 342). The mystery of the Trinity, for instance, is an article of faith that cannot be known by natural reason alone.[12] But if we are supernaturally illuminated by divine grace, we cannot but embrace those mysteries by dint of our absolute confidence that they have been revealed by God.[13]

The conviction arising from the supernatural light of divine grace is no less irresistible than that engendered by the natural light of reason, namely, the clear and distinct perceptions of the intellect.[14] Indeed, as the above quotation confirms, Descartes insists that whoever is granted the supernatural light of grace is blessed with an even higher degree of certainty than that granted by the natural light of reason.

For Descartes, then, to avoid sin or error in matters of faith, we must accept the articles of faith for the "right reasons," that is, through our absolute confidence, originating in divine grace, that these articles have been revealed to us by God. As he writes to Mersenne, "when truths depend on faith and cannot be proved by natural argument, it degrades them if one tries to support them by human reasoning and mere probabilities" (May 27, 1630, AT i 153: CSMK 26). Relying on this reasoning, Descartes holds that whoever accepts faith on grounds originating in natural reason, without being gifted by the light of grace, will not be saved:

One should note that what is known by natural reason – that [God] is all good, all powerful, all truthful, etc. – may serve to prepare infidels to receive the Faith, but cannot suffice to enable them to reach heaven. For that it is necessary to believe in Jesus Christ and other revealed matters, and that depends upon grace. (Letter to Mersenne, March 1642, AT iii 544: CSMK 211)

---

[12] Letter to Mersenne, October 28, 1640 (AT iii 215–16: CSMK 155). See also Descartes' letter to the same addressee of December 31, 1640 (AT iii 274: CSMK 166).
[13] AT vii 148: CSM ii 105. Note that Descartes does not dismiss the possibility that divine grace might allow us to know even the objects of faith, and not merely the formal reason at the root of our belief in them. In a letter to Hyperaspistes dated August 1641, he confirms this while addressing the excerpt just quoted from the Second Replies: "but there I was speaking not of human knowledge, but of faith. And I did not assert that by the light of grace we clearly know the very mysteries of faith – though I would not deny that this too may happen – but only that we are confident that they are to be believed" (AT iii 425–26: CSMK 191).
[14] The following paragraph from the Second Replies also implies this view: "Those who read my books will not be able to suppose that I did not recognize this supernatural light [*lumen supernaturale*], since I expressly stated in the Fourth Meditation, where I was looking into the cause of falsity, that it produces in our inmost thought a disposition to will, without lessening our freedom" (AT vii 148: CSM ii 106). The passage from the Fourth Meditation to which Descartes is referring here seems to be the following: "[T]he more I incline in one direction – either because I clearly understand that reasons of truth and goodness point that way, or because of a divinely produced disposition of my inmost thoughts – the freer is my choice. Neither divine grace nor natural knowledge ever diminishes freedom; on the contrary, they increase and strengthen it" (AT vii 58: CSM ii 40). See also Cottingham (2002: 356–57).

In the Second Replies, Descartes goes even further and argues that those who commit themselves to the principles of Christian faith for inappropriate reasons are to be considered *sinners* in no less measure than those who reject them:

Let us take the case of an infidel who is destitute of all supernatural grace and has no knowledge of the doctrines which we Christians believe to have been revealed by God. If, despite the fact that these doctrines are obscure to him, he is induced to embrace them by fallacious arguments, I make bold to assert that he will not on that account be a true believer, *but will instead be committing a sin by not using his reason correctly.* (AT VII 148: CSM II 106; my emphasis)

Descartes indicates that the sin committed by those who reject the principles of Christianity does not lie in the *content* of their beliefs but rather in their resistance to the impulses of divine grace within them, or in their being unworthy to be thus illuminated:

The sin that Turks and other infidels commit by refusing to embrace the Christian religion does not arise from their unwillingness to assent to obscure matters (for obscure they indeed are), but from their resistance to the impulses of divine grace within them, or from the fact that they make themselves unworthy of grace by their other sins. (AT VII 148: CSM II 105–06)

These passages clearly manifest Descartes' non-consequentialist attitude toward the nature of sin: the sin committed by infidels does not consist in the content of their beliefs but in the reasons that motivate them either to adhere to or to deny the articles of faith. Whoever embraces these articles for fallacious reasons is no less a sinner than one who rejects them. And even those who reject the tenets of faith are counted as sinners not because of their unwillingness to embrace obscure matters but because of their own responsibility for not being irresistibly inclined by divine grace to embrace them. This may occur either because they willfully turn their mind's eye away from the impulses of divine grace, or because they make themselves unworthy of grace by their other sins.[15]

---

[15] Descartes does not express a definite position on whether our being blessed with "efficacious" divine grace depends on our actions or prayers. As noted in previous chapters, he states that although free will and divine preordination are both self-evident, we can easily encounter great difficulties if we attempt to reconcile them, because the manner of their reconciliation is beyond human grasp (*Principles*, I, 39–40). And yet, in the *Conversation with Burman*, Descartes takes a stand in the theological controversies of his days about this issue, adhering to the Calvinist conception as represented by the Dutch theologian Franciscus Gomarus. He contends that, from the metaphysical point of view "it is quite unintelligible that God should be anything else but completely unalterable" (CB 50 = AT V 166: CSMK 348). Since there is no real distinction between God and his decrees, we cannot think of him as changing his decrees in response to the prayers of human beings (CB 50 = AT V 166: CSMK 348). Descartes acknowledges, however, that the

Descartes also brings his non-consequentialist reasoning into play regarding faith, when discussing the ethical-religious legitimacy of his method of doubt:

For if someone sets out to doubt about God with the aim of persisting in the doubt, then he sins gravely, since he wishes to remain in doubt on a matter of such importance. But if someone sets out to doubt as a means of acquiring a clearer knowledge of the truth, then he is doing something altogether pious and honourable, because nobody can will the end without willing also the means, and in Scripture itself men are often invited to seek this knowledge of God by natural reason. (Letter to Buitendijck, conjecturally dated 1643, AT iv 63: CSMK 229)

Besides implying the ethical-religious significance that Descartes assigns to the search for truth, this passage also indicates that the reasons for doubting God are constitutive in determining the value of doing so. Descartes expands on this point:

[T]ake the case of someone who imagines a deceiving god – even the true God, but not yet clearly enough known to himself or to the others for whom he frames his hypothesis. Let us suppose that he does not misuse this fiction for the evil purpose of persuading others to believe something false of the Godhead, but uses it only to enlighten the intellect, and bring greater knowledge of God's nature to himself and others. Such a person is in no way sinning in order that good may come. There is no malice at all in his action; he does something which is good in itself, and no one can rebuke him for it except slanderously. (AT iv 64: CSMK 230)

Here too, the contours of sin depend on the reasons motivating the agent's actions and beliefs. The rightness of one's reasons for doubting God (just in order to elicit a greater knowledge of God's perfection) renders the action *good in itself*, and definitely exonerates it from being sinful.

---

situation would appear differently from ethical and religious perspectives: "Concerning ethics and religion, on the other hand, the opinion has prevailed that God can be altered, because of the prayers of mankind; for no one would have prayed to God if he knew, or had convinced himself, that God was unalterable" (CB 50 = AT v 166: CSMK 348). To remove this difficulty, Descartes suggests the following scheme: God has foreordained not only human prayers and whether he would grant them, but also that acceding to prayers would be *inter alia* in virtue of them: "[W]e have to say that God is indeed quite unalterable, and that he has decreed from eternity either to grant me a particular request or not to grant it. Coupled with this decree, however, he has made a simultaneous decree that the granting of my request shall be in virtue of my prayers, and at a time when, in addition, I am leading an upright life" (CB 50 = AT v 166: CSMK 348). In his correspondence with Princess Elizabeth, however, Descartes' position seems to be closer to that of Jacobus Arminius and his followers, among them the Jesuits. Descartes claims that God foresaw and willed the manner in which we shall employ our free will, but did not thereby will that our will be constrained to the choice in question (January 1646, AT iv 353–54: CSMK 282). See also Gilson (1913: 394); Cottingham (1976: xxxvii–xxxix); Gibson (1987: 333–34).

In a letter to Mesland dated May 2, 1644, Descartes offers a view that is even more far-reaching. Barring the possibility of better knowledge, and for practical purposes only, a moral judgment will not count as erroneous even if its content is *false*, provided it is supported by a "good enough reason," such as an appeal to authority:

The moral error which occurs when we believe something false with good reason – for instance because someone of authority has told us – involves no privation provided it is affirmed only as a rule for practical action, in a case where there is no moral possibility of knowing better. Accordingly it is not strictly an error; it would be one if it were asserted as a truth of physics, because the testimony of an authority is not sufficient in such a case. (AT iv 115: CSMK 233)

In the pure theoretical arena, wherein justification is said to be infallible, an appeal to authority will not suffice to justify our judgments regarding the true or the good. The case is apparently different with respect to judgments we make only as a rule for practical action and when no better source for knowledge is within reach. Such a judgment, even if false, is not to be considered erroneous precisely because it involves no privation, namely, it does not constitute a misuse of free will.

Although matters of faith are to be excluded from the scientific inquiry commanded by our natural reason, they are subject to the same deontological approach whose key merit is the duty to make right use of the will.[16]

Descartes' earliest pronouncements on moral issues pertaining to the regime of our natural reason appear in the third part of the *Discourse*, where he presents his *morale par provision*. This text, which lacks the metaphysical backing of the doctrine of free will, does not yet exhibit the theory of virtue that would only appear in the 1645–49 correspondence and in the *Passions of the Soul* of 1649. Nevertheless, the *morale par provision* allows us to become acquainted with Descartes' earliest and most primal ethical motivations and outlook, which would accompany him until the end of his life. Preceding the analysis of Descartes' mature morality of virtue with an examination of the "provisional" morality of the *Discourse* may therefore prove significant.

---

[16] See also the discussion in Menn (1998: 322–36), about how Descartes' attitude toward faith and reason is related to Augustine's. Challenging the interpretation advanced by Étienne Gilson and Henri Gouhier on this issue, Menn argues that Descartes' doctrine of faith is indistinguishable from Augustine's. The two doctrines are naturally the same, he argues, "since Descartes' doctrine of faith is a consequence of his adoption of the Augustinian doctrine of the free exercise of will in judgment" (1998: 333).

In Part Three of the *Discourse*, Descartes lays out a "provisional moral code" (*morale par provision*, hereafter referred to as the *morale*), "consisting of just three or four maxims" that he found necessary to formulate for himself and follow while in the process of constructing his "permanent residence." Descartes explains why he found it necessary to adopt a "provisional" moral code at this juncture in his philosophical enterprise:

> Now, before starting to rebuild your house, it is not enough simply to pull it down ... you must also provide yourself with some other place where you can live comfortably while building is in progress. Likewise, lest I should remain indecisive in my actions while reason obliged me to be so in my judgments, and in order to live as happily as I could during this time, I formed for myself a provisional moral code consisting of just three or four maxims, which I should like to tell you about. (AT VI 22: CSM I 122)

In this passage, Descartes explains that he intended his *morale* to regulate the practical affairs of his everyday life that could not be settled by the first rule of method presented in Part Two of the *Discourse*. Aware of the danger of an excessive application of the first rule of method to practical affairs, Descartes feared that his reason would undesirably compel him to do so by obliging him to withhold judgment whenever he lacked evident knowledge of the matter in question. Descartes intended his *morale* to fill the lacuna created by the exclusion of the first rule of the method, in an attempt to escape the indecisiveness and unhappiness attendant on this interim period. Acknowledging that life often requires him to act without delay even in the absence of certain knowledge, he resolves to keep his mind peaceful and free from indecisiveness while devoting himself to establishing the foundations of his science.[17]

---

[17] Some scholars hold that Descartes had formed and embraced the *morale par provision* long before he decided on the rigorous application of the rule of evidence, and hence could not have derived the need for his *morale* from this rule. Marshall, for example, thinks that Descartes "adopted his *morale par provision* at the time he dedicated himself to the search for truth, which was in 1620," when he had not yet divested himself of all his previous opinions (1998: 11ff.). In Marshall's interpretation, the need for a *morale par provision* does not initially arise from a commitment to pure inquiry but from more commonplace skeptical considerations, prior to methodical doubt: "a battery of skeptical arguments bequeathed to him by Sextus Empiricus and vivified by Montaigne" (p. 22). It could prove challenging for this reading, however, to explain Descartes' explicit assertion in the opening paragraph of the *Discourse* that some of the moral rules he introduces in Part Three are "derived from his method" (AT VI 1: CSM I 111). What is more, in claiming that his reason obliged him to be indecisive in his judgments, Descartes probably points to the first rule of method that instructs him to suspend judgment on matters he does not clearly understand. Further evidence is found in a letter to Reneri of 1683, where Descartes writes that had he not formulated his *morale par provision* (in particular, the second maxim), people would have

In discussing his reasons for adopting a *morale par provision* in the *Discourse*, Descartes typically employs first-person language, referring in particular to his own intellectual journey. In the Preface to the French edition of the *Principles* published in 1647, however, he approaches this issue from a broader, normative perspective, referring to the order that whoever is engaged with self-instruction must follow. Descartes maintains that formulating a provisional moral code is the first course of action one must undertake when rebuilding the foundations of one's knowledge:

I would wish to explain here the order which I think we should follow when we aim to instruct ourselves. First of all, a man who still possesses only the ordinary and imperfect knowledge ... should try before anything else to devise for himself a code of morals which is sufficient to regulate the actions of his life. For this is something which permits no delay, since we should endeavour above all else to live well. (AT ixb 13: CSM i 185–86)

When Descartes states that each person should "devise for himself a code of morals which is sufficient to regulate the actions of his life," it is unlikely he means that each meditator should form his or her own "provisional" morality. Insofar as the "provisional" moral code constitutes a prerequisite for pure inquiry, it ought to be at least sufficiently adequate to regulate the actions of life and provide the meditator with the genuine tranquility he or she needs. Moreover, as shown below, rather than merely a stopgap device for solving current practical problems, Descartes considers some of the *morale* maxims to be a source for "true and certain" reasons for action (AT vi 25: CSM i 123). In addition, as John Marshall rightly observes, Descartes regards the four maxims as a genuine *morality*, even if amendable, viewing them as a set of fundamental values expressing his conception of the good life (1998: 18ff.). Morality thus emerges as both the initial and the final rung of Descartes' philosophical enterprise.

Before proceeding to inquire into the kind of justification that Descartes might have for his *morale par provision* in the *Discourse*, let me consider the sense in which the *morale* is "provisional" (*par provision*). In my understanding, in describing his *morale* maxims as "provisional," Descartes employs this term not in the sense of "temporal" but rather in the sense of "conditional." The full approval of the *morale* maxims is conditional on establishing the metaphysical and scientific foundations that might justify them. Indeed, as I show below, strong evidence supports the notion that Descartes believed at least some of his *morale* maxims were

---

objected that his universal doubt "could give rise to great indecision and moral chaos" (AT ii 35: CSMK 97).

true and certain "from a practical point of view," and hoped them to be sustained by his subsequent metaphysical and scientific investigation. But until this task was completed, Descartes could not rule out the possibility that his *morale* would eventually be found inadequate, or even false. As Marshall rightly points out, Descartes regards the *morale par provision* as imperfect precisely on these grounds, as opposed to the highest and most perfect moral system he envisages, which he intends to rest on firm metaphysical and scientific foundations (1998: 18, 30).

The view that Descartes regards his *morale* as no more than a temporary expedient destined to be abandoned as soon as the principles of the highest and most perfect moral system are established was, until recently, rather common.[18] Emphasizing the "stop-gap character" of the four maxims, Gibson maintains that Descartes specifically adopted them only for himself: "even as rules, they are not intended for anyone else; and much less are they to be taken as a guide to moral philosophy" (1987: 345; see also pp. 343–44). On the other side of the scale, we find recent interpretations holding that Descartes intended his *morale* to constitute a part of his projected definitive morality. Michèle Le Dœuff, for example, holds that nothing in the *Discourse* justifies the devaluation of the *morale* or its characterization as "a makeshift, a short term expedient which will have to be reconsidered later on." In her reading, "what Descartes says is not that he will content himself with it for the time being, but that he is content with it" (1989: 64). Le Dœuff finds the English translation of *par provision* as "provisional" misleading, since the former is "a juridical term meaning what a judgment awards in advance to a party." For example, "one can award *par provision* a sum of a thousand *livres* damages to a plaintiff suing for assault. The *provision* is not liable to be put in question by the final judgment; it is a first installment" (1989: 62). Le Dœuff therefore thinks that the expression "provisional morality" is inappropriate:

> The expression "provisional morality" is a devaluing one; it designates something which is destined to be replaced, something probably inadequate, to be invalidated once something better is found: something which awaits its own rejection. Whereas the word *provision* signifies the validity of this morality. (1989: 62)

---

[18] See, for instance, Espinas (1925: 16–18); Keefe (1972: 134–39 and the references therein). For further references, see Le Dœuff (1989: 59–60). As rightly noted, however, this line of interpretation has generally mistaken the *morale par provision* with a *morale provisoire*, a term that Descartes himself never employs. See, for example, Le Dœuff (1989: 57); Morgan (1994: 44); Marshall (1998: 57).

Embracing Le Dœuff's reading, Lisa Shapiro suggests that, in the *Discourse*, Descartes regards his *morale* maxims as "unconditional duties," designed to supplement his perfect moral system. She writes:

The maxims, as unconditional duties, are not to be called into question as we arrive at the perfect moral system, and indeed they frame the circumstantial duties we will arrive at with complete knowledge. That is, the Cartesian perfect moral system will consist in a comprehensive guide for action that includes all circumstantial duties as well as the framing unconditional duties or maxims. (2008: 453)

Among the reasons Shapiro suggests in support of her reading is Descartes' clear commitment to the four maxims of the *morale* in his later correspondence with Elizabeth and in the *Passions*. This commitment, she states, "argues against the view that the *morale* maxims are merely provisional" (p. 453).

Descartes does indeed adhere to the four maxims of his *morale* throughout his life. But this does not prove that he had already envisaged in the *Discourse* that his projected perfect moral system would include them as "framing unconditional duties." Only retrospectively can we affirm that his *morale* does constitute the basis for his later (and still imperfect) morality of virtue.

But what kind of justification might Descartes have for his commitment to his *morale* maxims in the *Discourse*? Even if he did not aspire to meet the strict standard of the first rule of his method when formulating these four maxims in particular, he had to justify his conviction that they could fulfill the practical function he intended for them. Moreover, he had to warrant their standing as *moral* maxims, even if conditional and revisable. Indeed, not only does Descartes not regard his adoption of these maxims as arbitrary, but he claims it rests on "true and certain" reasons.

At the opening of the *Discourse*, Descartes states that he derived his *morale par provision* from his method (AT vi 1: CSM i 111). But except for this challenging comment, he does not specify how the four maxims of his *morale* might be said to derive from his rules of method, and it is hard to see how this might be the case. I therefore agree with various scholars who claim that, in making this comment, Descartes did not imply any clear logical connection between the contents of his *morale* maxims and his method. A more promising explanation argues that the general *need* for a provisional moral code arises from the limited scope of the method, in the manner introduced above.[19] Beginning to pave his

---

[19] See, for example, Gilson (1947: 81); Rodis-Lewis (1970: 18); Coolidge (1991: 276, 279–81); Morgan (1994: 55). Though not addressing this solution, Beck also asserts that the *morale* maxims "cannot

moral path in the *Discourse*, Descartes appears to have no overwhelming, independent criteria to prefer one moral principle over another. And yet, as I will presently show, in shaping his views on practical reason at this early stage of his philosophical enterprise, he employs the first rule of method as a sort of model or ideal he aspires to imitate in various significant respects. This way of thinking, which he embraces only implicitly, allows him to develop the moral guidelines that he upheld for the rest of his life. Although Descartes does not introduce a full-fledged theory of judgment and conception of free will until the *Meditations*, a close kinship appears to link the *morale* maxims he places in the *Discourse* and his later morality of virtue.

Descartes does not directly confront the issue of justifying his *morale* as a whole, but does offer several reasons in support of each of his maxims in particular, which I examine below. Note that the four maxims are not intended to supply us with standards for the shaping of our moral beliefs. They provide us with evident second-order guidelines as to how we should act in situations requiring us to make concrete, first-order decisions in the absence of certainty. These maxims are intended to shape our attitude toward the choices we make in the practical domain and to help us build our self-esteem as rational and virtuous agents. To put this slightly differently, the main objective of the maxims is to allow us to master our lives as far as possible, even while walking in the dark. The grounds Descartes offers in support of these maxims, as I will show, do not differ in kind from those the maxims themselves provide to justify our conduct in concrete situations of choice. Accordingly, through the very formulation and adoption of the *morale*, Descartes exemplifies the contents of the maxims themselves (especially the second and the third). On top of this recursive feature of the *morale*, we must also take into consideration the hierarchical structure Descartes uses to set out the maxims, when each one exceeds its antecedent in generality and provides it with additional support.

---

be said to have any logical connection with the rules of method" (1952: 4). Robert Cumming emphatically challenges the above interpretation as overlooking that "it is only the first rule of method which requires complete doubt, and not 'cette méthode' without qualification" (1955: 209). The three remaining rules of method, in Cumming's reading, are rules of construction whose first implementation is precisely the *morale par provision* in Part Three of the *Discourse* (pp. 209, 217ff.).

4 THE FOUR *MORALE* MAXIMS

Maxim one

The first of the four maxims contains three key directives: "to obey the laws and customs of my country," "holding constantly to the religion in which by God's grace I had been instructed from my childhood," and "governing myself in all other matters according to the most moderate and least extreme opinions – the opinions commonly accepted in practice by the most sensible of those with whom I should have to live" (AT VI 23: CSM I 122). Whereas the first two directives seem to rest on Descartes' willingness to remain faithful to the institutional law and morality of the state and the Church, the third directive appears to run against Descartes' persistent endeavor to free himself from external authorities and trust only those opinions at which he arrives by using his own reasoning. Earlier in the *Discourse*, Descartes writes that the greatest benefit he derived from traveling around Europe in his youth, "mixing with people of diverse temperaments and ranks," was the lesson that many things, "although seeming very extravagant and ridiculous to us, are nevertheless commonly accepted and approved in other nations" (AT VI 10: CSM I 115–16). And so he learned "not to believe too firmly anything of which [he] had been persuaded only by example and custom" (AT VI 10: CSM I 116). A few paragraphs later, he observes even more forcefully:

I thought, too, how the same man, with the same mind, if brought up from infancy among the French or Germans, develops otherwise than he would if he had always lived among the Chinese or cannibals ... Thus it is custom and example that persuade us, rather than any certain knowledge. And yet a majority vote is worthless as a proof of truths that are at all difficult to discover; for a single man is much more likely to hit upon them than a group of people. I was, then, unable to choose anyone whose opinions struck me as preferable to those of all others, and I found myself as it were forced to become my own guide. (AT VI 16: CSM I 119)

Given these remarks, the first maxim supporting a strict social and cultural conformism might emerge as questionable and quite perplexing. In all matters not falling under the legal authority of the state and the articles of his own religious faith, Descartes resolves to follow the moderate opinions commonly accepted by sensible people in his own community.

Yet a closer look at the first maxim reveals that in resolving to govern himself *according* to the opinions of local custom, Descartes does not resolve to *accept* these opinions as the most probable. He is only determined to govern his *actions* in accordance with them, namely, to act or function in line with them within the social dimension of his life. Descartes finds it more useful to adjust his conduct to prevailing practices and customs so as to attain the peace of mind he is seeking. While explaining his preference for the example of the sensible people with whom he lives, he clarifies that he does not regard their opinions as more probable than those of sensible people living elsewhere: "although there may be men as sensible among the Persians or Chinese as among ourselves, I thought it would be most useful for me to be guided by those with whom I should have to live" (AT vi 23: CSM i 122). Seeking to exclude active social reform from any application of his philosophical enterprise, as Morgan points out (1994: 45), Descartes might be willing to put his enterprise on the right track as aiming not at external reform but rather at the transformation of the individual self. Cottingham also relates the first maxim to Descartes' characteristic reluctance to enter the arena of public controversy, so as to be "a spectator rather than an actor in all the comedies that are played out there" (AT vi 28: CSM i 125; see Cottingham 1998: 67). Indeed, while explaining his allegiance to the moderate opinions of the sensible people of his community, Descartes states they have a greater chance than the extreme ones of being *true*, and they are also the easiest to correct.[20] Nevertheless, this allegiance does not entail that he believed the moderate opinions accepted in his own society to be any truer than those common in other cultures.[21]

---

[20] AT vi 23–24: CSM i 122–23. This call for moderation becomes particularly important when one must choose between opinions enjoying equal measures of support. Descartes writes that he will then choose the most moderate opinions since they "are always the easiest to act upon and probably the best (excess being usually bad), and also so that if I made a mistake, I should depart less from the right path than I would if I chose one extreme when I ought to have pursued the other" (AT vi 23–24: CSM i 122–23).

[21] By contrast, some scholars hold that in expressing his allegiance to views of sensible people in the first maxim, Descartes accepts certain beliefs as morally certain. Adhering to this view, Marshall states that the first maxim covers not only the "normal range of duties to self, to others, and within social institutions, such as the duty not to steal," but also "the full range of beliefs about ourselves and the world of which we can claim moral certainty" (1998: 26 and n. 24). But practical opinions that are accepted and implemented in one's community – even if the most sensible and moderate – are not necessarily such that "we never normally doubt," nor such that whoever doubts them would be considered extravagant. In Part Four of the *Discourse*, Descartes states that we have a moral certainty about things "that it seems we cannot doubt them without being extravagant," such as our having a body, there being stars and an earth, and the like (AT vi 37–38: CSM i 130). And in the French version of the *Principles*, recall, he states that "moral certainty is certainty which is sufficient to regulate our behaviour, or which measures up to the certainty we have on matters relating to the conduct of life *which we never normally doubt*, though we know that it is possible, absolutely speaking, that they may be false" (AT iv, 205; my emphasis).

Later in the *Discourse*, moreover, Descartes clarifies that the first maxim's directive to rest content with the opinions of others is meant to be abandoned at a later stage of his inquiry. Aware of the genuine tension between its content and his enduring combat against external authorities and custom, he writes: "For since God has given each of us a light to distinguish truth from falsehood, I should not have thought myself obliged to rest content with the opinions of others for a single moment if I had not intended in due course to examine them using my own judgment" (AT VI 27: CSM I 124). The third directive of the first maxim, therefore, differs in status from the remaining three maxims in being "provisional" not only in the sense of "conditional" but also in the sense of *temporal*.

Descartes concludes his first maxim with a remark that applies to his *morale* as a whole. Since nothing in the world remains stable, he states, it would be a sin against good sense, and therefore a vice, to go on supporting opinions we had once decided to follow even though we no longer find them worthy:

I saw nothing in the world which remained always in the same state, and for my part I was determined to make my judgments more and more perfect, rather than worse. For these reasons I thought I would be sinning against good sense if I were to take my previous approval of something as obliging me to regard it as good later on, when it had perhaps ceased to be good or I no longer regarded it as such. (AT VI 24: CSM I 123)

Descartes here underscores that the edict to follow the opinions of other people, however sensible, does not exempt him from the responsibility to keep correcting his moral judgments in particular, and his *morale* maxims in general, so as to make them "more and more perfect" in accordance with his increasing knowledge of the world.[22] In his 1638 letter to Reneri, Descartes further indicates that we are obliged not only to change our opinions as soon as we find better ones but also "to lose no opportunity of looking for them" (AT II 35: CSMK 97). Descartes places the virtue of decisiveness, which is the main issue of the second *morale* maxim, "between its two contrary vices, indecision and obstinacy" (AT II 35: CSMK 97).

---

[22] A few lines earlier in the *Discourse*, Descartes writes: "I counted as excessive all promises by which we give up some of our freedom" (AT VI 24: CSM II 123). This may imply, as Morgan notes, that in refraining from correcting our moral judgments in accordance with the growth of our knowledge, we are committing a sin against good sense because we give up our freedom to correct them (1994: 46).

Maxim two

The second maxim, which will later develop into Descartes' definition of virtue, is a second-order rule for action, applicable to any particular situation of choice where knowledge is either incomplete or absent: "My second maxim was to be as firm and decisive in my actions as I could, and to follow even the most doubtful opinions, once I had adopted them, with no less constancy than if they had been quite certain" (AT VI 24: CSM I 123). Descartes proceeds:

Since in everyday life we must often act without delay, it is a most certain truth that when it is not in our power to discern the truest opinions, we must fol-low the most probable. Even when no opinions appear more probable than any others, we must still adopt some; and having done so we must then regard them not as doubtful, from a practical point of view, but as most true and certain, on the grounds that the reason which made us adopt them is itself true and certain. (AT VI 25: CSM I 123)

The principal role of the second maxim is thus to provide a true and certain basis for practical action in situations where certainty regarding the first-order choice is lacking. In such cases, we must first do our best to choose the most probable course of action to pursue. But even in the face of outright ignorance as to the more probable or otherwise prefer-able alternative, we must not withhold judgment but instead adopt some option. Having done so, we should then regard our decision as the truest and most certain and should carry it out firmly and resolutely, with no less resolve than we would if our judgment was indubitable.[23] The moral value of our actions, according to this second maxim, does not depend on the truthfulness of our first-order choices or on their resulting con-sequences. Barring certainty regarding the object of our choices, all we should do is act resolutely and firmly on the basis of our best judgment "on the ground that the reason which made us adopt them is itself true and certain." But what might ground Descartes' conviction that the sec-ond-order directive – to base our choices on the best knowledge available and to act upon them resolutely – is itself true and certain and, as such, may warrant our first-order (fallible) decisions?

---

[23] Descartes reinforces the second maxim of the *Discourse* several years later when he writes: "As far as the conduct of life is concerned, I am very far from thinking that we should assent only to what is clearly perceived. On the contrary, I do not think that we should always wait even for probable truths; from time to time we will have to choose one of many alternatives about which we have no knowledge, and once we have made our choice, so long as no reasons against it can be produced, we must stick to it as firmly as if it had been chosen for transparently clear reasons" (Second Replies, AT VII 149: CSM II 106).

In the second maxim, what we find as Descartes' main justification for its adoption is that it allows him to escape indecisiveness, which is the source of regret and remorse – the principal obstacles to happiness. "By following this maxim," he concludes, "I could free myself from all the regret and remorse which usually trouble the consciences of those weak and faltering spirits who allow themselves to set out on some supposedly good course of action which later, in their inconstancy, they judge to be bad" (AT VI 25: CSM I 123). This theme, formative to Descartes' moral thinking, appears in later writings as well. Descartes writes to Princess Elizabeth, for example, that "nothing can impede our contentment except desire and regret or repentance" (August 4, 1645, AT IV 266: CSMK). In the *Passions of the Soul*, he defines remorse as "a kind of sadness which results from our doubting that something we are doing, or have done, is good." As such, "it necessarily presupposes doubt" (art. 177). Regret is also a kind of sadness, which is joined to some despair and to a memory of a pleasure that gave us joy – one which is so completely lost that we have no hope for recovering it at the time in which we regret it (art. 209). In connection with practical judgment, both passions arise from the passion of irresolution, an "anxiety of choosing wrongly," which in turn stems from our unrealistic assessment of our prospects to attain the truth or the good (art. 170).

Granted this, the main rationale of the second maxim may be portrayed as follows: when absolute certainty is unattainable, our greatest mistake would be to approach and evaluate our choices in terms of consequences. This attitude would result in the paralyzing passion of irresolution accompanied by remorse and regret, which we should strive to avoid. Obviously, we must do our utmost to reach the best (truest) judgment available. But having done so, the moral value of any particular decision we make does not depend on the truth of our judgment or on its outcomes, but on the manner in which we reach this judgment and act on it. Insofar as we are confident that we have made the best possible judgment under the circumstances, we should execute our decision firmly and resolutely, knowing that the moral certitude of our action would not be detracted even if we later realize that it was bad in itself. This theme becomes explicit later in the *Passions of the Soul*:

[A]n excess of irresolution results from too great a desire to do well and from a weakness of the intellect, which contains only a lot of confused notions, and none that are clear and distinct. That is why the remedy against such excess is to become accustomed to form certain and determinate judgments regarding everything that comes before us, and *to believe that we always do our duty when we do what we judge to be best, even though our judgment may perhaps be a very bad one.* (art. 170; my emphasis)

Yet a higher-order justification for the second maxim is given in the third maxim of the *morale*, whose main merit is that of self-mastery. The second maxim's metaphor of the traveler lost in the woods might be helpful to illustrate this point:

In this respect I would be imitating a traveller who, upon finding himself lost in a forest, should not wander about turning this way and that, and still less stay in one place, but should keep walking as straight as he can in one direction, never changing it for slight reasons even if mere chance made him choose it in the first place; for in this way, even if he does not go exactly where he wishes, he will at least end up in a place where he is likely to be better off than in the middle of a forest. (AT VI 24–25: CSM I 123)

The traveler who keeps walking along a straight line, even if he fails to arrive exactly where he wished, "will at least end up in a place where he is likely to be better off that in the middle of a forest." Surely, if we consider the situation only in terms of consequences, we can envision cases where the consequences of inaction are preferable to those of random action. But the traveler who stays in the middle of the forest wondering which way he should take is not behaving rationally, not only because of the distress caused by his indecisiveness but also because, passively awaiting external salvation, he fails to channel his aspirations and actions to things he has the power to change. The motif of walking slowly but resolutely along a straight path is formative in Descartes' reasoning. Earlier in the *Discourse* he writes: "those who proceed but very slowly can make much greater progress, if they always follow the right path, than those who hurry and stray from it" (AT VI 2: CSM I 111).

 Preoccupied with constructing his permanent abode, Descartes is himself the wanderer in the woods trying to find the right destination to pursue: "like a man who walks alone in the dark, I resolved to proceed so slowly, and to use such circumspection in all things, that even if I made but little progress I should at least be sure not to fall" (AT VI 16–17: CSM I 119). In the very decision to formulate and adopt the *morale par provision*, Descartes is indeed in active compliance with the second and third maxims. At this point in his journey, he has no conclusive justification for preferring one guiding rule for action over another. But even when lacking a guarantee of the truth, he must judge as best as he can, and then regard the maxims chosen with no less constancy than he would if all doubts were eliminated. Instead of remaining in the middle of the forest, Descartes formulates these particular *morale* maxims and follows them just as if they were proved to be true. Like any other practical decision, these maxims are open to later refutation and change; but although they may later be revised, whoever rejects them as invalid must rest his rejection on sufficient, reasonable grounds.

Maxim three

The third maxim is of a higher order and greater generality than the two previous ones, anticipating Descartes' later ideal of the hegemony of reason over the passions through the right use of free will. The principal objective of this maxim is to help us control our desires by limiting them to those goods entirely within our power, and avoid desiring things that are not in our dominion:

My third maxim was to try always to master myself rather than fortune, and change my desires rather than the order of the world. In general I would become accustomed to believing that nothing lies entirely within our power except our thoughts, so that after doing our best in dealing with matters external to us, whatever we fail to achieve is absolutely impossible so far as we are concerned. This alone, I thought, would be sufficient to prevent me from desiring in future something I could not get, and so to make me content. (AT VI 25: CSM I 123–24)

Striving to control ourselves rather than fortune and shaping or altering our desires rather than the order of the world requires that we first distinguish properly between what is in our power and what is not. Descartes holds that if we become accustomed to believing that only our thoughts are in our absolute dominion, we shall not feel guilty or responsible when we fail to achieve an external good that is not subject to our control: "after doing our best in dealing with matters external to us, whatever we fail to achieve is absolutely impossible so far as we are concerned."

For Descartes, a proper assessment of the limits of our power is not only necessary but also sufficient for our ability to control and regulate our desires, because "our will naturally tends to desire only what our intellect represents to it as somehow possible" (AT VI 25–26: CSM I 124). Thus, insofar as we distinguish adequately between things that depend on us and things that do not, we can be assured that we shall not yearn for things we cannot attain. To free ourselves from unrealistic desires, which are a source of unhappiness and frustration, all we must do is "become accustomed to believe that nothing lies entirely within our power except our thoughts." This belief is not the result of a momentary insight but one we can only become *accustomed* to through persistent practice: "it takes long practice and repeated meditation to become accustomed to seeing everything in this light" (AT vi 26: CSM i 124). And insofar as we become habituated to consider all external goods as equally beyond our power, "we shall not regret the absence of goods which seem to be our birthright when we are deprived of them through no fault of our own" (AT vi 26: CSM i 124).

In the letter to Reneri mentioned earlier, Descartes elaborates on the idea he considers self-evident ("a truth which nobody should deny") that "there is nothing entirely in our power except our thoughts." He writes that by the word "thought," he intended "to cover all the operations of the soul, so that not only meditations and acts of the will, but the activities of seeing and hearing and deciding on one movement rather than another, so far as they depend on the soul, are all thoughts" (AT ii 36: CSMK 97). The term "thought" in this context thus signifies the mind's activity, as opposed to the "activities" pertaining to the body alone, which "are said to take place in a man rather than to be performed by him" (AT ii 36: CSMK 97). Although external things might be in our control, "they are in our power only in so far as they can be affected by our thoughts, and not *absolutely* or *entirely* in our power because there are other powers outside us which can frustrate our designs" (AT ii 36: CSMK 97–98). Therefore, when setting out our specific ends, we must be realistic as far as possible in identifying those external things that our own mental activity might change or affect, including our body-dependent desires.[24]

In this third maxim, the influence of Stoic ethics is evident. Alluding to his Hellenistic predecessors, Descartes writes:

In this, I believe, lay the secret of those philosophers who in earlier times were able to escape from the dominion of fortune and, despite suffering and poverty, rival their gods in happiness. Through constant reflection upon the limits prescribed for them by nature, they became perfectly convinced that nothing was in their power but their thoughts, and this alone was sufficient to prevent them from being attracted to other things. Their mastery over their thoughts was so absolute that they had reason to count themselves richer, more powerful, freer and happier than other men who, because they lack this philosophy, never achieve such mastery over all their desires, however favoured by nature and fortune they may be. (AT vi 26–27: CSM i 124)

---

[24] Descartes also acknowledges that not all our thoughts are subject to our command. Several years later, he writes to Mersenne that he had never said "that all our thoughts are in our power, but only that if there is anything absolutely in our power, it is our thoughts, that is to say, those which come from our will and free choice." Descartes adds that he wrote it "only in order to show that our free will has no absolute jurisdiction over any corporeal thing" (December 3, 1640, AT iii 249: CSMK 160).

But whereas the Stoic ideal of living in accordance with reason is tantamount to "living in agreement with nature," with the cosmic *logos*, Descartes' vision of the hegemony of reason is considerably different. What is incumbent on the virtuous person, according to the Stoic conception, is to be harmoniously attuned to the meaningful and unalterable order of the universe, of which human beings are a natural part. But Descartes, equipped with his new mechanical science, believes in the human capacity to control and manipulate the alien, physical universe, including the mechanism of the human body itself.[25] In Part Six of the *Discourse*, Descartes sets out his expectations from his new physics. He first expresses his hope of discovering a practical philosophy that would be "very useful in life" (AT VI 61: CSM I 142). Indeed, as shown below, in his later years he develops a new physiological account of how reason may control and regulate the passions. Descartes then proceeds to specify an extensive range of scientific objectives, among them knowledge of "the power and action of fire, water, air, the stars, the heavens and all the other bodies in our environment." He also mentions the invention of innumerable experimental devices to facilitate our welfare, and the development of a new science of medicine by which "we might free ourselves from innumerable diseases, both of the body and of the mind, and perhaps even from the infirmity of old age" (AT VI 62: CSM I 143). Descartes holds that his projected philosophy could enable human beings to render themselves, as it were, "the lords and masters of nature" (AT VI 62: CSM I 142–43).

Before I proceed to the fourth and last maxim, which places the *morale par provision* within the broader context of Descartes' philosophical enterprise, I wish to remark on the crucial role that the third maxim plays for the *morale* as a whole and, in particular, for the applicability of the second maxim.

Making infallible practical judgment about a concrete good when circumstances permit only probable ones is not, as noted, within our power. Descartes writes in the *Passions* that "an excess of irresolution results from too great a desire to do well and from a weakness of the intellect" (art. 170). When we yearn excessively and unrealistically to make infallible practical judgments, evaluating them from a consequentialist point of view, we may fall into a paralyzing indecisiveness accompanied by guilt, regret, and remorse over the loss of goods that had been beyond our reach in the first place. But if we become accustomed to believing that this good

---

[25] For illuminating discussions of this issue, see Cottingham (1998: 68–80); Taylor (1989: 147–53).

(arriving at infallible practical decision) is beyond our control, we shall no longer desire it. Regulating our desires in this manner, as the third maxim prescribes, enables us to follow the second maxim's command to act resolutely according to our best judgment available. In such cases, even if we fail to attain what we had hoped, we shall not feel responsible for the consequences and shall not experience guilt or remorse: "if we consider all external goods as equally beyond our power, we shall not regret the absence of goods which seem to be our birthright when we are deprived of them through no fault of our own, any more than we regret not possessing the kingdom of China or of Mexico" (AT vi 26: CSM i 124).

The third maxim's distinction between what depends entirely on us and what depends on external causes is fundamental to Descartes' later morality of virtue and to his theory of the passions. As he writes in the *Passions of the Soul*, the chief utility of morality lies in our controlling our desires, directing them to things whose attainment depends only on us, on our free will (art. 144). But what the third maxim, and the *morale* as a whole, leave undetermined, is whether the merit of self-mastery has an independent value of its own – as the later morality will explicitly assert – or rather constitutes a mere means for precluding distress, remorse, or regret, and their resultant unhappiness. However, even at this early stage, when Descartes had not yet fully developed his theory of judgment and of free will, he is convinced that a proper understanding of the scope of our power is the key to our virtuousness, rationality, and happiness.

Maxim four

Finally, to conclude this moral code, I decided to review the various occupations which men have in this life, in order to try to choose the best. Without wishing to say anything about the occupations of others, I thought I could do no better than to continue with the very one I was engaged in, and devote my whole life to cultivating my reason and advancing as far as I could in the knowledge of the truth, following the method I had prescribed for myself. Since beginning to use this method I had felt such extreme contentment that I did not think one could enjoy any sweeter or purer one in this life. Every day I discovered by its means truths which, it seemed to me, were quite important and were generally unknown by other men; and the satisfaction they gave me so filled my mind that nothing else mattered to me. Besides, the sole basis of the foregoing three maxims was the plan I had to continue my self-instruction. (AT vi 27: CSM i 124)

The personal tone Descartes uses at the opening of this passage may explain his initial hesitation to include it in his *morale* ("consisting of three or four maxims"). "Without wishing to say anything about the occupations of others," he simply appears to be reporting his own reasons for deciding to devote his whole life to the cultivation of reason and the search for truth. Descartes' expounding on the extreme contentment he has gained by practicing his method and by discovering new truths may lend further credence to this initial impression. But any such interpretation is precluded by Descartes' further statement that his plan to continue his philosophical investigation is "the sole basis" of the foregoing three maxims, thereby hinting that whoever wishes to attain any benefit from practicing his *morale* must follow the same course. To support this statement, he proceeds to spell out how the validity and efficiency of each of the three maxims is conditional on his resolve to keep developing his inquiry. The first maxim's prescription to rest content with the opinions of others would have been unjustifiable had he not "intended in due course to examine them using [his] own judgment"; the second maxim's command to pursue resolutely whatever direction he considers the most probable would not have exempted him from having scruples about it, unless he had undertaken to correct his provisional judgments by discovering better ones. Last, he could not have limited his desires or been content had he not been determined to increase his knowledge of the true goods within his reach (AT VI 27–28: CSM I 124–25).

We thus see that, for Descartes, advancing knowledge and embracing the *morale* are mutually dependent. Just as one needs to follow the *morale* in order to keep the mind untroubled while devoted to the search for truth, so also, in order to warrant the *morale* maxims and gain any benefit from adopting them, one must keep making progress in the pure intellectual inquiry. Descartes concludes his *morale par provision* with a general explanation of how the acquisition of knowledge is imperative for attaining the two principal merits of his ethics – virtuousness and self-contentment:

> For since our will tends to pursue or avoid only what our intellect represents as good or bad, we need only to judge well in order to act well, and to judge as well as we can in order to do our best – that is to say, in order to acquire all the virtues and in general all the other goods we can acquire. And when we are certain of this, we cannot fail to be happy [*content*]. (AT VI 28: CSM I 125)

Descartes anticipates here a prominent principle of his later theory of judgment, claiming that the will has a natural tendency toward goodness and truth in proportion to the clarity and distinctness of the intellect's perceptions.[26] But Descartes goes even further, indicating that to judge

---

[26] Second Replies (AT VII 166: CSM II 117); Sixth Replies (AT VII 432: CSM II 292); *Principles*, I, 43; *Passions*, art. 177.

well is sufficient in order to act well, and thus be both virtuous and content. A clear and distinct apprehension of the good, then, compels the will not only to assent to it but also to pursue it by doing what is right. Descartes' reference to this remark in a letter to Mersenne of the same year supports this reading. Facing the charge of Pelagianism, he endorses the "common Scholastic doctrine" that "the will does not tend towards evil except in so far as it is presented to it by the intellect under some aspect of goodness." Descartes insists that the weakness of the will is only possible when the intellect's perceptions are not clear:

[T]hat is why they say that "whoever sins does so in ignorance" – so that if the intellect never represented anything to the will as good without its actually being so, the will could never go wrong in its choice. But the intellect often represents different things to the will at the same time; and that is why they say "I see and praise the better, but follow the worse", which applies only to weak minds, as I said on page 26. (AT 1 366: CSMK 56)[27]

In the above quotation from the *Discourse* (maxim four, AT vi 28: CSM 1 125), however, Descartes also indicates that we need not judge indubitably in order to judge well in practical matters: "we need only to judge well in order to act well, and to judge as well as we can in order to do our best – that is to say, in order to acquire all the virtues and in general all the other goods we can acquire. And when we are certain of this, we cannot fail to be happy [*content*]."

---

[27] References in this passage are to Ovid's *Metamorphoses* (7, 20), and to the *Discourse*, apparently to the passage quoted above (AT vi 28: CSM 1 125). Descartes repeats this view in a letter to Mesland dated May 2, 1644, where he contends that "wherever there is an occasion for sinning, there is indifference" (AT iv 117: CSMK 234). Not only is it not *necessary* that sinners see clearly that what they are doing is evil, but for them to have this clear understanding is also *impossible*: "For if we saw it clearly, it would be impossible for us to sin, as long as we saw it in that fashion" (ibid.). See also AT iv 116: CSMK 233; CB 32 = AT v 159: CSMK 342; *Passions*, arts. 177, 191. Echoing Plato in *Protagoras* (358d, 345e1) and Socrates in *Meno* (77–78b1), Descartes rejects the possibility of *akrasia* or weakness of will. And akin to Aristotle, he endorses the view that any moral weakness must be bound up with a certain degree of ignorance (Aristotle 1985: 111, 1110b28, 1147a11). But Descartes' adherence to the traditional intellectualistic conception of moral action does not mean that he endorses some sort of "ethical determinism," a phrase used by Alanen (2003: 226). Acknowledging our freedom to detract the mind's attention from a clearly perceived good, he admits our power to control our moral activity indirectly. As Cottingham points out, "Descartes' philosophical psychology does allow for weakness of will, in the sense of a willful disregarding of the manifest perceptions of the intellect ... however, the only way in which one may do this, it emerges, is by refusing to attend to or concentrate on the relevant proposition" (1976: 89). See also Cottingham (2002: 354–56). Byron Williston also maintains that what allows us to attribute a theory of *akrasia* to Descartes is the possibility of "a prior withdrawal of attention from the good in favour of a less worthy alternative, which is itself then seen (delusively) as the good" (1999: 41–42).

The *morale par provision* thus culminates in the two key objectives of Descartes' ethics: the practice of virtue, which is the resolute exercise of the will in accordance with one's best judgment, and the acquisition of happiness through the practice of virtue. But it is not until his later correspondence and the *Passions of the Soul* that Descartes specifies and elaborates on the relationship between the two merits of virtue and happiness, which the *morale par provision* leaves indeterminate.

CHAPTER 6

Descartes' deontological ethics of virtue

When Descartes becomes preoccupied with ethics in his later years, he is furnished with the metaphysics of the *Meditations* and the physics of the *Principles*. In the Preface to the 1647 French edition of the *Principles*, he specifies the tasks still remaining so as to complete his philosophical edifice:

[I]n order to bring the plan to its conclusion I should have to go on to explain in the same manner the nature of all the particular bodies which exist on the earth, namely minerals, plants, animals and, most importantly, man. And then to conclude, I should have to give an exact account of medicine, morals and mechanics. This is what I should have to do in order to give to mankind a body of philosophy that is quite complete. (AT IXB 17: CSM I 188)

Descartes realizes he will not be able to bring his philosophical enterprise to an end during his lifetime. Although he does not feel "so old, or so diffident about [his] powers, or so far away from knowledge of these remaining topics," he recognizes that making all the scientific observations needed in order to back up and justify his arguments

would require great expense – too great for an individual like myself unless he were assisted by the public. And since I do not see that I can expect such assistance, I think that in future I should be content to study for my own private instruction and that future generations will forgive me if from now on I give up working on their behalf. (AT IXB 17: CSM I 188)

These passages indicate, *inter alia*, that Descartes did not regard the morality he lays out in his correspondence of 1645–49 and in the *Passions of the Soul* as tantamount to what he envisaged as the highest and most perfect moral system, which "presupposes a complete knowledge of the other sciences" (AT IXB 14: CSM I 186). And yet, although the principles of his "mature" morality are not set within a thoroughly systematic and perfectly established moral system, he does regard them as definitive and final, since they are anchored in his physical and metaphysical doctrines (notably the dualism of body and soul and the theory of free will).

In previous chapters, I emphasized the crucial standing that Descartes' epistemology, from the *Meditations* onward, accords to the right use of free will, considering it an independent end. I also explained in what sense the freedom of our will constitutes for Descartes the most significant mark of our rationality and sense of godlikeness. In the present chapter, I attempt to accomplish this task by delving into Descartes' more developed ethical writings from the years 1645–49, showing the deep connection between his epistemology and his ethics. Whereas the *morale par provision* of the *Discourse* does not introduce a definite outlook on the hierarchy between virtue and happiness, the later moral writings are unequivocal on this point. Although happiness is the natural outcome of our virtuous behavior, Descartes insists that the practice of virtue itself, which he reduces to the good use of the will, *ought* to be the ultimate end for which we should strive in all our actions.

Descartes may thus be viewed as a successor of a long-enduring tradition of ethical theory holding that the good consists in practicing virtue. Like his Stoic predecessors, he considers virtue not merely a means to happiness but rather our supreme good (*summum bonum*).[1] On these grounds, I support Lisa Shapiro's view of Descartes as a virtue ethicist.[2] But what I take to be the striking dimension in Descartes' ethical reasoning is that he approaches virtue in deontological terms. In equating the pursuit of virtue with our supreme good, he endows it with obligatory force as "the final end or goal towards which our actions *ought* to tend."[3] My endeavor, therefore, is to defend the claim that Descartes' ethics of virtue is deontological, and to dismiss the inner tension that this claim ostensibly entails.

I THE UNITY OF VIRTUE

An important aspect of Descartes' attitude toward his own morality is his conviction of its uniqueness. On the one hand, he does not conceal his admiration for the ancient ethicists, especially the Stoics, stressing their immense influence on his own thinking. Early in his correspondence with Princess Elizabeth, he writes that it would be most useful to examine what the ancients have written on ethics and "try to advance beyond them by adding something to their precepts." Accordingly, Descartes

---

[1] See, e.g., letter to Princess Elizabeth, October 6, 1645 (AT IV 305: CSMK 268); letter to Queen Christina, November 20, 1647 (AT V 82–83: CSMK 324–25).
[2] Shapiro (2007: 32–34; 2008: 445, 449ff.).
[3] Letter to Princess Elizabeth, August 18, 1645 (AT IV 275: CSMK 261; my emphasis).

suggests to Elizabeth that Seneca's *De Vita Beata* (On the Happy Life) be their main topic of discussion (July 21, 1645, AT IV 252–53: CSMK 256). On the other hand, he keeps expressing his discontent with the Aristotelian, Stoic, and Epicurean treatments of key traditional notions and with the ways they establish their main ethical tenets. Therefore, in employing key traditional terms such as "virtue," "supreme good," "happiness," or "generosity," Descartes typically endows them with a new meaning, appropriate to his own philosophical enterprise.[4] In a letter to Elizabeth dated August 4, 1645, he presents his own definition of "virtue" (*la vertu*) as "a firm and constant resolution to carry out whatever reason recommends without being diverted by … passions or appetites" (AT IV 265: CSMK 257–58). Emphasizing the originality of this definition he adds: "Virtue, I believe, consists precisely in sticking firmly to this resolution; though I do not know that anyone has ever so described it. Instead, they have divided it into different species to which they have given various names, because of the various objects to which it applies" (AT IV 265: CSMK 258).

This remark provides an important insight into the general direction of Descartes' ethical thinking. He does not propose an extensive set of ideals of character and first-order rules for action, with a view to govern the particular decisions we make in the various circumstances of our lives. Instead, Descartes places at the center of his moral system a single, second-order duty to practice virtue, namely, to carry out resolutely and constantly whatever reason recommends on the basis of the best knowledge available. Descartes speaks of one single virtue, which he identifies with the good use of free will, from which all other perfections proceed. The exercise of virtue, moreover, is not merely a means to an end but rather *is itself* our supreme good, which Descartes characterizes in normative terms as "the final end or goal towards which our actions *ought* to tend."[5]

Descartes' view of the unity of virtue is closely connected to his fundamental conception of the unity of wisdom. Just as, in pure inquiry, we should "consider simply how to increase the natural light of [our] reason,

---

[4] Note that shortly after suggesting to Elizabeth that they should read Seneca's *De Vita Beata*, Descartes expresses reservations about this choice: "When I chose Seneca's *On the Happy Life* to suggest to Your Highness as an agreeable topic of discussion, I took account only of the reputation of the author and the importance of his topic, without thinking of his manner of treating it. I have since given some thought to this and find it not sufficiently rigorous to deserve to be followed" (August 4, 1645, AT IV 263: CSMK 256–57). On the relationship between Cartesian and Stoic morality see, e.g., Rodis-Lewis (1970: 22); Gueroult (1984: II, 184–88); Alanen (2003: 214–24, 250); Rutherford (2004).

[5] Letter to Princess Elizabeth, August 18, 1645 (AT IV 275: CSMK 261; my emphasis).

not with a view to solve this or that scholastic problem" (AT x 361: CSM 1 10), so also, in the practice of virtue, our practical reason demands that we set ourselves the good exercise of free will as the ultimate goal of all our actions. I therefore suggest that we read Descartes' account of virtue in light of his general conception of rules, and particularly in light of his rejection of the notion of subjecting the mind to a plurality of rules for thinking or action teaching us "how to hold forth on all subjects" (CB 77 = AT v 175: CSMK 350).[6] Recall that neither in the *Rules* nor in the *Discourse* does Descartes furnish a comprehensive "theory of method." Rather, he suggests a relatively limited set of "reliable rules" designed to properly direct us in the use we make of our mental capacities through persistent self-training and exercise. The full intension of these rules of method depends on practice, that is, on their application to concrete contents. Descartes accordingly writes to Mersenne that his method "is concerned more with practice than with theory" (AT 1 349: CSMK 53).[7]

Descartes' conception of the nature of moral rules is no different, though anchored in distinctive reasons. There is a single virtue, irrespective of the plurality of objects to which it is applied. Descartes reinforces this view in the dedicatory letter to Elizabeth that preceded the French edition of the *Principles*, when he writes:

[T]he pure and genuine virtues, which proceed solely from knowledge of what is right, all have one and the same nature and are included under the single term "wisdom." For whoever possesses the firm and powerful resolve always to use his reasoning powers correctly, as far as he can, and to carry out whatever he knows to be best, is truly wise, so far as his nature permits. And simply because of this, he will possess justice, courage, temperance, and all the other virtues; but they will be interlinked in such a way that no one virtue stands out among the others. (AT viiia 2–3: CSM 1 191)

---

[6] In *The Search for Truth*, Eudoxus (Descartes' spokesman) contends: "I cannot but stop you here, not to lead you off the road but to encourage you and make you consider what good sense can achieve if given proper direction ... When [the light of reason] operates on its own, it is less liable to go wrong than when it anxiously strives to follow the numerous different rules, the inventions of human ingenuity and idleness, which serve more to corrupt it than render it more perfect" (AT x 521: CSM II 415). See also *Rules*, Rule 4 (AT x 371–72: CSM 1 16); *Discourse*, Part Two (AT vi 17–18: CSM 1 119–20).

[7] In Part One of the *Discourse*, Descartes famously presents the pragmatic feature of his method: "My present aim, then, is not to teach the method which everyone must follow in order to direct his reason correctly, but only to reveal how I have tried to direct my own. One who presumes to give precepts must think himself more skilful than those to whom he gives them; and if he makes the slightest mistake, he may be blamed. But I am presenting this work only as a history or, if you prefer, a fable in which, among certain examples worthy of imitation, you will perhaps also find many others that it would be right not to follow" (AT vi 4: CSM 1 112). See also the discussion in Garber (2001: 283–88).

It is against this background, I suggest, that we should read Descartes' insistence that all the concrete goods we can attain should be valued or esteemed not for themselves, but rather according to the extent to which they can be acquired through our good use of the will, namely, by the exercise of virtue. As he writes to Queen Christina, "I shall not hesitate to express my opinion that nothing except virtue really deserves praise. All other goods deserve only to be esteemed and not to be honoured or praised, except in so far as they are supposed to have been acquired or obtained from God by the good use of free will" (AT v 84: CSMK 325). Characterizing virtue in pragmatic terms as the good use of the will, Descartes asserts that only those goods that depend entirely on us, on our free will, deserve to be pursued. And "regarding the things which do not depend on us in any way, we must never desire them with passion, however good they may be" (*Passions*, art. 145).

Viewed from this perspective, Descartes' moral outlook, no less than his conception of method, emerges as being concerned more with practice than with theory. Descartes holds that we all possess the ability to use free will well, that is, rationally and resolutely (*Passions*, arts. 50, 154, 161). Actualizing this ability, however, requires the acquisition of "good habits" through constant training and practice. As Descartes tells Elizabeth, "virtues are habits; for in fact our failings are rarely due to lack of theoretical knowledge of what we should do, but to lack of practical knowledge – that is, lack of a firm habit of belief" (September 15, 1645, AT iv 295–96: CSMK 267).[8] These considerations must be taken into account when dealing with the moral rules that Descartes sets out in his later moral writings. Far from being a comprehensive set of first-order duties governing the particular decisions we make in our lives, these rules amount to a limited set of constitutive conditions that are both necessary and sufficient for the fulfillment of our ultimate and unconditional duty – to practice virtue, namely, to make good use of the will.[9] My main purpose in what follows is to offer a more explicit analysis of Descartes'

---

[8] See also *Passions*, art. 161. Likewise, as noted, Descartes writes in the *Discourse* that to free ourselves from unrealistic desires, we must become *accustomed* to considering all external goods as equally beyond our power. Descartes emphasizes that "it takes long practice and repeated meditation to become accustomed to seeing everything in this light" (AT vi 26: CSM i 124).

[9] On these grounds, I disagree with Shapiro's suggestion that "we should expect Descartes' perfect moral system to include not only a set of unconditional duties which frame our general approach to life, but also a complete set of rules governing the particular decisions we make in the course of life, that is, a complete set of circumstantial duties" (2008: 452). More plausibly, I think, Descartes intended his envisaged perfect moral system to fully establish and justify the second-order moral principles he sets out in his later writings.

account of virtue. In particular, I wish to explain why I take him to regard the practice of virtue as a moral imperative, thereby defending my above suggestion that Descartes' ethics of virtue is indeed deontological.

2 VIRTUE AS THE RIGHT USE OF THE WILL

Throughout his 1645–49 correspondence and in the *Passions of the Soul*, Descartes consistently adheres to the definition of virtue presented above in his letter to Princess Elizabeth of August 4, 1645, as "a firm and constant resolution to carry out whatever reason recommends." In a later letter to Elizabeth, he asserts that "in order to achieve a contentment which is solid, we need to pursue virtue – that is to say, to maintain a firm and constant will to bring about everything we judge to be the best, and to use all the power of our intellect in judging well" (August 18, 1645, AT IV 277: CSMK 262). Likewise, Descartes writes to Queen Christina that to practice virtue is to hold "a firm and constant resolution to carry out to the letter all the things which one judges to be best, and to employ all the powers of one's mind in finding out what these are" (November 20, 1647, AT V 83: CSMK 325).[10]

To exercise virtue, we must meet two main conditions. The first is to strive to judge well, namely, to use all the powers of our intellect to find the best course of action to pursue. The second condition is to execute resolutely and firmly whatever course of action we have decided to follow relying on our best available knowledge. Firmness and resolution are thus insufficient for virtue. Just as the right use of free will in speculative matters depends on the exercise of the will in accordance with the intellect's distinct perceptions, so also the good use of the will in the practice of virtue demands a firm resolve to always use our reason as best we can and to act in accordance with our best judgments. To judge well in the conduct of life and thereby meet the first condition of virtue, however, we need not judge indubitably and infallibly. Even when we fail to choose what is best, we can still be virtuous (and thus escape blame for vice and error) provided that when making our decision, we strive to employ our mind in the best possible manner so as to reach the best judgment available and act resolutely on it.[11]

---

[10] See also letter to Princess Elizabeth, September 1, 1645 (AT IV 284: CSMK 263); *Passions*, art. 148.

[11] See e.g. letter to Princess Elizabeth, August 4, 1645 (AT IV 266–67: CSMK 258); letter to Princess Elizabeth, October 6, 1645 (AT IV 307: CSMK 269); letter to Queen Christina, November 20, 1647 (AT V 83–84: CSMK 325); *Passions*, art. 170.

When explaining this non-consequentialist feature of his notion of virtue, Descartes stresses the internal connection between wisdom and resolution as two conditions for virtue. In practicing virtue, as he writes to Queen Christina, our resolution must not stem from mere stubbornness but from our conviction that we have done our utmost to reach the best judgment available under the circumstances. Only then, Descartes states, can we be sure of having done our duty and, consequently, be absolved of feelings of guilt, regret, and remorse, even when our judgment turns out to be false:

[V]irtue consists only in the resolution and vigour with which we are inclined to do the things we think good – this vigour, of course, must not stem from stubbornness, but from the knowledge that we have examined the matter as well as we are normally able. What we do after such examination may be bad, *but none the less we can be sure of having done our duty.* (Letter to Queen Christina, November 20, 1647, AT v 83–84: CSMK 325; my emphasis)

The non-consequentialist nature of Descartes' moral thinking lies in the view that actions are good or bad depending on how they are chosen and elicited, not on their intrinsic features or resulting consequences. Descartes elaborates on this point in a letter to Elizabeth, emphasizing the scope of our moral responsibility:

I think also that there is nothing to repent of when we have done what we judged best at the time when we had to decide to act, even though later, thinking it over at our leisure, we judge that we made a mistake. There would be more ground for repentance if we had acted against our conscience, even though we realized afterwards that we had done better than we thought. For we are responsible only for our thoughts, and it does not belong to human nature to be omniscient, or always to judge as well on the spur of the moment as when there is plenty of time to deliberate. (October 6, 1645, AT iv 307: CSMK 269)

To support his non-consequentialist outlook in this passage, Descartes invokes his fundamental distinction between things that depend only on us, on our free will, and things that do not. Since we can be morally responsible only for matters that are in our dominion, there would be no grounds for regret or repentance when we realize later that, despite our best efforts, we have failed to obtain what we had hoped, provided we know we have done our utmost to reason well. Only if we acted against our conscience would we have grounds for repentance, however expedient the outcome of our action.

Descartes encapsulates this point in the *Passions*, stating that "we always do our *duty* when we do what we judge to be best, even though our judgment may perhaps be a very bad one" (art. 170; my emphasis).[12] His use of the term "duty" (*devoir*) while speaking of the practice of virtue is in line with his deontological approach, regarding the practice of virtue as a command of reason, as a constitutive moral imperative that we must fulfill for its own sake. The deontological dimension of Descartes' account of virtue becomes apparent in his doctrine that virtue constitutes our supreme good, which he characterizes in obligatory terms as "the final end or goal towards which our actions *ought* to tend" (AT iv 275: CSMK 261; my emphasis). The normative import of this definition suggests that the practice of virtue is not only the highest good we *might* attain, but also the highest good we *ought* to set ourselves as the ultimate end of all our actions. To act virtuously, as the next section will show, we must not only act rationally and resolutely but also strive for virtue as our ultimate end. To defend this reading, I will now consider more closely Descartes' position on the relationship between virtue, the supreme good, and happiness.

3 VIRTUE, THE SUPREME GOOD, AND HAPPINESS

In the autumn of 1647, Descartes was informed by a friend, the French diplomat Hector-Pierre Chanut, of Queen Christina's interest in his view of the supreme good. Descartes writes to Queen Christina in November 1647, expounding "all that [he has] been able to discover on the topic" (AT v 82: CSMK 324). He begins by presenting his main criterion for identifying something as good: "we should not consider anything as good, in relation to ourselves, unless we either possess it or have the power to acquire it" (ibid.). Since the only thing absolutely "within our disposal" and entirely dependent on us is our good use of free will, a firm will to do well is our supreme good, the greatest of all the goods we can possess:

[T]he supreme good of each individual … consists only in a firm will to do well and the contentment which this produces. My reason for saying this is that I can discover no other good which seems so great or so entirely within each man's power. For the goods of the body and of fortune do not depend absolutely upon us; and those of the soul can all be reduced to two heads, the one being to know, and the other to will, what is good. But knowledge is often beyond our powers; and so there remains only our will, which is absolutely within our disposal. (AT v 82–83: CSMK 324–25)

---

[12] See also the passage cited above from the letter to Queen Christina, November 20, 1647 (AT v 83–84: CSMK 325).

Descartes goes on to identify the good use of free will, which constitutes our supreme good, with the exercise of virtue:

And I do not see that it is possible to dispose [the will] better than by a firm and constant resolution to carry out to the letter all the things which one judges to be best, and to employ all the powers of one's mind in finding out what these are. This by itself constitutes all the virtues; this alone really deserves praise and glory; this alone, finally, produces the greatest and most solid contentment in life. So I conclude that it is this which constitutes the supreme good. (AT v 83: CSMK 325)

The good use of the will, or, what comes to the same, the practice of virtue, is not simply a means to an end but rather our supreme good, namely, "the final end or goal toward which our actions ought to tend" (AT IV 275: CSMK 261). And since we cannot be praised or blamed except for what depends entirely on us, on our free will, the practice of virtue *qua* the good use of the will is also the only thing which deserves praise and glory. "[N]othing except virtue," Descartes adds, "really deserves praise. All other goods deserve only to be esteemed and not to be honoured or praised, except in so far as they are supposed to have been acquired or obtained from God by the good use of free will. For … only what depends on the will provides grounds for reward or punishment" (AT v 84: CSMK 325).

Descartes' next step is "to prove that the good use of free will is what produces the greatest and most solid contentment in life" (AT v 84: CSMK 325). Although virtue, not happiness, is the final end for which we should strive in all our actions, happiness is the immediate and natural consequence of being virtuous. Proving this does not seem difficult, Descartes says, "if we consider carefully what constitutes pleasure, or delight, and in general all the sorts of contentment we can have" (AT v 84: CSMK 325). Among the points he raises in this context, the following two deserve special attention: (1) "there is nothing that can make the soul content except its belief that it possesses some good"; (2) "if it knew the just value of its goods," its contentment would always be in proportion to the greatness of the good from which it proceeded" (AT v 84–85: CSMK 325–26). Granted this, our awareness of the good use to which we put our will in practicing virtue, the greatest of all the goods we can attain, is evidently the source of our greatest contentment:

Now free will is in itself the noblest thing we can have, since it makes us in a way equal to God and seems to exempt us from being his subjects; and so its correct use is the greatest of all the goods we possess; indeed there is nothing that is more our own or that matters more to us. From all this it follows that nothing but free will can produce our greatest happiness. (AT v 85: CSMK 326)

This account sheds light on my above suggestion that, for Descartes, to act virtuously and attain the resulting contentment, we ought to aim for virtue as our ultimate end. Descartes addresses this point early in his correspondence with Elizabeth. In a letter dated August 18, 1645, he rejects the Epicurean conception of happiness as the supreme good, maintaining that happiness is the contentment or satisfaction of the mind that results from possessing the supreme good:

My first observation is that there is a difference between happiness, the supreme good, and the final end or goal towards which our actions ought to tend. For happiness is not the supreme good, but presupposes it, being the contentment or satisfaction of the mind which results from possessing it. The end of our actions, however, can be understood to be one or the other; for the supreme good is undoubtedly the thing we ought to set ourselves as the goal of all our actions, and the resulting contentment of the mind is also rightly called our end, since it is the attraction which makes us seek the supreme good. (AT iv 275: CSMK 261)

In this passage, Descartes explicitly asserts that happiness does *not* constitute our supreme good, which means that happiness is not "the thing we ought to set ourselves as the goal of all our actions." Yet Descartes acknowledges that aspiring to happiness plays a significant motivational role in our striving for virtue as our ultimate *moral* end. To illustrate this point, he uses a target-range situation:

Suppose there is a prize for hitting a bull's-eye: you can make people want to hit the bull's-eye by showing them the prize, but they cannot win the prize if they do not see the bull's-eye; conversely, those who see the bull's-eye are not thereby induced to fire at it if they do not know there is a prize to be won. So too virtue, which is the bull's-eye, does not come to be strongly desired when it is seen all on its own; and contentment, like the prize, cannot be gained unless it is pursued. (AT iv 277: CSMK 262)

Seeing the bull's-eye is not enough to induce a marksman to fire; he needs also to know that success will be rewarded. But he will not win the prize unless he aims his weapon at the bull's-eye, regarding it as his final target (and succeeding in shooting it with the greatest precision). Similarly, Descartes appears to assume that human beings will not be motivated to aim for virtue unless they expect to attain some benefit (contentment) by so doing. Virtue, he states, "does not come to be strongly desired when it is seen all on its own." But this is not to suggest that the virtuous agent strives for contentment as her ultimate moral end. Whoever sets out to acquire contentment as the ultimate goal of action will not act virtuously and, therefore, will not attain the desired reward either. To attain true and solid contentment, the agent must aim for virtue as her ultimate, self-rewarded moral end, even though what drives the agent to aspire to virtue as an ultimate end might be her expectation of reward.[13]

But even if this reading is correct, Descartes' conception could still face a problem when attempting to explain what exactly the virtuous agent strives for. How can the agent's final end be to judge well and act in accordance with the best judgment and, at the same time, be motivated by a desire to gain some benefit (contentment) from it? If attaining contentment through the practice of virtue constitutes the virtuous agent's ultimate end, this would mean that the agent treats the practice of virtue as merely a means to that end, in which case the agent would neither be considered "virtuous" nor be able to attain any solid contentment. But then, if the supreme good that should be the agent's ultimate end is virtue itself, what would induce the agent to act virtuously, given that virtue "does not come to be strongly desired when it is seen all on its own"?

To make sense of Descartes' position on this issue we need to recall that he considers our virtuous behavior inherently and necessarily pleasurable: "we cannot ever practice any virtue – that is to say, do what our reason tells us we should do – without receiving satisfaction and pleasure from so doing" (letter to Elizabeth, September 1, 1645, AT IV 284: CSMK 263). Since virtue is something advantageous in itself, to say that we can aim for virtue for its own sake while also expecting to be rewarded for it is not self-contradictory. To aim for virtue as our final, self-rewarding moral end is not the same as to strive for virtue on account of its resulting contentment, and Descartes adheres only to the first of these positions.[14]

Descartes defines happiness (*béatitude*) as "a perfect contentment of mind and inner satisfaction, which is not commonly possessed by those who are most favoured by fortune, and which is acquired by the wise

---

[13] The distinction suggested here between the psychological and the strictly ethical (deontological) levels is also implicit in Descartes' statement, some lines earlier in the same letter, that "although the mere knowledge of our duty might oblige us to do good actions, yet this would not cause us to enjoy any happiness if we got no pleasure from it" (AT IV 276: CSMK 261). See also letter to Princess Elizabeth, October 6, 1645 (AT IV 305: CSMK 268), cited in n. 17 below; cf. Rutherford (2004: 184).

[14] Long makes a similar point in connection with Stoic ethics, which he takes to be a hybrid of Bentham's utilitarianism and Kant's deontology (1996: 144–45). In Long's notably interesting reading, the pursuit of virtue for the Stoics proves to be a moral obligation, independent of the fact that it is also advantageous (p. 145).

without fortune's favour."[15] Although things not entirely within our power, such as honors, riches, and health, can contribute to our contentment, they cannot provide solid contentment and, therefore, to seek them in order to find happiness "would be a waste of time" (AT IV 265: CSMK 257). The only sort of contentment we should seek is the one that depends solely on us, which we can achieve without external assistance. Everyone can attain this contentment, even those least blessed by nature and fortune:

A small vessel may be just as full as a large one, although it contains less liquid; and similarly if we regard each person's contentment as the full satisfaction of all his desires duly regulated by reason, I do not doubt that the poorest people, least blest by nature and fortune, can be entirely content and satisfied just as much as everyone else, although they do not enjoy as many good things. (AT IV 264–65: CSMK 257)[16]

Since our free will is the only thing that depends entirely on us, our awareness of having used our free will well is the only source of solid contentment or happiness in our life. As Descartes writes to Elizabeth, "in order to achieve a contentment which is solid, we need to pursue virtue – that is to say, to maintain a firm and constant will to bring about everything we judge to be the best, and to use all the power of our intellect in judging well" (August 18, 1645, AT IV 277: CSMK 262). Virtuous activity, which requires that we consciously and deliberately aim for virtue as our ultimate end, is essentially and inseparably intertwined with happiness.

Although Descartes considers the practice of virtue both necessary and sufficient for true happiness, he does not credit them with the same ethical value, as evidenced by his insistence that only virtue constitutes the supreme good for which we ought to strive as our final moral end.[17] "Nothing except virtue," he writes, "really deserves praise" (AT V

15 Letter to Princess Elizabeth, August 4, 1645 (AT IV 264: CSMK 257); see also a letter to the same addressee of August 18, 1645 (AT IV 277: CSMK 262).
16 See also letter to Princess Elizabeth, September 1, 1645 (AT IV 281–82: CSMK 262).
17 See also AT V 83: CSMK 325. Explaining to Elizabeth his reasons for refusing to treat contentment or joy as our supreme good, Descartes writes: "If I thought joy the supreme good, I should not doubt that one ought to try to make oneself joyful at any price ... But I make a distinction between the supreme good – which consists in the exercise of virtue, or, what come to the same, the possession of all those goods whose acquisition depends upon our free will – and the satisfaction of mind which results from that acquisition" (October 6, 1645, AT IV 305: CSMK 268). Cf. Morgan (1994: 105, 111); Marshall (1998: 68–70); Rutherford (2004, esp. pp. 181–84); Shapiro (2007: 32; 2008: 454ff.). Martial Gueroult holds a considerably different understanding of Descartes' morality, which he takes to be a mere technique "comparable to medicine" and therefore only a means to attain "happiness in the present life" (1984: II, 178). In Gueroult's reading, "morality is therefore the technique that must determine in what way I must act in this life in order for my soul to be full of contentment, in spite of the fact that this soul is not only pure

84: CSMK 325). Independently of our expectation of reward for our virtuous activity, then, we must desire virtue not just for its resulting contentment but also because it is morally obligatory and commendable in its own right.

Expounding to Elizabeth the essential connection between virtue and happiness, Descartes addresses the principle noted above whereby our contentment is always proportionate to the greatness of the good from which it proceeded. "According to the rule of reason," he writes, "each pleasure should be measured by the size of the perfection which produces it" (September 1, 1645, AT IV 283–84: CSMK 263). The more perfect the cause of our contentment, the greater our resulting contentment. Since virtue consists in the right exercise of free will, which is the greatest of all the goods we can possess, we cannot attain a greater contentment than the one we acquire through the exercise of virtue itself.[18] But Descartes recognizes the distorting influence of the passions for our estimation of the goods: "often passion makes us believe certain things to be much better and more desirable than they are; then, when we have taken much trouble to acquire them, and in the process lost the chance of possessing other more genuine goods, possession of them brings home to us their defects; and thence arise dissatisfaction, regret and remorse" (AT IV 284: CSMK 263–64).[19] Since a proper evaluation of possible goods is crucial for our moral activity, Descartes regards this deceitful effect of the

mind, but is also substantially united to a body that plunges it into a natural and social world whose vicissitudes are infinite" (p. 179). See also Davies (2001: 44, 51), who follows Gueroult on this point. For a critical discussion of Gueroult's interpretation, see Marshall (1998: 85–95).

[18] The essential nexus that Descartes draws between virtue and happiness leads him to present his three rules of morality, which he relates to the three *morale* maxims of the *Discourse*, as the conditions for attaining contentment without any external assistance: (1) to try always to employ our mind as well as we can to discover what we should or should not do in all the circumstances of life; (2) to have "a firm and constant resolution to carry out whatever reason recommends without being diverted by [our] passions or appetites"; (3) to bear in mind that while we thus guide ourselves as far as we can, by reason, all the good things which we do not possess are one and all entirely outside our power. In this way we will become accustomed not to desire them (August 4, 1645, AT IV 265–66: CSMK 257–58). The first two moral rules (echoing the second *morale* maxim) encapsulate Descartes' definition of virtue, whereas the third rule, which traces the line of the third *morale* maxim, prescribes control of our desires by limiting them to objects entirely within our power. The practice of virtue is intrinsically self-rewarding and also prevents indecisiveness and the resultant regret and remorse. If we bear in mind that things we have failed to attain are not in our power, we will cease desiring them and thus be content: "For nothing can impede our contentment except desire and regret or repentance; but if we always do whatever our reason tells us, even if events show us afterwards that we have gone wrong, we will never have any grounds for repentance, because it was not our own fault" (AT IV 266: CSMK 258).

[19] See also letter to Princess Elizabeth, September 15, 1645 (AT IV 294–95: CSMK 267); letter to Queen Christina, November 20, 1647 (AT V 85: CSMK 326); *Passions*, art. 138.

passions as "the source of all the evils and all the errors of life."[20] The true function of reason in the conduct of life, he tells Elizabeth, is "to examine and consider without passion the value of all the perfections, both of the body and of the soul, which can be acquired by our conduct." But this does not imply that the passions should be despised altogether or even that we should entirely free ourselves from them: "It is enough to subject one's passions to reason; and once they are thus tamed they are sometimes the more useful the more they tend to excess" (AT IV 287: CSMK 265). This theme becomes dominant in the *Passions of the Soul*, where the passions are shown to be not just impediments to our virtuousness and happiness but also an indispensable source of both, provided we subject our passions to reason by tuning them and channeling them to our rational goals.

4 VIRTUE AS SELF-MASTERY IN THE *PASSIONS OF THE SOUL*

Descartes opens the *Passions of the Soul* by remarking on his new approach to the topic. He asserts that "the defects of the sciences we have from the ancients are nowhere more apparent than in their writings on the passions." Given that their teachings about the passions "are so meagre and for the most part so implausible," he cannot hope to approach the truth "except by departing from the paths they have followed." He is therefore obliged to write on the passions as if he were considering a topic that no one had discussed before him (*Passions*, art. 1). Descartes sought to replace the traditional account of the passions as belonging to the appetitive faculty with a systematic, mechanistic account of their physiological origin congruent with his new physics and with the metaphysical dualism of body and soul. To stress the novelty of his treatment of the passions in this treatise, he understates its significant ethical dimension, asserting his intention "to explain the passions only as a natural philosopher, and not as a rhetorician or even as a moral philosopher" (Prefatory letter to Egmont, August 14, 1649, AT XI 326: CSM I 327).

Descartes defines the passions as "those perceptions, sensations or emotions of the soul which we refer particularly to it, and which are caused, maintained and strengthened by some movement of the spirits" (art. 27).[21]

---

[20] AT IV 284: CSMK 263. See also *Passions*, art. 144.
[21] The "animal spirits," in Descartes' terminology, are a very fine gas ("a certain very fine wind, or rather a very lively and pure flame") transmitted to the brain through the nervous system. See *Treatise on Man* (AT XI 129ff.: CSM I 100ff.); *Discourse*, Part Five (AT VI 49ff.: CSM I 135ff.);

Cartesian passions are thus body-dependent mental states, resulting from the mind's union with the body. As such, they are contrasted with the actions of the mind, namely, the thoughts caused solely by the mind and dependent on the will.[22] Early in the *Passions*, Descartes differentiates between three classes of thoughts that are not produced by the activity of the soul, of which he only undertakes to explain the third in this treatise (arts. 23–25). The first class contains sense perceptions such as light, sounds, and the like, which refer to the external objects causing them. The objects of our senses produce certain movements in the brain, which cause the soul, via the nerves, to have sensory perceptions of these objects (art. 23). The second class of body-dependent thoughts contains those that refer to our body, such as hunger, thirst, pain, cold, heat, and all other states we feel are in our body and not in objects outside us (art. 24). Last are emotions such as joy, anger, fear, and the like, which refer only to our soul. The distinctive character of these perceptions is that although we feel their effects in the soul, "we do not normally know any proximate cause to which we can refer them." Sometimes they are aroused in us "by the objects which stimulate our nerves and sometimes also by other causes" (art. 25). Ignorant of their genuine causes, we mistakenly perceive these passions as inclinations of our will, as if they were actions or volitions originated by the soul (Alanen 2003: 185–89).

The passions are in fact passively aroused in the soul by specific movements in the pineal gland, originated by a perception of some object that is immediately represented as beneficial or harmful. For example, when we see an animal approaching us, the light reflected from its body forms an image in our eyes that, in turn, by means of the optic nerve, causes specific movements in the brain. If this image resembles those of animals that have previously been harmful to us, it excites the passion of fear,

---

Optics (AT VI 130–31: CSM I 167–68); *Principles*, IV, 189ff.; *Passions*, arts. 7, 9–16, 30ff. *passim*. See also Cottingham (1998: 88).

[22] In article 17, Descartes draws a distinction between actions and passions in the thoughts of our soul: "Those I call its actions are all the volitions, for we experience them as proceeding directly from our soul and as seeming to depend on it alone. On the other hand, the various perceptions or modes of knowledge present in us may be called its passions, in a general sense, for it is often not our soul which makes them such as they are." He likewise writes to Elizabeth that "the term 'passion' can be applied in general to all the thoughts which are thus aroused in the soul by cerebral impressions alone, without the concurrence of its will, and therefore without any action of the soul itself; for whatever is not an action is a passion" (October 6, 1645, AT IV 310: CSMK 270).

which may dispose us to flee (*Passions*, arts. 35–36). Descartes enumerates six primitive passions – wonder, love, hatred, desire, joy, and sadness – of which all others are either compositions or species (art. 69). Although different passions arise from different movements of the gland, the principal effect of all the human passions is the same: "they move and dispose the soul to want the things for which they prepare the body. Thus the feeling of fear moves the soul to want to flee, that of courage to want to fight, and similarly with the others" (art. 40). The passions are therefore crucial for the preservation of the mind–body union. They are all by nature good, and we have nothing to avoid but their misuse or their excess (art. 211). Just like sensations and appetites, they inform the soul of the value of external things, disposing it to "want the things which nature deems useful for us, and to persist in this volition" (art. 52; see also arts. 40, 137–39).

The passions dispose the soul to will certain things by means of the desires they produce (arts. 143–44). Desire (*désir*) is "an agitation of the soul caused by the spirits, which disposes the soul to wish, in the future, for the things it represents to itself as agreeable" (art. 86). Although desire is itself a passion, all other passions "govern our behaviour by producing desire in us" (art. 143). In the sequence of our psycho-physiological mechanism, desire is the passion closest to action. Reinforcing the effect of the passions from which it is produced, desire prompts us to act. A feeling of pain, for example, "produces in the soul first the passion of sadness, then hatred of what causes the pain, and finally the desire to get rid of it" (art. 137).[23] Now, since the passions "cannot lead us to perform any action except by means of the desire they produce," Descartes clarifies, "it is this desire which we should take particular care to control; and here lies the chief utility of morality" (art. 144).

---

[23] As Deborah Brown remarks, desire is the passion that acts directly on the will, and is thus the last passion prior to action (2006: 52, 177). See also James (1997: 258, 269). Another peculiarity of desire is that it has no opposite (art. 87). Unlike his scholastic predecessors, Descartes regards desire and aversion as one and the same passion. The same movements of the animal spirits that cause us to pursue some good, cause us, at the same time, to avoid the opposite evil (art. 87). "In pursuing riches, for example, we necessarily avoid poverty, while in avoiding illness we pursue health, and likewise in other cases" (art. 87). For the difficulties embedded in this approach, in light of the possibility of avoiding evil *without* thereby pursuing good, and vice-versa, see James (1997: 265–68). Descartes' view, however questionable, implies significant ramifications for our understanding of his conviction that someone's desire to make right use of the will is tantamount to her desire to avoid misusing the will (see Chapter 2, section 7, above). Brown makes a similar point in connection with Descartes' idea that the desire for happiness is one and the same as the desire to avoid regret and repentance, which militate against happiness (2006: 177).

A primary task of reason is to deal with conflicting desires that the passions produce in us, which in turn cause conflicting inclinations of the will. Just as brain movements yield passions in the soul, so also the soul, by willing something, produces movements in the brain.[24] This often results in conflicting impulses affecting the pineal gland, "pushed to one side by the soul and to the other side by the animal spirits" (art. 47). But since the soul is one and indivisible, Descartes insists that these conflicts do not involve different parts of the soul (meaning rational and irrational forces originating in the soul) but rather rational volitions and bodily movements pushing the pineal gland in contrary directions.[25] These conflicts make the soul "feel itself impelled, almost at one and the same time, to desire and not to desire one and the same thing" (art. 47). Such opposing desires, Descartes states, "pull the will first to one side and then to the other, thus making it battle against itself and so putting the soul in the most deplorable state possible" (art. 48).

Each person can recognize the strength or weakness of his soul, Descartes explains, by its success in settling these conflicts. The strongest souls "belong to those in whom the will by nature can most easily conquer the passions and stop the bodily movements which accompany them" (art. 48). As Alanen remarks, however, it is not merely a matter of stopping these bodily movements but of stopping them in the right manner, by using the soul's own weapons (2003: 204). The proper weapons against undesirable passions are "firm and determinate judgments bearing upon the knowledge of good and evil, which the soul has resolved to follow in guiding its conduct" (art. 48). But since these judgments are often false, being themselves based on passions, "we may judge souls to be stronger or weaker according to their ability to follow these judgments more or less closely and resist the present passions which are opposed to them" (art. 49). The most common error we commit with regard to our desires is the "failure to distinguish adequately the things which depend wholly on us from those which do not depend on us at all" (art. 144).

---

[24] By willing something, Descartes explains, our soul "brings it about that the little gland to which it is closely joined moves in the manner required to produce the effect corresponding to this volition" (art. 41; see also art. 47).

[25] For Descartes' conception of the indivisible unity of soul see also art. 68, and the discussion in Chapter 4, section 4, above. See also Voss (1989: 44–45 n. 47). As Susan James rightly observes, however, Descartes' conception of the passions as mental experiences of bodily motions might pose difficulties to his doctrine of the unity of the soul. Although Descartes describes the conflict between volitions and passions as one between the soul and the body taking place in the pineal gland, it would be more accurate to say that this conflict is between states of the soul (mental actions) and states of the soul–body composite, which cannot be attributed to either the soul or the body alone (James 1997: 259; 1998: 25–26).

This distinction, which is no less formative in the *Passions* than in the correspondence and in the *Discourse*, is the key to our virtuous activity and happiness:

Regarding those [things] which depend only on us – that is, on our free will – our knowledge of their goodness ensures that we cannot desire them with too much ardour, since the pursuit of virtue consists in doing the good things that depend on us, and it is certain that we cannot have too ardent a desire for virtue. Moreover, what we desire in this way cannot fail to have a happy outcome for us, since it depends on us alone, and so we always receive from it all the satisfaction we expected from it. (art. 144)

Since the soul's virtuousness and happiness are both embedded in its good use of the will, "all the troubles coming from elsewhere are power-less to harm it." Such troubles, moreover, increase the joy of the soul; "for on seeing that it cannot be harmed by them, it becomes aware of its per-fection" (art. 148).

Descartes is optimistic about the power of the soul to regulate the pas-sions in the pursuit of virtue: "Even those who have the weakest souls could acquire absolute mastery over all their passions if we employed sufficient ingenuity in training and guiding them" (art. 50). But he also recognizes that because of the mind's union with the body, we cannot control our physiological states directly through the mere exercise of our will. Our passions, he writes, "cannot be directly aroused or suppressed by the action of our will, but only indirectly through the representation of things which are usually joined with the passions we wish to have and opposed to the passions we wish to reject" (art. 45). Descartes appears to be applying here what is commonly called his "principle of habituation" (e.g., Voss 1989: viii, 42 n. 43), which he counts as "the principle which underlies everything I have written about [the passions]" (art. 136). This principle alone, he adds "can account for any particular phenomenon involving the passions" (art. 136). According to this principle, "nature or habit has joined certain movements of the gland to certain thoughts" or passions, but we may join them to others through habit (arts. 44, 50; see also arts. 107, 211).

Descartes thus holds we can control our well-established patterns of emotional response indirectly. Although nature or habit joins certain brain movements to certain passions, we can rehabituate ourselves to make new associations between recurrent stimuli and other passions or emotions we find more desirable: "although the movements … which represent certain objects to the soul are naturally joined to the movements which produce certain passions in it, yet through habit the former can be separated from the latter and joined to others which are very different" (art. 50).²⁶ Such a change in our habitual or natural patterns of psycho-physical response may occur either accidentally or deliberately. When we unexpectedly eat something foul, for example, our surprise may change the disposition of our brain in such a way that "we cannot afterwards look upon any such food without repulsion, whereas previously we ate it with pleasure" (art. 50). In such cases, a new habitual pattern of emotional response is acquired by a single action and does not require long practice. But we can also initiate a process of this kind, and only then will our free will come into play. Our first step must be to inquire into the genuine cause of the particular passion we wish to suppress. Bearing in mind that we must seek only those things entirely dependent on our free will that we judge worthy of being desired, the very knowledge that the stimulus that causes our passion affected us against our will suffices to stop us from being affected by it in the same manner. Descartes illustrates this point by an example from his personal experience:

[W]hen I was a child I loved a little girl of my own age who had a slight squint. The impression made by sight in my brain when I looked at her cross-eyes became so closely connected to the simultaneous impression which aroused in me the passion of love that for a long time afterwards when I saw persons with a squint I felt a special inclination to love them simply because they had that defect. At that time I did not know that was the reason for my love; and indeed as soon as I reflected on it and recognized that it was a defect, I was no longer affected by it. (Letter to Chanut, June 6, 1647, AT v 57: CSMK 322)²⁷

This therapeutic model is in line with the principles so far introduced, which also dominate the correspondence and the *Discourse*. For Descartes, virtuous individuals are those who wield power over their emotions and are not enslaved by their passions. Our main task as moral agents, which is also the key to our acquisition of happiness, is to accustom ourselves to

---

²⁶ As several commentators have remarked, this account anticipates what we now recognize as the theory of conditioned response (e.g., Voss 1989: 49 n. 54; Cottingham 1998: 90; Sutton 1998: 133–34). Descartes notes that this kind of mechanism may be observed even in animals, which lack reason or thought, allowing us to train them by changing the habitual associations between their brain movements and their pattern of conditioned response (art. 50). See also letter to Mersenne, March 18, 1630 (AT I 134: CSMK 20).

²⁷ Descartes' explanation of this psycho-physical mechanism in this letter is striking. He states that sensory stimuli cause certain "folds" in the brain (what we might now regard as a "neural pathway"), which in turn produce in us certain patterns of emotional response: "The objects which strike our senses move parts of our brain by means of the nerves, and there make as it were folds, which undo themselves when the object ceases to operate; but afterwards the place where they were made has a tendency to be folded again in the same manner by another object resembling even incompletely the original object" (AT v 57: CSMK 322).

seek and desire only those goods entirely dependent on our free will that our reason judges worthy of pursuit, and free ourselves from all others. In the correspondence with Queen Christina, as noted, Descartes explains that all the concrete goods we can attain are to be valued not for themselves but according to the extent to which they can be obtained through the good use of the will (AT v 84: CSMK 325). Hence, only things whose acquisition depends solely on us deserve to be pursued. Regarding things that do not depend on us in any manner "we must never desire them with passion, however good they may be" (art. 145). This prescription holds, Descartes explains, not only because of the frustration we may suffer when such vain desires are not fulfilled, "but chiefly because in occupying our thoughts they prevent our forming a liking for other things whose acquisition depends on us" (art. 145).

In article 145, Descartes proceeds to offer two general remedies for "vain" desires, directed to objects beyond our power. The characteristic feature of these remedies is that both are intended to help us *habituate* ourselves to desire only things within our control, namely, to acquire a *habitual desire for virtue*. The first remedy is generosity, which Descartes discusses only in the third part of the treatise, and the second is "frequent reflection upon divine Providence: we should reflect upon the fact that nothing can possibly happen other than as Providence has determined from all eternity." Descartes' point of departure is that we can desire only what we consider in some way to be possible, a principle that structures the third *morale* maxim of the *Discourse*. Granted this, Descartes believes that frequent reflection on the immutable necessity with which God has determined all things to happen from all eternity will strengthen our recognition that external things are beyond our power and will enable us to stand back from desiring them:

And we must recognize that everything is guided by divine Providence, whose eternal decree is infallible and immutable to such an extent that, except for matters it has determined to be dependent on our free will, we must consider everything that affects us to occur of necessity and as it were by fate, so that it would be wrong for us to desire things to happen in any other way. But most of our desires extend to matters which do not depend wholly on us or wholly on others, and we must therefore take care to pick out just what depends only on us, so as to limit our desire to that alone. (art. 146)

To acquire a *habitual* desire for virtue, however, we must also have a proper sense of our own nature as free agents. This proper self-esteem consists in generosity (*générosité*), the second of Descartes' two remedies for vain desires, which he considers to be the crowning virtue: "the key to all the other virtues and a general remedy for every disorder of the passions" (art. 161).

5 CARTESIAN GENEROSITY

Descartes' discussion of generosity in Part Three of the treatise is, in some significant respects, the culmination of his ethical thinking and the thread binding his epistemology and his ethics. He defines generosity as follows:

> Thus I believe that true generosity, which causes a person's self-esteem to be as great as it may legitimately be, has only two components. The first consists in his knowing that nothing truly belongs to him but this freedom to dispose his volitions, and that he ought to be praised or blamed for no other reason than his using this freedom well or badly. The second consists in his feeling within himself a firm and constant resolution to use it well – that is, never to lack the will to undertake and carry out whatever he judges to be best. To do that is to pursue virtue in a perfect manner. (*Passions*, art. 153)

True generosity contains two elements, one cognitive and the other affective. Its cognitive element is the knowledge that nothing truly belongs to us but our free will, and that the way we use this freedom is the only reason for our deserving moral praise or blame. This self-understanding, as noted in Chapter 4 above, involves our *experience* of freedom (see also Shapiro 1999: 254–58), which Descartes regards as part of our constitution,[28] but it also requires metaphysical knowledge of the nature of our free will and of how our using it well or badly determines our moral worth. The second, affective element of generosity is the feeling we experience within ourselves of a firm and constant resolution to use this freedom well. The intimate connection between the two elements is apparent. To be *constantly disposed* to act virtuously, we must first understand the distinctive value of our free will, namely, the manner in which this power relates to us and determines our moral evaluation. It is only on account of this self-knowledge that we then feel committed to the duty of using this power correctly. Descartes characterizes this commitment as a *feeling* of firm and constant resolve to use the free will well – a *habitual passion for virtue*.

Generosity for Descartes is both a passion and a virtue (arts. 54, 160). The passion of generosity – the *feeling* within ourselves of a firm and

---

[28] See the textual references given above, in Chapter 3, section 1, and in Chapter 4, sections 3 and 4, where I discussed the self-evident experience we have of our freedom and its formative role.

constant resolve to pursue virtue – becomes an active, particular virtue on its own, when we develop it into a habit, a habitual passion to use free will well.[29] Descartes characterizes the particular virtues as habits: "what we commonly call 'virtues' are habits in the soul which dispose it to have certain thoughts: though different from the thoughts, these habits can produce them and in turn can be produced by them" (art. 161). Although our thoughts may be produced by the soul alone, "it often happens that some movement of the spirits strengthens them, and in this case they are both actions of virtue and at the same time passions of the soul" (art. 161).

Descartes asserts that "generosity causes us to esteem ourselves in a justified manner, in accordance with our true value" (arts. 153, 161). To explain the internal connection between the passion of generosity and proper self-esteem, he analyzes this passion into its three primitive components: the passions of wonder, of joy, and of love (art. 160). Esteem is a species of wonder (art. 150), which in turn is "a sudden surprise of the soul which brings it to consider with attention the objects that seem to it unusual and extraordinary" (art. 70). Wonder arises when we first encounter some object surprising us, one we find novel or very different from what we formerly knew (art. 53). Being "the first of all the passions," wonder occurs "before we know whether or not the object is beneficial to us" (art. 53). Unlike the other passions, wonder is not accompanied by any change in the heart or in the blood, but only by changes in the brain. As such, "it has as its object not good or evil, but only knowledge of the thing that we wonder at" (art. 71). When joined with other passions, it "augments almost all of them" (art. 72), directing our attention to objects we find worthy of special consideration, and making us learn them and retain them in our memory (arts. 70, 75).

In generosity, what we wonder at is ourselves, our own worth and, in particular, our "marvellous" power to make good use of the will, which causes us to value ourselves in a justified manner (art. 160). Explaining the element of surprise in connection to our good use of the will, Descartes indicates that the infirmities of the subject possessing this power cause us not to esteem ourselves too highly, so that "each time we consider them afresh they are a source of new wonder" (art. 160). As Shapiro points out, what we ought to wonder at and esteem is not our faculty of willing as such, but rather our *having willed well* (1999: 259).

Apart from wonder, as noted, the passion of generosity is composed of the passion of joy (which originates in the same cause as our self-esteem,

---

[29] See also Brown (2006: 188, 191).

namely, our good use of the will) and of the passion of love ("self-love
as much as the love we have for the cause of our self-esteem") (art. 160).
The passion of generosity is caused by the same movements of the animal
spirits as the passion of vanity. Both these passions are made up of a combination of the three noted primitive passions, and consist simply in the
good opinion we have of ourselves. The sole difference between them is
that this opinion is justified in one case and unjustified in the other (art.
160). Descartes claims that the only thing that can justify our self-esteem
is our good use of the will, the highest perfection we can attain:

> I see only one thing in us which could give us good reason for esteeming our-
> selves, namely, the exercise of our free will and the control we have over our voli-
> tions. For we can reasonably be praised or blamed only for actions that depend
> upon this free will. It renders us in a certain way like God by making us masters
> of ourselves, provided we do not lose the rights it gives us through timidity.
> (art. 152)

In forming our proper attitude toward ourselves, the virtue of generosity
also forms our proper attitude toward others. Descartes writes that those
who possess this knowledge and this feeling about themselves never have
contempt for anyone, for they "readily come to believe that any other person can have the same knowledge and feeling about himself, because this
involves nothing which depends on someone else" (art. 154). While not
everyone enjoys the same amount of wealth, or the same degree of honor,
intelligence, knowledge, or beauty, all human beings are capable of possessing a virtuous will since they are all endowed with an equal power to
use free will well (ibid.).[30]

Descartes thus holds that the virtue of generosity, which causes us to
esteem ourselves in accordance with our true value, is within everyone's
reach. Accordingly, when explaining his reasons for preferring the French
term *"générosité"* over the Aristotelian–scholastic "magnanimity" (*magna-
nimitas*), he says that although this virtue depends more than any other
virtue on good birth, proper upbringing and, even more importantly, self-
education, can correct defects of birth.[31] To acquire this supreme virtue,

---

[30] Recall that in the *Discourse*, what Descartes takes to be naturally equal in all men is "the power
of judging well and of distinguishing the true from the false – which is what we properly call
'good sense' or 'reason'" (AT VI 2: CSM I 111). I ascribe this shift in his position (from 1637 to
1649) to the fact that in the *Discourse*, he had not yet worked out his mature distinction between
the faculty of judgment and the faculty of knowledge, nor had he developed its metaphysical
groundwork – the doctrine of free will. Cf. Rodis-Lewis (1990).

[31] For helpful discussions of the ancient and scholastic origins of Cartesian *générosité* and its relation
to "magnanimity," see, e.g., Taylor (1989: 152–55); Voss (1989: 109 n. 12); Brown (2006: 189–94).

we must first arouse the passion of generosity in ourselves, by reflecting time and again on the merits of our good use of the will: "if we occupy ourselves frequently in considering the nature of free will and the many advantages which proceed from a firm resolution to make good use of it – while also considering, on the other hand, the many vain and useless cares which trouble ambitious people – we may arouse the passion of generosity in ourselves and then acquire the virtue" (art. 161).

To be generous, however, it is not enough that we merely reflect on the many advantages of using free will well,[32] nor that we simply *experience* our freedom. We must also understand the nature and distinctive value of this freedom: that nothing truly belongs to us but this freedom to dispose our volitions, and that we ought to be praised or blamed for no other reason than our using this freedom well or badly (art. 153). Descartes' account of generosity thus reveals how our moral growth depends on our metaphysical knowledge. But it also reveals how the passions, when adequately tuned by the application of the proper ethics, contribute to our moral and intellectual development. To become *habituated* to act virtuously, in both the practical and the intellectual domains, we need not disengage ourselves from the emotive-passionate dimension of our lives but rather acquire a habitual *desire for virtue*, for the good use of the will. Our intellectual understanding of the value of our free will is strengthened by some movement of the spirits and becomes an active rational emotion (which is both an action of virtue and a passion of the soul) – a habitual feeling, so to speak, of a steadfast resolve to always use free will well.

This account applies not only to our practical affairs but also to scientific inquiry. Indeed, the principal theme I have put forward throughout this book is that acquiring the habit of using free will correctly is, *mutatis mutandis*, the highest, self-sufficient merit in Descartes' ethics and epistemology. In both domains, we are *obliged* – not only encouraged or advised – to cultivate our freedom by developing a firm resolve to use free will well. When we develop this attitude within us to a point where it becomes a habit, we situate ourselves at the highest level in the hierarchy of perfections. In the closing passage of the Fourth Meditation, recall, Descartes states that acquiring the *habit* of avoiding error, of retaining the will so that it extends to what the intellect clearly and distinctly reveals, is "man's greatest and most important perfection" (AT vii 62:CSM ii

---

[32] Rather, I suggest, frequent consideration of "the many advantages which proceed from a firm resolution to make good use of free will" may strengthen our willingness to awaken in ourselves the passion of generosity and then develop it into a virtue.

43). Here too, the acquisition of this virtue-habit of using free will correctly is conditional on the meditator's metaphysical and epistemological knowledge (notably, the Fourth Meditation's theory of free will and error in judgment as well as the method for attaining clear and distinct ideas exemplified in the first three Meditations). But to be *habitually* and *passionately* committed to the duty to avoid misusing the will, as the *Passions'* account of generosity makes clear, the meditator must also *feel* a firm and constant resolve to use free will well, namely, have a rational and active *desire* for virtue, for the good use of the will. We see, then, that the later ethical writings' account of generosity and virtue may be properly extended to the realm of intellectual inquiry whose highest merit, I argue, is the right use of the will.

From a broader perspective, moreover, our scientific inquiry demands a *voluntary* intellectual effort, constant practice, and good habits or virtues.[33] Accordingly, Descartes writes to Elizabeth that our scientific inquiry is conditional, above all, on the acquisition of good "habits of belief":

I said above that besides knowledge of the truth, practice also is required if one is to be always disposed to judge well. We cannot continually pay attention to the same thing; and so, however clear and evident the reasons may have been that convinced us of some truth in the past, we can later be turned away from believing it by some false appearances unless we have so imprinted it on our mind by long and frequent meditation that it has become a settled disposition with us. In this sense the scholastics are right when they say that virtues are habits; for in fact our failings are rarely due to lack of theoretical knowledge of what we should do, but to lack of practical knowledge – that is, lack of a firm habit of belief. (September 15, 1645, AT IV 295–96: CSMK 267)

Our moral development is thus both a condition for, and the result of, our metaphysical knowledge. Viewed from this perspective, Descartes' moral thinking is not only founded on the metaphysics of the *Meditations*, but also nourishes and enriches its own roots.[34]

It now becomes apparent why generosity is, for Descartes, the crowning virtue – "the key to all the other virtues and a general remedy for every disorder of the passions" (art. 161). Whereas all the particular virtues, both intellectual and practical, are reduced to the good use of the will, which Descartes equates with the practice of virtue in his peculiar sense, the particular virtue-habit of generosity forms our proper attitude toward the practice of virtue itself and, through it, toward ourselves.

---

[33] See esp. Chapter 1, section 5, and Chapter 2, section 6, above.
[34] Cf. the discussions in Rodis-Lewis (1987); Brown (2006: 23–27); Shapiro (2008: 459–61).

Being inclined to feel within oneself a firm resolve to use free will well, the generous agent is disposed to pursue virtue "in a perfect manner" (art. 161). Generosity may be viewed, moreover, as the affective-ethical counterpart of the Cogito (cf. Marion 1993: 65–70). The Cartesian agent is autonomous in recognizing herself to be the sole, self-sufficient source for her moral worth, proper self-esteem, dignity, and happiness.

An assessment of the emotional mechanism associated with the virtue of generosity, which Descartes counts as "a general remedy for every disorder of the passions," seems a fitting ending for this book. "Those who steadfastly pursue virtue," he asserts, enjoy habitual peace of mind or "tranquility," which is distinguishable from the immediate, recurrent satisfaction (passion of joy) they gain afresh whenever they perform an action they think good – "a kind of joy which I consider to be the sweetest of all joys, because its cause depends only on ourselves" (art. 190). Descartes explains how the life of virtue is both necessary and sufficient for tranquility and enduring happiness:

[I]f anyone lives in such a way that his conscience cannot reproach him for ever failing to do something he judges to be the best (which is what I here call "pursuing virtue"), he will receive from this a satisfaction which has such power to make him happy that the most violent assault of the passions will never have sufficient power to disturb the tranquility of his soul. (art. 148)

Besides the self-satisfaction or happiness resulting directly from the practice of virtue, as well as the enduring tranquility possessed by generous souls, Descartes says that feeling the passions arousing in us, even those of sadness and grief, is itself an independent source of pleasure and joy (arts. 147, 148).[35] He characterizes this kind of pleasure as "intellectual joy," which is an instance of what he calls "internal emotions" (*émotions intérieures*) (art. 147). The latter "are produced in the soul only by the soul itself" and, in this respect, they differ from the passions, which always originate in some movement of the animal spirits (art. 147).[36] These internal emotions affect us more intimately than the passions occurring within them and, consequently, have much more power over us (art. 148).[37]

---

[35] A similar idea appears in a letter to Queen Christina: "the soul is pleased to feel passions arise in itself no matter what they are, provided it remains in control of them" (AT v 309: CSMK 270).

[36] In Part One of the treatise, accordingly, Descartes regards these internal emotions as volitions (art. 29). For the role played by these internal emotions in prompting us to engage in scientific inquiry, see James (1997: 196–200).

[37] See the astonishing example Descartes gives in article 147 of a husband mourning his dead wife, who might be sorry to see her brought back to life. Besides the sadness evoked in him by the funeral display and by her absence, he might feel "at the same time a secret joy in his innermost

To be immune to the disturbances of the passions, however, the soul needs to "always [have] the means of happiness within itself," for which it needs to be disposed "to pursue virtue diligently" (art. 148).[38] Once it has met this condition, "all the troubles coming from elsewhere are powerless to harm it. Such troubles will serve rather to increase its joy; for on seeing that it cannot be harmed by them, it becomes aware of its perfection" (art. 148). Since the generous souls always derive their means for happiness from their mastery over their passions, the more powerful the effect of the passions on them, the stronger the pleasure they gain from recognizing their own perfection or independence.

With this theme, Descartes closes the *Passions of the Soul*: "persons whom the passions can move most deeply are capable of enjoying the sweetest pleasures of this life." Indeed, when they fail to put these passions to good use or when fortune works against them, they may also experience the most bitterness. "But the chief use of wisdom lies in its teaching us to be masters of our passions and to control them with such skill that the evils which they cause are quite bearable, and even become a source of joy" (art. 212).

---

soul, and the emotion of this joy has such power that the concomitant sadness and tears can do nothing to diminish its force." Similarly, reading a book or seeing a play can arouse different passions in us, including sadness or hatred, "but we also have pleasure in feeling them aroused in us, and this pleasure is an intellectual joy which may as readily originate in sadness as in any of the other passions" (art. 147).

38 The exercise of virtue, Descartes writes, "is a supreme remedy against the passions" (art. 148). In article 91, he marks off the passion of joy, which is caused by cerebral movement, from "the purely intellectual joy that arises in the soul through an action of the soul alone. The latter may be said to be a pleasant emotion which the soul arouses in itself whenever it enjoys a good which its understanding represents to it as its own." Intellectual joy is thus the natural sequel of the practice of virtue.

References

Alanen, L. 1990. "Cartesian Ideas and Intentionality," *Acta Philosophica Fennica* 49: 344–69.

1994. "Sensory Ideas, Objective Reality, and Material Falsity," in Cottingham (ed.), pp. 229–50.

2003. *Descartes's Concept of Mind*, Cambridge, MA and London: Harvard University Press.

2008. "Omnipotence, Modality, and Conceivability," in Broughton and Carriero (eds.), pp. 353–71.

Alquié, F. 1950. *La découverte métaphysique de l'homme chez Descartes*, Paris: Presses Universitaires de France.

Alquié, F. (ed.) 1967. *Oeuvres philosophiques de Descartes*, vol. ii, Paris: Éditions Garnier Frères.

Aquinas, St. Thomas. 1975. *Summa Contra Gentiles* [1259–1264/54], ed. and trans. V. J. Bourke, Notre Dame and London: University of Notre Dame Press.

Ariew, R., and Garber, D. (eds. and trans.) 1989. *G. W. Leibniz: Philosophical Essays*, Indianapolis and Cambridge, MA: Hackett Publishing Company.

Aristotle. 1985. *Nicomachean Ethics* [c. 325 BC], trans. T. Irwin, Indianapolis: Hackett Publishing Company.

Ayers, M. 1998. "Ideas and Objective Being," in Garber and Ayers (eds.), pp. 1062–107.

Beck, L. J. 1952. *The Method of Descartes: A Study of the Regulae*, Oxford University Press.

Beyssade, J.-M. 1992. "Descartes on Material Falsity," in Cummins and Zoeller (eds.), pp. 5–20.

1993. "On the Idea of God: Incomprehensibility or Incompatibilities?," in Voss (ed.), pp. 85–94.

Beyssade, M. 1994. "Descartes's Doctrine of Freedom: Differences between the French and Latin Texts of the Fourth Meditation," in Cottingham (ed.), pp. 191–206.

Bolton, M. B. 1986. "Confused and Obscure Ideas of Sense," in Rorty (ed.), pp. 389–403.

Bordo, S. R. 1987. *The Flight to Objectivity: Essays on Cartesianism and Culture*, Albany: State University of New York Press.

Broughton, J. 2002. *Descartes's Method of Doubt*, Princeton University Press.

2008. "Self-Knowledge," in Broughton and Carriero (eds.), pp. 179–95.

Broughton, J. and Carriero, J. (eds.) 2008. *A Companion to Descartes*, Malden, MA and Oxford: Blackwell.

Brown, D. J. 2006. *Descartes and the Passionate Mind*, Cambridge University Press.

2008. "Descartes on True and False Ideas," in Broughton and Carriero (eds.), pp. 196–215.

Butler, R. J. (ed.) 1972. *Cartesian Studies*, Oxford: Blackwell.

Campbell, J. K. 1999. "Descartes on Spontaneity, Indifference, and Alternatives," in R. J. Gennaro and C. Huenemann (eds.), *New Essays on the Rationalists*, Oxford University Press, pp. 179–99.

Carriero, J. 2008. "The Cartesian Circle and the Foundations of Knowledge," in Broughton and Carriero (eds.), pp. 302–18.

Caton, H. 1975. "Will and Reason in Descartes's Theory of Error," *Journal of Philosophy* 72: 87–104.

Chappell, V. 1986. "The Theory of Ideas," in Rorty (ed.), pp. 177–98.

1994. "Descartes's Compatibilism," in Cottingham (ed.), pp. 177–90.

1997. "Descartes's Ontology," *Topoi* 16: 111–27.

Clarke, D. M. 1982. *Descartes' Philosophy of Science*, Manchester University Press.

2003. *Descartes's Theory of Mind*, Oxford: Clarendon Press.

Clatterbaugh, K. C. 1980. "Descartes' Causal Likeness Principle," *Philosophical Review* 89: 379–402.

Coolidge, F. P. 1991. "The Insufficiency of Descartes' Provisional Morality," *International Philosophical Quarterly* 31: 275–93.

Costa, M. J. 1983. "What Cartesian Ideas Are Not," *Journal of the History of Philosophy* 21: 537–49.

Cottingham, J. 1996. "Cartesian Ethics: Reason and the Passions," *Revue Internationale de Philosophie* 50: 193–216.

1997. "Descartes, Sixth Meditation: The External World, 'Nature' and Human Experience," in V. Chappell (ed.), *Descartes's Meditations: Critical Essays*, Lanham, MD: Rowman and Littlefield, pp. 207–23.

1998. *Philosophy and the Good Life: Reason and the Passions in Greek, Cartesian and Psychoanalytic Ethics*, Cambridge University Press.

2002. "Descartes and the Voluntariness of Belief," *Monist* 85: 343–60.

2008a. "The Role of God in Descartes's Philosophy," in Broughton and Carriero (eds.), pp. 288–301.

2008b. *Cartesian Reflections: Essays on Descartes's Philosophy*, New York: Oxford University Press.

Cottingham, J. (ed.) 1992. *The Cambridge Companion to Descartes*, Cambridge University Press.

1994. *Reason, Will, and Sensation: Studies in Descartes's Metaphysics*, Oxford: Clarendon Press.

Cottingham, J. (trans. with Introduction and Commentary) 1976. *Descartes' Conversation with Burman*, Oxford: Clarendon Press.

Cover, J. A., and Kulstad, M. (eds.) 1990. *Central Themes in Early Modern Philosophy*, Indianapolis: Hackett Publishing Company.

Cress, D. 1994. "Truth, Error, and the Order of Reason: Descartes' Puzzling Synopsis of the Fourth Meditation," in Cottingham (ed.), pp. 141–55.

Cronin, T. J. 1966. *Objective Being in Descartes and Suárez*, Rome: Gregorian University Press.

Cumming, R. 1955. "Descartes' Provisional Morality," *Review of Metaphysics* 9: 207–235.

Cummins, P. D., and Zoeller, G. (eds.) 1992. *Minds, Ideas and Objects: Essays on the Theory of Representation in Modern Philosophy*, Atascadero, CA: Ridgeview Press.

Cunning, D. 2003. "True and Immutable Natures and Epistemic Progress in Descartes's *Meditations*," *British Journal for the History of Philosophy* 11: 235–48.

Curley, E. M. 1975. "Descartes, Spinoza and the Ethics of Belief," in M. Mandelbaum and E. Freeman (eds.), *Spinoza, Essays in Interpretation*, LaSalle, IL: Open Court, pp. 159–89.

1978. *Descartes against the Skeptics*, Cambridge, MA: Harvard University Press.

1986. "Analysis in the *Meditations*: The Quest for Clear and Distinct Ideas," in Rorty (ed.), pp. 153–76.

1993. "Certainty: Psychological, Moral, and Metaphysical," in Voss (ed.), pp. 11–30.

Curley E. M. (ed. and trans.) 1985. *The Collected Works of Spinoza*, Princeton University Press.

Danto, A. 1978. "The Representational Character of Ideas and the Problem of the External World," in Hooker (ed.), pp. 287–98.

Davies, R. 2001. *Descartes: Belief, Scepticism and Virtue*, London and New York: Routledge.

Della Rocca, M. 2005. "Descartes, the Cartesian Circle, and Epistemology without God," *Philosophy and Phenomenological Research* 70: 1–33.

2006. "Judgment and Will," in Gaukroger (ed.), pp. 142–59.

2008. "Causation without Intelligibility and Causation without God in Descartes," in Broughton and Carriero (eds.), pp. 235–50.

Doney, W. 2005. "True and Immutable Natures," *British Journal for the History of Philosophy* 13: 131–37.

Espinas, A. 1925. *Descartes et la morale*, Paris: Éditions Brossard.

Evans, J. L. 1963. "Error and the Will," *Philosophy* 38: 136–48.

Field, R. W. 1993. "Descartes on the Material Falsity of Ideas," *Philosophical Review* 102: 309–33.

Frankfurt, H. 1970. *Demons, Dreamers, and Madmen: The Defense of Reason in Descartes's Meditations*, Indianapolis: Bobbs-Merrill.

1977. "Descartes on the Creation of Eternal Truths," *Philosophical Review* 86: 36–57.

1978. "Descartes on the Consistency of Reason," in Hooker (ed.), pp. 26–39.

Friedman, M. 2008. "Descartes and Galileo: Copernicanism and the Metaphysical Foundations of Physics," in Broughton and Carriero (eds.), pp. 69–83.

Garber, D. 1992. *Descartes' Metaphysical Physics*, University of Chicago Press.
  1993. "Descartes and Experiment in the *Discourse* and *Essays*," in Voss (ed.), pp. 288–310 (repr. in Garber 2001, pp. 85–110).
  2001. *Descartes Embodied: Reading Descartes through Cartesian Science*, Cambridge University Press.
Garber, D. and Ayers, M. (eds.) 1998. *The Cambridge History of Seventeenth-Century Philosophy*, 2 vols., Cambridge University Press.
Garber, D. and Nadler, S. (eds.) 2006. *Oxford Studies in Early Modern Philosophy*, Oxford University Press.
Gaukroger, S. 1995. *Descartes: An Intellectual Biography*, Oxford: Clarendon Press.
Gaukroger, S. (ed.) 1998. *The Soft Underbelly of Reason: The Passions in the Seventeenth Century*, London and New York: Routledge.
  2006. *The Blackwell Guide to Descartes' Meditations*, Oxford: Blackwell.
Gebhardt, C. (ed.) 1925. *Spinoza Opera*, 4 vols., Heidelberg: Carl Winter.
Gewirth, A. 1941. "The Cartesian Circle," *Philosophical Review* 50: 368–95.
  1943. "Clearness and Distinctness in Descartes," *Philosophy* 18: 17–36. Page numbers refer to reprinting in W. Doney (ed.) 1967. *Descartes: A Collection of Critical Essays*, New York: Doubleday, pp. 250–77.
  1970. "The Cartesian Circle Reconsidered," *Journal of Philosophy* 67: 668–85.
Gibson, A. B. 1987. *The Philosophy of Descartes*, New York and London: Garland Publishing.
Gilbert, C. 2005. "Grades of Freedom: Augustine and Descartes," *Pacific Philosophical Quarterly* 86: 201–24.
Gilson, É. 1913. *La liberté chez Descartes et la théologie*, Paris: Alcan.
  1967. *Études sur le rôle de la pensée médiévale dans la formation du système cartésien*, Paris: Vrin.
Gilson, É. (ed.) 1947. *Discours de la Méthode: texte et commentaire*, Paris: Vrin.
Grene, M. 1985. *Descartes*, Minneapolis: University of Minnesota Press.
Gueroult, M. 1984. *Descartes' Philosophy Interpreted according to the Order of Reasons*, 2 vols., trans. R. Ariew, Minneapolis: University of Minnesota Press.
Hatfield, G. 1986. "The Sense and the Fleshless eye: The Meditations as Cognitive Exercise," in Rorty (ed.), pp. 45–80.
Hobbes, Thomas. 1840. "Of Liberty and Necessity" [1654], in W. Molesworth (ed.), *The English Works of Thomas Hobbes*, vol. iv, London: John Bohn, pp. 229–78.
Hoffman, P. 1996. "Descartes on Misrepresentation," *Journal of the History of Philosophy* 34: 357–81.
  2002. "Direct Realism, Intentionality, and the Objective Being of Ideas," *Pacific Philosophical Quarterly* 83: 163–79.
  2003. "The Passions and Freedom of Will," in Williston and Gombay (eds.), pp. 261–99.
  2009. *Essays on Descartes*, New York: Oxford University Press.

Hooker, M. (ed.) 1978. *Descartes: Critical and Interpretative Essays*, Baltimore: Johns Hopkins University Press.

Imlay, R. A. 1982. "Descartes and Indifference," *Studia Leibnitiana* 14: 87–97.

James, S. 1997. *Passion and Action: The Emotions in Seventeenth-Century Philosophy*, Oxford: Clarendon Press.

1998. "Explaining the Passions: Passions, Desires, and the Explanation of Action," in Gaukroger (ed.), pp. 17–33.

Jolley, N. 1990. *The Light of the Soul: Theories of Ideas in Leibniz, Malebranche, and Descartes*, Oxford University Press.

Kaufman, D. 2000. "Descartes on the Objective Reality of Materially False Ideas," *Pacific Philosophical Quarterly* 81: 385–408.

2003a. "*Infimus gradus libertatis*? Descartes on Indifference and Divine Freedom," *Religious Studies* 39: 391–406.

2003b. "Divine Simplicity and the Eternal Truths in Descartes," *British Journal for the History of Philosophy* 11: 553–79.

2005. "God's Immutability and the Necessity of Descartes's Eternal Truths," *Journal of the History of Philosophy* 43: 1–19.

Keefe, T. 1972. "Descartes's 'Morale Provisoire': A Reconsideration," *French Studies* 26: 129–33.

Kenny, A. 1968. *Descartes: A Study of His Philosophy*, New York: Random House.

1970. "The Cartesian Circle and the Eternal Truths," *Journal of Philosophy* 57: 685–700.

1972. "Descartes on the Will," in Butler (ed.), pp. 1–31.

Larmore, C. 1984. "Descartes' Psychologistic Theory of Assent," *History of Philosophy Quarterly* 1: 61–74.

Le Dœuff, M. 1989. *The Philosophical Imaginary*, trans. C. Gordon, London: Athlone Press.

Locke, John. 1995. *An Essay Concerning Human Understanding* [1689], New York: Prometheus Books.

Loeb, L. E. 1990. "The Priority of Reason in Descartes," *Philosophical Review* 99: 3–43.

1992. "The Cartesian Circle," in Cottingham (ed.), pp. 200–35.

Loemker, L. E. 1969. *G. W. Leibniz: Philosophical Papers and Letters*, 2nd edn., Dordrecht: Reidel.

Long, A. A. 1996. *Stoic Studies*, Cambridge University Press.

MacKenzie, A. W. 1994. "The Recognition of Sensory Experience," in Cottingham (ed.), pp. 251–72.

Marion, J.-L. 1991. *Sur la théologie blanche de Descartes*, 2nd edn., Paris: Presses Universitaires de France.

1993. "Generosity and Phenomenology: Remarks on Michel Henry's Interpretation of the Cartesian Cogito," in Voss (ed.), pp. 52–74 (repr. in Marion, J.-L. 1999. *Cartesian Questions: Method and Metaphysics*, University of Chicago Press, pp. 96–117).

Markie, P. 1986. *Descartes's Gambit*, Ithaca, NY: Cornell University Press.

Marshall, J. 1998. *Descartes' Moral Theory*, Ithaca, NY: Cornell University Press.

2003. "Descartes' *Morale par Provision*," in Williston and Gombay (eds.), pp. 191–238.

McRae, R. 1972. "Descartes' Definition of Thought," in Butler (ed.), pp. 55–70.

Menn, S. 1998. *Descartes and Augustine*, Cambridge University Press.

Morgan, V. 1994. *Foundations of Cartesian Ethics*, Atlantic Highlands, NJ: Humanities Press.

Moyal, G. J. D. 1987. "The Unity of Descartes' Conception of Freedom," *International Studies in Philosophy* 19: 33–51.

Mullin, A. 2000. "Descartes and the Community of Inquirers," *History of Philosophy Quarterly* 17: 1–27.

Naaman-Zauderer, N. 2000. "Descartes: Error without Falsity," in Y. Senderowicz and Y. Wahl (eds.), *Descartes: Reception and Disenchantment*, Tel Aviv: University Publishing Projects, pp. 173–93.

2004. "The Loneliness of the Cartesian Thinker," *History of Philosophy Quarterly* 21: 43–62.

2007. *Descartes: The Loneliness of a Philosopher*, Tel Aviv University Press [in Hebrew].

2008. "The Place of the Other in Leibniz's Rationalism," in M Dascal (ed.) *Leibniz: What Kind of Rationalist?* Dordrecht: Springer, pp. 315–27.

Nadler, S. 1989. *Arnauld and the Cartesian Philosophy of Ideas*, Princeton University Press.

2006. "The Doctrine of Ideas," in Gaukroger (ed.), pp. 86–103.

Nelson, A. 1996. "The Falsity in Sensory Ideas: Descartes and Arnauld," in E. J. Kremer (ed.), *Interpreting Arnauld*, University of Toronto Press, pp. 13–32.

1997. "Descartes' Ontology of Thought," *Topoi* 16: 163–78.

2008. "Cartesian Innateness," in Broughton and Carriero (eds.), pp. 319–33.

Newman, L. 1999. "The Fourth Meditation," *Philosophy and Phenomenological Research* 59: 559–91.

2008. "Descartes on the Will in Judgment," in Broughton and Carriero (eds.), pp. 334–52.

Nolan, L. 1997. "The Ontological Status of Cartesian Natures," *Pacific Philosophical Quarterly* 78: 169–94.

Normore, C. 1986. "Meaning and Objective Being: Descartes and His Sources," in Rorty (ed.), pp. 223–41.

Patterson, S. 2008. "Clear and Distinct Perception," in Broughton and Carriero (eds.), pp. 216–34.

Perin, C. 2008. "Descartes and the Legacy of Ancient Skepticism," in Broughton and Carriero (eds.), pp. 52–65.

Ragland, C. P. 2006a. "Descartes on the Principle of Alternative Possibilities," *Journal of the History of Philosophy* 44: 377–94.

2006b. "Alternative Possibilities in Descartes's Fourth Meditation," *British Journal for the History of Philosophy* 14: 379–400.

2006c. "Is Descartes a Libertarian?," in Garber and Nadler (eds.), pp. 57–90.

Rodis-Lewis, G. 1970. *La morale de Descartes*, Paris: Presses Universitaires de France.

1987. "Le dernier fruit de la métaphysique cartésienne: la générosité," *Etudes Philosophiques* 1: 43–54.

1989. "Introduction," in Voss (ed. and trans.), pp. xv–xxv.

1990. "Liberté et égalité chez Descartes," *Archives de Philosophie* 53: 421–30.

1998. *Descartes: His Life and Thought*, trans. J. M. Todd, Ithaca, NY and London: Cornell University Press.

Rorty, A. O. (ed.) 1986. *Essays on Descartes' Meditations*, Berkeley: University of California Press.

Rosenthal, D. M. 1986. "Will and the Theory of Judgment," in Rorty (ed.), pp. 405–34.

Rubin, R. 1977. "Descartes's Validation of Clear and Distinct Apprehension," *Philosophical Review* 86: 197–208.

Rutherford, D. 2004. "On the Happy Life: Descartes vis-à-vis Seneca," in S. K. Strange and J. Zupko (eds.), *Stoicism: Traditions and Transformations*, New York: Cambridge University Press, pp. 177–97.

Schmaltz, T. M. 1991. "Platonism and Descartes' View of Immutable Essences," *Archiv für Geschichte der Philosophie* 73: 129–70.

1994. "Human Freedom and Divine Creation in Malebranche, Descartes and the Cartesians," *British Journal for the History of Philosophy* 2: 3–50.

2000. "The Disappearance of Analogy in Descartes, Spinoza, and Regis," *Canadian Journal of Philosophy* 30: 85–114.

Secada, J. 2000. *Cartesian Metaphysics: The Late Scholastic Origins of Modern Philosophy*, Cambridge and New York: Cambridge University Press.

Shapiro, L. 1999. "Cartesian Generosity," in T. Aho and M. Yrjonsuuri (eds.), *Norms and Modes of Thinking in Descartes*, Acta Philosophica Fennica 64: 249–75.

2008. "Descartes's Ethics," in Broughton and Carriero (eds.), pp. 445–63.

Shapiro, L. (ed. and trans.) 2007. *The Correspondence between Princess Elisabeth of Bohemia and René Descartes*, University of Chicago Press.

Simmons, A. 1999. "Are Cartesian Sensations Representational?," *Nous* 33: 347–69.

Smith, K. 2001. "A General Theory of Cartesian Clarity and Distinctness Based on the Theory of Enumeration in the *Rules*," *Dialogue* 40: 279–309.

Suárez, Francisco. 1965. *Disputationes metaphysicae* [1597], Hildesheim: Olms (repr. from *Opera omnia*, vols. xxv–xxvi, Paris: Louis Vivès, 1856–59).

Sutton, J. 1998. "Controlling the Passions: Passions, Memory, and the Moral Physiology of Self in Seventeenth-Century Neurophilosophy," in Gaukroger (ed.), pp. 115–46.

Taylor, C. 1989. *Sources of the Self: The Making of the Modern Identity*, Cambridge, MA: Harvard University Press.

Tierno, J. T. 1997. *Descartes on God and Human Error*, Atlantic Highlands, NJ: Humanities Press.

Van De Pitte, F. 1988. "Intuition and Judgment in Descartes's Theory of Truth," *Journal of the History of Philosophy* 26: 453–70.

Vinci, T. C. 1998. *Cartesian Truth*, New York: Oxford University Press.

Voss, S. (ed.) 1993. *Essays on the Philosophy and Science of René Descartes*, New York and Oxford: Oxford University Press.

Voss, S. (ed. and trans.), 1989. *René Descartes: The Passions of the Soul*, Indianapolis and Cambridge, MA: Hackett Publishing Company.

Wee, C. 2006a. *Material Falsity and Error in Descartes's Meditations*, London and New York: Routledge.

2006b. "Descartes and Leibniz on Human Free Will and the Ability to Do Otherwise," *Canadian Journal of Philosophy* 36: 387–414.

Wells, N. J. 1984. "Material Falsity in Descartes, Arnauld, and Suárez," *Journal of the History of Philosophy* 22: 25–50.

1990. "Objective Reality of Ideas in Descartes, Caterus and Suárez," *Journal of the History of Philosophy* 28: 33–61.

Williams, B. 1973. *Problems of the Self,* Cambridge University Press.

1978. *Descartes: The Project of Pure Inquiry*, New York: Penguin.

Williston, B. 1997. "Descartes on Love and/as Error," *Journal of the History of Ideas* 58: 429–44.

1999. "Akrasia and the Passions in Descartes", *British Journal for the History of Philosophy* 7: 33–55.

Williston, B. and Gombay, A. (eds.) 2003. *Passion and Virtue in Descartes*, Amherst, NY: Humanity Books.

Wilson, C. 2008. "Descartes and Augustine," in Broughton and Carriero (eds.), pp. 33–51.

Wilson, M. D. 1978. *Descartes*, London: Routledge and Kegan Paul.

1990. "Descartes on the Representationality of Sensation," in Cover and Kulstad (eds.), pp. 1–22.

1993. "Descartes on the Perception of Primary Qualities," in Voss (ed.), pp. 162–76.

1994. "Descartes on Sense and 'Resemblance'," in Cottingham (ed.), pp. 209–28.

Yolton, J. W. 1984. *Perceptual Acquaintance from Descartes to Reid*, Minneapolis: University of Minnesota Press.

Index